The Corporate Campus

Other books in CAUT Series

Neil Tudiver, Universities for Sale (1999)

James L. Turk (ed.)

The Corporate Campus:
Commercialization and the Dangers to Canada's
Colleges and Universities

A CAUT Series Title
James Lorimer and Company Ltd., Publishers
Toronto, 2000

James Lorimer & Company Ltd. acknowledges the support of the Ontario Arts Council. We acknowledge the financial support of the Government of Canada through the Book Publishing Industry Development Program (BPIDP) for our publishing activities. We acknowledge the support of the Canada Council for the Arts for our publishing program..

Canadian Cataloguing in Publication Data

Main entry under title:

The corporate campus: commercialization and the dangers to Canada's colleges and universities

Co-published by the Canadian Association of University Teachers.
"A CAUT series title"
ISBN 1-55028-696-X

1. Universities and colleges – Canada. 2. Academic freedom – Canada. 3. Industry and education – Canada. I. Turk, James, 1943- . II. Canadian Association of University Teachers.

LC1085.4.C3C67 2000   378.71   C00-930191-7

A CAUT Series Title
James Lorimer & Company Ltd., Publishers
35 Britain Street
Toronto, ON   M5A 1R7

Printed and bound in Canada

For Ursula Franklin
who has set an example for all of us

Contents

Preface

The articles in this book began as presentations to the Canadian Association of University Teachers's Conference, *Universities and Colleges in the Public Interest.* CAUT had several objectives in sponsoring the conference. One was to draw attention to the extent and nature of commercialization in post-secondary education in Canada. A second was to explore how commercial pressures are changing universities and colleges and what are the implications for the institutions' ability to serve the public interest. A third was to examine what should be done.

Many people made the CAUT conference possible. In particular I would like to thank Bill Graham, Bill Bruneau, Jan Newson, David Noble, and David Robinson for their advice and guidance. Tom Booth, Victor Catano, David Clipsham, Ken Field, Jeanette Lynes, Shirley Mills, Pat O'Neill, and Diane Peters played important roles in chairing sessions and workshops. Kevin Albert, Louise D'Anjou, Louise Desjardins, Nancy Gordon, Robert Léger, Peggy Richer, and Johanne Smith provided vital staff assistance before and during the conference.

In preparation for this book, the conference speakers turned their presentations into revised and expanded chapters. I wrote the introductory chapter to provide an overview of the issues explored at greater length in the rest of the book

Any book is a collective effort. I would like to thank Russell Woodell and Bill Bruneau who provided invaluable editorial assistance. Neil Tudiver's comments were helpful, as always. Louise Desjardins did her usual fine job of proofreading, and Diane Young of James Lorimer & Company was patient and helpful throughout the process.

James L. Turk

The junk merchant doesn't sell his product to the consumer,
he sells the consumer to the product.
He does not improve and simplify his merchandise.
He degrades and simplifies the client.

William S. Burroughs
Naked Lunch

INTRODUCTION

Introduction - *What Commercialization Means for Education*

JAMES L. TURK

It is hard to miss signs of the growing commercialization of universities and colleges across North America. From advertisements carefully placed on washroom walls to corporate names on buildings and corporate research partnerships, commercial interests have staked their claims to post-secondary education. The consequences are grave.

The basic role of universities in democratic society is at risk. Alone among social institutions, the university's mission is the unqualified pursuit and public dissemination of knowledge and truth. The university serves the broad public interest by treasuring informed analysis and uncompromising standards of intellectual integrity. Through teaching, research, and community service, the people who make up the university struggle to push beyond the conventional, refusing to be constrained by "what everybody knows."

This creates an uneasy relationship with the rest of society, especially with those in power who invariably want to harness the university to their wagon so that the university serves power and the status quo, not threatens it. Over centuries, the church, the state, and the corporate sector have sought to command the university.

In the most recent period, it has been the private sector's siren song that has beseeched the university to draw closer. The tune has been similar for many years. In a 1988 report, Science Council of Canada Chair, Geraldine Kenney-Wallace, issued "a call to intellectual arms" stating her belief "that destiny includes closer university-industry interaction...It is imperative that the university's knowledge be put to work for winning in a world economy."[1] Currently, the Prime Minister's Advisory Council on Science and Technology is considering an almost identical message from the Expert Panel on the Commercialization of University Research.[2]

For community colleges, corporate pressures are attempting to make them little more than outposts of industry – places that turn out job-ready workers on a just-in-time basis. Being lost are commitments to general education and

3

visions of colleges as places that educate the whole person for all aspects of their lives.

"Commercialization" is the term most commonly used to designate the attempt to hitch universities and colleges to the private sector. But commercialization has several forms that are usefully distinguished.

MARKETING SITES

The first form of commercialization is the most familiar: turning educational institutions into marketing sites for brand name products. In a highly commercialized society, educational institutions have been largely virgin territory. This, coupled with their huge captive audience of young consumers, has sparked the desire of corporations to finds ways of getting through the doorway.

Marketing people are not shy about touting the attractiveness of getting into educational institutions. For example, promotional material for *Kids World Magazine* lured advertisers a few years ago by noting "Competition and clutter can kill the chances of great advertising creative being noticed by kids. *Kids World Magazine* stands out from all other kids' media because our publication is enjoyed in the non-cluttered, non-competitive and less commercial classroom environment."

That environment is changing. Cutbacks in public funding have helped open the door to "great [and not so great] advertising creative" penetrating our educational institutions as never before. Corporate logos abound. Advertising is popping up in the most likely and unlikely places. Corporate banners hang outside university buildings named after corporate benefactors who topped up the public funding.

Coke and Pepsi have created the greatest controversy with "exclusivity" deals in which a university or college signs a multi-year contract with a soft drink company to allow the sale of only that company's products. The secret deals tie the institution's payment to the sale of a specified amount of the "product" – turning each university or college into a merchant with a vested interest in persuading students, faculty, administrators, and visitors to drink up. On many campuses, vending machines are popping up faster than dandelions so that the "product" will be readily available to the thirsty scholar.

Recently students at McGill University in Montreal held a referendum on whether to support an exclusive deal with Coke. In the largest student vote in memory, a strong majority voted against the deal – rejecting the advice of the administration and the urging of their own student association. At the University of Ottawa, following its exclusive agreement to sell Coke products, the editor of the student newspaper exposed attempts by Coke to persuade the newspaper to make reference to Coke in newspaper stories.

SELLING GOODS AND SERVICES TO UNIVERSITIES AND COLLEGES

Unpleasant as the adornment of the university with corporate logos and corporate advertising may be, turning educational institutions into marketing sites is arguably the least damaging form of commercialization. Far more pernicious is the corporate drive to alter how education is delivered so there will be greater usage of privately supplied goods and services.

Much of the non-academic side of universities and colleges has already beenprivatized – often at the expense of the quality of goods and services to students and faculty, not to mention the loss of jobs and lower pay for workers providing the newly privatized services.

The main market potential for corporate interests lies selling more private goods and services for the academic side. In a report to investors in 1996, the large American investment advisory firm, Lehman Brothers, forecast:

> "The shift we see is a system going from a government-run monopoly with little accountability and, by definition, no competition, to a market-driven system that competes on price and quality. As in health care, the delivery of service and the change in funding sources will be critically interactive as an investment driver. Shifts such as we are forecasting do not occur overnight, but with the increasing discussion, consideration and implementation of charter schools, school choice, private management of public schools and vouchers, we are certain that the traditional way that education and childcare have been delivered and funded will continue to change and there is no going back. We believe that companies that offer innovative solutions in this changing environment will offer significant opportunities to investors."[3]

Assessing the potential for the private sector in the educational industry four years later, a leading American business publication, *Business Week*, notes:

> "Although education is a huge part of the U.S. economy, until recently it wasn't much of a business...But as the millennium dawns, the private sector is poised to play a much larger role...fueled by an explosion in the money available to education start-ups."[4]

Business Week's optimism was confirmed in May 2000, when more than 2,200 people and 647 corporate exhibitors attended the first "World Education Market Forum" in Vancouver "to engage in four productive days of business and relationship-building among the international who's who of education."[5]

Already, in American elementary and secondary schools, a growing number of private companies have been contracted to provide administrative and teaching services for public institutions. But the most significant private intervention, at all levels of education in Canada and the United States, has been persuading administrators, faculty and students that computer hardware and software must be incorporated into the learning process. Cash-strapped universities and colleges are investing millions in new hardware and software to tap the educational potential of what is variously called technologically mediated instruction, on-line learning, and virtual education.

There is little evidence that the proliferation of virtual education technologies has enriched the quality of education for students or faculty. But as universities and colleges are devoting ever increasing resources to adding on-line capabilities, they are certainly enriching the economic prospects of hardware, software, and educational service companies.

BECOMING PRIVATE – IN PRACTICE

Adopting Corporate Language

The third form of commercialization is the most serious: driving public educational institutions to operate as if they were private. One sign of this change is when corporate language starts creeping into common usage. "Customers," "clients," and "products" become institutional jargon for students. Teachers become "service providers," "learning guides," or "education managers." Evaluation becomes "quality control," and the whole process becomes "production."

Since language is never neutral, this change is more than an irritation. It suggests a fundamental misunderstanding of the nature of education and of the teacher-student relationship. Unlike a retail clerk, the teacher's role is not to sell a product or please customers. It is to challenge students, to provoke new ways of thinking, to make students uneasy with what they have taken for granted. Education should engage students in a dialogue in which both teacher and student are partners in learning. The measure of success is not "customer satisfaction" but intellectual growth. This can be a difficult and unsettling process – the opposite of what is to happen to a retail customer who is to be placated and soothed into buying a product.[6]

Moving to User-Pay

The approach to financing education also changes. User-pay increasingly replaces public funding. Post-secondary education is redefined as a private good that primarily benefits those who attend the institution. The public interest and benefit from having a well-educated citizenry are ignored, as governments focus on individual benefits to justify significant increases in student tuition and fees to compensate for cuts in public funding. Charity replaces public responsibility as universities are told to seek private donors to top up their depleted coffers.

The consequences are significant. For students, their family income, not ability to benefit from further education, increasingly determines whether they can attend university. For the university, itself, growing dependence on private money allows donors to steer the institution in different directions, as will be discussed below.

Taking Control of the Labour Process

Management practices also change as public institutions adopt a private sector mentality. Presidents and principals become chief executive officers, not lead educators. They are increasingly chosen for their managerial skills, not their experience and knowledge as educators. In universities, collegial governance comes to be seen as an impediment to efficient management. In universities and colleges, educational managers assume the historic preoccupation of industrial managers – how to change an artisan-based labour process into one controlled by management.

The fathers of corporate managerialism, such as Charles Babbage and Frederick Taylor, set the agenda for "management science." Babbage identified the advantage of subdividing each part of a job so employers would not have to pay skilled workers to undertake less skilled tasks. Careful motion and time studies were advocated so no time or effort was wasted. Technology was designed to replace labour wherever productivity gains, cost reduction, or managerial control would result.

We can see the results of managerial science consistently in industry and in diverse non-industrial sectors from retail operations to nursing. One "failure" has been in education where management has not been able to control and reorganize the educational labour process. Fragmentary attempts to manage by lesson plans, inspectors and standardized curriculum have failed to take away teachers' ability to maintain control of their craft.

But with tightening budgets and a growing commitment to corporate managerialism, new efforts are being made to impose management practices on education that are common in most other sectors. As elsewhere, this means casualization and the introduction of labour-replacing technology.

Using Casual Labour

Redesigning work to use more part-time and contract employees has proven a boon for employers. Part-time and contract employees are paid less money, receive fewer benefits, have fewer legal rights, and are less likely to unionize. The contingent nature of their jobs makes them vulnerable.

In the United States, the proportion of university faculty working part-time grew from 22 percent in 1970 to 42.5 percent in 1997.[7] The American Association of University Professors notes that part-time and non-tenure-track contract appointments now constitute more than half of all faculty in the United States.[8] Equivalent data are not available for Canada because, for almost a decade, too few universities have completed Statistics Canada's annual survey on part-time faculty to allow publication of data on part-timers. Anecdotal evidence suggests that the Canadian pattern is similar to the American, with a number of Canadian universities employing as many part-time and contract staff as tenured and tenure-track faculty.

Some university administrations are going much further. Royal Roads University in Victoria, British Columbia, employs less than a dozen "core" faculty, hired on renewable fixed term appointments, and a much larger number of "associate faculty" who teach a single course each. This is a model pioneered by the University of Phoenix which has almost 70,000 students at 64 campuses across North America. Only about 3 percent of their faculty are full-time. None has tenure.

In Britain's college sector, the British Further Education Sector Educational Lecturing Service has established a cadre of about 400,000 individuals who are available to work part-time in further education. Colleges are encouraged to have a core staff and then hire part-timers at lower rates to round out their complement of teachers.[9]

Introducing Labour-Replacing Technologies

As in industry, educational administrators are coming to see that casualization must be complemented by labour-replacing technologies if they are to be successful in reshaping the labour process in education. Two of North America's most distinguished experts on higher education, William F. Massy and Robert Zemsky,[10] provide a careful exploration of this issue.

Massy and Zemsky point out that information technologies (IT) offer the possibility of "a departure from the traditional handicraft mode of education, where faculty learning curves (for the production of learning) are shallow and capital offers little leverage beyond the traditional physical plant."[11] In language strikingly similar to that of Charles Babbage a century and a half earlier, Massey and Zemsky argue that academic work can be subdivided and cheapened through the use of information technologies, allowing productivity gains.[12]

They add that this requires using information technologies to replace labour:

> "Using IT for more-with-less productivity enhancement requires that technology replace some activities now being performed by faculty,

8

teaching assistants, and support personnel. With labor accounting for 70 percent or more of current operating cost, there is simply no other way. Faculty will have to re-engineer teaching and learning processes to substitute capital for labor on a selective basis."[13]

Proper use of IT in post-secondary education, according to Massy and Zemsky, means substituting capital for labour even where there is no justification in terms of immediate cost advantages.[14] Massy and Zemsky note that this re-engineered post-secondary educational system is not for everyone: the elite will still have access to "traditional handicraft-oriented instruction that has been the hallmark of our system" – an approach "too expensive for massified higher education."[15]

Massey and Zemsky lay bare the corporate vision of what IT can do for post-secondary education. Without such a vision, why would underfunded universities and colleges be pouring vast resources into their IT projects? The answer certainly is not the conventional claim that they want to provide better access to single mothers in Sioux Lookout and other remote communities. Nor is the answer that IT is simply a wonderful supplement to current academic staff practices. Massey and Zemsky refer to the latter dismissively as the "more for more" approach.

In a document prepared for The World Bank, Bruce Johnstone warns against viewing technologies simply as a supplement to existing teaching practices:

> "There is a risk that technology continues to be incorporated by individual faculty, mainly as 'add-ons' to conventional teaching and curricula, without the accompanying changes in the instructional production function that are required to realize useful productivity gains."[16]

In the current economic and political context, the only way to understand the large and growing investment in IT is its potential to facilitate the restructuring of post-secondary education to increase "productivity" by reducing the role of teachers and other academic staff. The World Bank document is very clear about the meaning of university restructuring:

> "Radical change, or restructuring, of an institution of higher education means either fewer and/or different faculty, professional staff, and support workers. This means lay-offs, forced early retirements, or major retraining and reassignment, as in: the closure or inefficient or ineffective institutions; the merger of quality institutions that merely lack the critical mass of operations to make them cost-effective; and the radical alteration of the mission and production function of an institution – which means radically altering who the faculty are, how they behave, the way they are organized, and the way they work and are compensated."[17]

SERVING PRIVATE INTERESTS

Corporate interests are also pushing universities and colleges to redefine whom they exist to serve. Education has always been contested territory. From the introduction of compulsory education in the 19th Century to today, business has often asserted the right to set objectives for education. In a presentation to the Ontario Standing Committee on Social Development, Robert Wilson typified the corporate claim:

> "Business is the prime user of the 'product' of education–the skill sets, or lack thereof, of the graduates. It has an inherent right, as any investor, to determine the return on its investment. And the right to determine the cost of the infrastructure that creates the return."[18]

As governments cut public funds, educational institutions are forced to rely more heavily on corporate funding. This makes it easier for the corporate sector to steer the educational process. Even Canada's largest and most richly endowed university, the University of Toronto, signed secret deals with the Joseph Rotman Foundation ($15 million for the Faculty of Management Studies), Peter Munk of Barrick Gold and Horsham corporations ($6.4 million for the Centre for International Studies) and Nortel ($8 million for the Nortel Institute for Telecommunications) that allowed those corporations unprecedented influence over the academic direction of University of Toronto programs.[19] There is every reason to believe that such cases are the small tip of a very large iceberg.

There are warning signs that commercialization is steering academic research as well. Government funding programs are opening the door to private direction by requiring "partners" as a condition of researchers getting public funding. One of the Canadian government's newest and most richly endowed programs, the Canada Foundation for Innovation, requires researchers to raise 60 cents from partners for every 40 cents they receive from the CFI's $1.8-billion public endowment. A growing number of Canadian granting council programs also require researchers to find partners as a condition of getting public support. This gives the "partners" effective veto power over what research is publicly funded. In many areas, insufficient public funding means the private sector may be a researcher's sole source of support.

A recent Canadian government panel recommended putting a greater emphasis on research with a commercial orientation, and even urged that commercialization become one of the central missions of the university.[20] More than 1,400 Canadian scientists and researchers wrote to the Prime Minister pointing out the Report's recommendations would mean "important research questions that lack the promise of short-term commercial profits would be marginalised [and] scientists would be perceived as beholden to special interests."[21]

Nobel laureate John Polanyi has decried the Canadian government's "commercialization" of science, saying that it is ruining Canada's universities and driving the best young scientists out of the country. "At a certain point...we don't have universities any more, but outlying branches of industry. Then all the things industry turns to universities for – breadth of knowledge, far time horizons and independent voice – are lost."[22]

The growing dependence on private funding for university research shapes what gets studied. Basic research, the groundwork for all intellectual advances, receives decreasing attention because it offers few prospects of short-term commercial return. Nobel Prize-winning biochemist Paul Berg, who laid the groundwork for splicing DNA to make hybrid molecules and whose discovery propelled a billion-dollar industry that is now cited as a model of university-industry linkage, pointed out the irony of the situation: "The biotech revolution itself would not have happened had the whole thing been left up to industry. Venture-capital people steered clear of anything that didn't have obvious commercial value or short-term impact. They didn't fund the basic research that made biotechnology possible." [23]

Likewise, there is little corporate interest in fields that hold little promise of generating profit; for example, research about child poverty, the causes of diseases common to the poor in Third World countries, the history of Western Canadian populism, or the antecedents of Shakespeare's tragedies.

With inadequate public research funding, private funders can more easily impose strings on the researchers they do support, such as requirements that researchers sign over rights to any discoveries, that findings be kept secret, and that data belong to the funder. Such requirements interfere with normal scientific exchange and graduate student education. As in the case of Dr. Nancy Olivieri, such strings can threaten human safety and jeopardize researchers' careers.[24]

Corporate sponsorship of research can also have less visible effects, such as introducing biases into the conclusions of the work. Henry Thomas Stelfox and colleagues, for example, reviewed research on the safety of calcium-channel antagonists as a treatment for cardiovascular disorders. Of those researchers who found the medication safe, 96 percent had financial relationships with manufacturers of the products. This compared with 60 percent of the researchers whose results were neutral on the question of safety, and 37 percent of those who were critical of the use of the medication. The authors conclude, "The results demonstrate a strong association between authors' opinions about the safety of calcium-channel antagonists and their financial relationship s with pharmaceutical manufacturers."[25]

COUNTERING COMMERCIALIZATION?

The challenge for Canada's public educational institutions is how to serve the public interest and not be captured by the commercial pressures that are coming to dominate society. Several things can be done.

The first is resisting the notion that providing education is like making widgets. Real education has no "products," no "clients," no "raw material," no "customers." There are only co-participants in a learning process–a human process and an interactive process. What is remarkable is not the occasional failure of this process but the remarkable success. Learning is a collective activity, not an individual one. We learn in community–from our fellow students, from our teachers, from our friends, from the thought and writing of those who have gone before and in response to the realities of our own lives. Bill Readings tells the story of a Nobel laureate in physics who was asked his understanding of the goal of an undergraduate education in physics. He replied that it was to introduce students to 'the culture of physics'. Readings added that "undergraduates learn things that they will later discard if they pursue their studies...[this] requires a model of knowledge as a conversation among a community rather than as a simple accumulation of facts."[26]

Secondly, we must vigorously reaffirm that our educational system should not be judged by superficial "measureables", such as standardized test scores and employer satisfaction ratings, but by how well it prepares an informed, active, and socially-conscious citizenry that is productive in all aspects of their lives.

George Martell summarized this vision:

> "Secretaries and plumbers, steelworkers and retail workers, mechanics and clerks must also be historians and economists, poets, intellectuals and artists. It is only through these activities that they can be full citizens...In the end a serious curriculum means linking the work students do in school with the larger fight to make a better world. It means telling the whole truth about the way things are and acting on that truth."[27]

Thirdly, we must vigorously defend the autonomy and integrity of post-secondary educational institutions – where the quest for knowledge and truth is paramount – so that society receives the fullest possible analysis and the broadest range of critical recommendations regarding policies, technologies, programs and products.

Achieving these goals requires adequate public funding to assure our educational institutions are not beholden to private interests. Strong teacher and faculty associations are necessary to defend the integrity of educational work and its commitment to serving the broader public interest. We must work actively to ensure public education is nothing less than the foundation for a democratic, egalitarian, just, and humane society.

PART 1

What Is At Stake?

What is at Stake? Universities in Context

URSULA FRANKLIN

I have worked in and around universities long enough to appreciate their context and their complexities. I know too that they are important parts of every society and that there is deep concern about the changes in Canada's social fabric and in the university's place within it.

There are things that are easier to do and to say when one is old and has no longer job or reputation to loose; and this holds certainly true for those associated with universities. Throughout the years the vision of tenure has been a contribution to self-censorship as well as a contribution to academic freedom.

I want, therefore, to use the gift of my independence and my persistent love for and belief in the importance of the work of universities, to consider the social function of universities and colleges. I want to indicate how these institutions have grown, evolved and mutated within our social ecology and then offer some thoughts on how to respond to the commercial threats to higher education in Canada.

But first I want to share a turn of phrase I learned from my husband. Sometimes he characterizes reports or pronouncements as "awfulizing", indicating the piling of one horror story upon the next with no analysis or resolution in sight. I do not want to use this occasion to awfulize, I want to address the question of "what is at stake ?" because I believe that Canadian universities and colleges must continue to operate in the public interest and that this cannot be taken for granted.

Let me start out from the premise that to remain silent on crucial issues is to make a conscious decision. It is therefore pointless to remain silent in order to avoid accountability. We will be held responsible for our silence, as well as for our activities, just as the university teachers of the Germany of my childhood were held responsible – morally and fraternally -- for their silence and their collaboration with an evil system. We need to think clearly and to speak out together with insights coming from the collective knowledge, experience and conviction of our community.

Historically, the social function of the university has remained basically the same: It is the place or institution where the ruling apparatus of the time transfers to the next generation the attitudes, skills and knowledge needed to cope with the future. Changes in social relations, in beliefs or power structures always had their impacts on the universities, because questions of what is most needed to cope with the future had to be constantly re-visited: Was it still Latin or law, science or management knowledge that was needed? And who needed and deserved this vital coping knowledge? The sons of the rich? Their daughters? The children of workers, of aboriginal peoples, of new immigrants?

Every change in society has resonated through the university communities and the communities have usually responded well, though often slowly. In the end, universal literacy and public education, including public post-secondary education, has to be regarded as one of the major social achievements of the past century.

From all this emerged the concept of **Knowledge as a common good** and the modern understanding of universities as **major national resources,** resources that include not only physical facilities, such as laboratories, libraries and hospitals, but also staff with valuable expertise and skills.

The potential of universities to generate new knowledge on request was realized by modern nations mainly, though not exclusively, as it relates to war and its conduct. The activity of research itself – this focused and concerted pursuit of a scientific or technical question, so treasured in contemporary society – was greatly perfected during war time (you will remember the rise of operations research and systems analysis in WWII).

The growing importance of research as a university-based activity changed the nature and functions of colleges and universities drastically. Beyond the training of knowledgeable people, the research function, i.e. the creation and assessment of new knowledge, began to define the economic and political role of the institution itself. The increased emphasis in the selection and promotion of faculty on the basis of research success (including success in attracting research funding) that occurred during my academic life, is as much a social and political development as it is an intellectual one.

Today, one needs to think of universities and colleges basically as knowledge-, or maybe more appropriately information-production sites in the full meaning of industrial production. Yet, even with this image in mind, two open questions remain: (1) What kind of knowledge is being produced and (2) who receives the products? After all, universities and colleges are publicly funded institutions and knowledge is a public good, rather than a private possession.

The war time experience had demonstrated to national governments the potential of focussed research in the pursuit of national objectives, and at the same time, universities and colleges began to count on research funding as sources of income. The gradual shift within the academic communities from doing "interesting" research to looking for "fundable" research topics was subtle, but very important, signaling the increasing obvious steering effect of research financing upon university policies, such as hiring and promotion and thus upon teaching and curriculum choices.

These developments affected the individual faculty members as well as their institutions and raised a number of fundamental questions. For instance, should - in times of peace - individual scholars engage in secret or classified research? Should universities and colleges, as public institutions, permit the use of their facilities for such endeavours?

A number of my colleagues and I struggled in the immediate post-war period to persuade our respective universities to refuse their approval of classified research contracts. In some instances our actions were successful, in others camouflage manoeuvers allowed compliance with the letter of regulations, yet negating their spirit.

Much, of course, was left to the decisions of the individual faculty member; I remember well that I was the only member of my department who, as a matter of conviction, did not seek support from sources such as the Defense Research Board (though they often offered unclassified research funding), AECL or Ontario Hydro. I also remember some not too friendly discussions with my Dean, who pointed out to me how my views not only impacted on my own research career, but deprived students of "relevant" research training and the department of much needed contributions to their equipment and supplies. It was clear to me that his understanding of the university as a production site meant that as long as the funding source was respectable and the project within the law, faculty members should compete for all appropriate research funds, to bring in business and put the faculty on the map, so to speak.

I have delineated these relatively recent changes in the social and political role of our universities and colleges in order to put the current problems in an appropriate context. Yet, I need to mention one more significant sea change that occurred in the mid to late 1970s. Up to this time, grants-in-aid of research, usually called 'operating grants' were awarded by the federal granting agencies on the basis of the researchers' merit and reputation. The quality of past research, judged mainly by peer assessment, publication record etc., rather than the subject matter of the research itself, determined the access to public funds.

This changed, first for the Sciences and Engineering sector, then for the Social Sciences, the Humanities as well as Medicine, when strategic or thematic grants began to be awarded. Suddenly, the subject matter of the research proposal became a factor in its adjudication: Was the problem relevant and worthy of public support? This became a decision to be made by those providing the funds, not by the researchers.

A similar development had occurred earlier in the United States, where significant public research funds were tied to end uses of national priority. My colleagues in the States would call it "nose cone research" when their grant applications for crystallographic studies had to be justified by hopes of finding materials resistant to thermal shock and thus suitable for the nose cones of rockets. And we Canadians felt quite superior, since we did not have to engage in such packaging techniques.

When Canada began to award **strategic grants,** the changes did not occur on the insistence of the granting agencies or the Federal government, but in response to pressures from the universities and from university-based researchers who were hoping for access to new funds. In my view, this development shifted the decision on the nature of the knowledge, to be produced at the university, even more towards outside influences.

Let me return now to the questions I asked earlier: If universities and colleges have turned into publicly equipped knowledge-production sites, what kind of knowledge is being produced and who will receive it? In other words, who can ask questions, who gets answers?

Elementary, dear Watson, the funders ask or approve of the research questions and will receive the results; the results may become publicly available through publications and reports, although the research strategies and the context of the questions may limit the general usefulness of the findings

Worse still, many significant problems remain unresearched or underexplored because of lack of recognition and funding. Just compare the fate of peace research at Canadian universities over the past decades to the growth of business schools in the same time span and at the same institutions.

Where does this leave us, as teachers and as citizens? Our long and hard fight for public investment into higher education has yielded industrial scale production sites, that are essentially assembly plants for economically useful knowledge and training facilities for skilled practitioners. They are profitable plants, but not universities or colleges in terms of the definitions offered earlier. These plants are not places to transmit to the young, values, knowledge, insights, skills and critical abilities to cope with the future – unless one believes that the global future is solely profitable commerce and business as usual.

Those of us who consider teaching and research a form of stewardship for the future, find that the essential academic decision-making is taken out of our hands. What we are to teach and how to teach it appears no longer a subject of academic and social discourse, but has become a "market decision". What then can we do if we want to retain Canadian universities and colleges as institutions serving the public interest?

Let me urge a concerned response on three levels:

The first level is **clarity:** We need to analyse, discuss and be clear on the new economic and political structures imposed today on universities and colleges. Much of this work is being done, though it needs to reach wider circles.

Second is **solidarity:** What we are discussing here is not so much a university problem, but the university manifestation of a general, technologically facilitated shift of power and accountability. The impact of this new mis-distribution of power is felt in many other public institutions in Canada; solidarity with them should be part of our response.

The third level is **politics:** We are citizens of Canada and have the legitimate right to be governed, rather than to be administered on behalf of global commerce. The protection of public institutions from interferences is in the end a matter of governance, a matter of establishing and safeguarding public/private boundaries. As history has shown over and over again, there is no substitute for good government. It has to be part of the present response, so that it may be part of the future.

Academic Freedom or Commercial License?

WILLIAM GRAHAM

In December of 1996, a seriously flawed agreement passed without challenge through a series of governing bodies of the University of Toronto: the Executive Committee of the Governing Council, the Planning and Budget Committee, and the Business Board. The donor agreement between the Joseph L. Rotman Charitable Foundation and the University of Toronto in fact conflicted with the University's own policies and its Statement of Institutional Purpose. It was only stopped at a meeting of the senate-like Academic Board in the face of heated objections from the U of T Faculty Association, individual faculty, including the Dean of Medicine, and the student newspaper *The Varsity*.[1]

The Rotman Foundation had pledged $15 million to the University's faculty of management for the laudable purpose of creating "the pre-eminent school of business in Canada and one of the most distinguished in the world"—called "the vision." For its part the University would contribute endowed adjustment funds (money saved by not contributing to the employees' pension plan because the plan is in surplus) as matching funds to create six new endowed chairs.

"The vision" required

> the unqualified support for and commitment to the principles and values underlying the vision by the members of the faculty of management as well as the central administration . upon the continuing ongoing support demonstrated by the members of the faculty.

Such language blatantly violated the University's policy commitment to academic freedom:

> Within the unique university context, the most crucial of all human rights are the rights of freedom of speech, academic freedom, and freedom of research. And we affirm that these rights are meaningless unless they entail the right to raise deeply disturbing questions and provocative challenges to the cherished beliefs of society at large and of the university itself. It is this human right to radical, critical teaching and research with which the university has a duty above all

> to be concerned; for there is no one else, no other institution and no other office, in our modern liberal democracy, which is the custodian of this most precious and vulnerable right of the liberated human spirit.[2]

Despite its clear violation of academic freedom, the Rotman donation agreement had passed without objection through three of the University's top governing bodies. The acting provost even stated with pride that

> given the magnitude and importance of the gift, the University is prepared to make a number of undertakings that in a number of ways involve new commitments or variances from previously approved allocations or from University policy.

These "undertakings" allowed the donor, if dissatisfied with progress toward "the vision," to redirect to some other purpose not only the donor's investment but the matching funds from the University; allowed for an advisory committee of external business people to "be consulted by all search committees constituted at any time in the future of faculty of management appointments;" and committed significant amounts of the University's future resources to the vision designs of the donor—a promise the University has never been willing to make to its own faculties and departments.[3]

Even more scandalous in many ways was the donor agreement between the University of Toronto and Mr. Peter Munk, together with his corporations, Horsham and Barrick Gold, which preceded the Rotman agreement but came to light at the same time. This too passed through the same University oversight committees without objection; even though it explicitly created a "business-academic relationship," it was not even sent to the Academic Board for perusal. Munk agreed to donate $6.4 million over 10 years to the Centre for International Studies. In return, the University promised Munk's project would "rank with the University's highest priorities for the allocation of its other funding, including its own internal resources." No mention was made of the need to protect academic freedom or any other basic University policy.[4]

Instead, an advisory board including former Prime Minister Brian Mulroney and advised by former U.S. President George Bush was set up to "provide such assistance and resources . as the board in its discretion considers appropriate, and the council (of the Centre) will be receptive thereof." Since Munk, like Rotman, could withdraw funding at any time over the 10 years if dissatisfied with the progress of the Centre, he was in a position to exert enormous influence over the teaching and research activities of the Centre. What, for example, might happen to an untenured faculty member of the Centre who spoke out in ways perceived as contrary to the interests of Horsham or Barrick Gold corporations?

In January of 1997, the University signed another donor agreement with Northern Telecom Ltd. (Nortel) for $8 million to set up the Nortel Institute for

Telecommunications, including two matching-fund chairs and three junior tenure-track positions, all to be appointed "in consultation with Nortel." Notably absent were any references to University policies and any commitment to academic freedom and freedom of research for the appointees. Would Nortel's opinions about the usefulness of an appointee's research play any role in promotion and tenure procedures? Since the agreement provides for certain Nortel technicians as well as a permanent oversight Nortel representative to work at the University, there are sufficient grounds for serious concern. Moreover, the secret section of the agreement concerning intellectual property rights has never been disclosed.[5]

Such secrecy pervades the whole realm of university-corporate donor agreements. None of the above agreements was voluntarily disclosed by the University even to its own Academic Board. Only after they were ferreted out by the Faculty Association and *The Varsity* did anyone take them seriously.

A March 1999 conference on "Secrecy in Science" at M.I.T. addressed threats to the scientific integrity and academic freedom of university scientists who speak out freely about their research: scientists such as David Kern at Brown University, Betty Dong at the University of California, San Francisco, and Nancy Olivieri at the University of Toronto. Long attributable mainly to governmental-military research, secrecy has in our era moved to corporate-industrial sponsored research, as governments promote university-industry partnerships for commercializable research as engines for national economic growth while shielding them from public scrutiny. Faculty associations will be challenged to defend academic freedom, scholarly integrity, and publicly accessible research.

That universities are involved in the practicalities of the world is, of course, nothing new. Basic and applied research, contemplation and practicality have coexisted as long as there have been universities, perhaps as far back as Plato's academy. But the balance between them has never been easy to identify or maintain. The CAUT's Information Paper on University-Business Relationships in Research and Development states:

> Universities are not monasteries. Each generation has to seek the balance anew because each epoch poses new problems.

This is demonstrated by the 1999 Report of the Expert Panel on the Commercialization of University Research, "Public Investments in University Research: Reaping the Benefits," written at the behest of the Prime Minister's Advisory Council on Science and Technology. It recommends that universities redefine their missions, adding to teaching, research, and service to the community a fourth mission: "innovation," defined narrowly as "the process of bringing new goods and services to market, or the result of that process"—or, in the words of the Report, "commercialization."

> We have no time to lose in establishing the conditions necessary to
> enable universities to perform to their full potential in commercial-
> izing the results of publicly funded research.

If the Expert Panel has its way, commercialization as an integral mission
is to become a condition for federal research funding.

> All intellectual property created from research supported in any part
> by federal funding . must be assigned to the university for possible
> commercialization.

Indeed, "universities must provide incentives to encourage their faculty,
staff and students engaged in research to create intellectual property,"
incentives such as "recognition of innovative researchers in tenure and
promotion policies." In other words, faculty members must become entrepreneurs. There are to be wholesale changes in federal tax policies to support
commercialization of research by reducing "the top rates of marginal tax on
personal income" for entrepreneurs, reducing "the arm's length restrictions on
RRSPs," amending "the tax treatment of employee share options," and
amending "the $500,000 lifetime capital gains exemption" for university
entrepreneurs.[6]

The Expert Panel included no experts from among university personnel
actually involved in the kind of research which has led to commercializable
results. John Polanyi, U of T Professor of Chemistry and Nobel Laureate, said
of this attempt to turn over control of the results of publicly funded research
to the private sector:

> This is the major threat to universities in the coming decade. . . Even
> in an era of commerce we need enclaves where the views of
> researchers have not been purchased. . . There is a cultural shift under-
> way. This relates to the university's attitudes to their central product,
> knowledge. This used to be regarded as a common good, but is in the
> process of being reappraised as intellectual property, and intellectual
> property is being narrowed down to commercial property.[7]

Crass commercialization of knowledge encourages or mandates secrecy in
partnered research and donor agreements. It ties publicly provided university
resources to private, commercial interests, upsets the delicate balance between
basic and applied knowledge and research, and undermines academic freedom
in favour of commercial license. In short, it cheats the public. The bias of
money steers research topics as well as approaches and, because university
teaching is so intimately wed to research, it steers teaching programs and
course content as well. Commercialization of knowledge in the present context
is emphatically not in the public interest.

Those who claim market forces themselves ensure the public interest is
looked after are dead wrong. When public funding becomes linked to partnerships with industry in favour of whatever is commercially exploitable, what
happens to areas of human life and experience not for sale or not exploitable

for profit research? UNESCO has designated the year 2000 as the International Year of the Culture of Peace. Will research into peace garner profits? What of research into homelessness, hunger, racism, sexism, general health, or clean water and air? Who, if not the public purse, will fund such research and knowledge?

Who shall protect the public interest against the encroachments of market forces when governments too are compromised? The federal Health Protection Branch, mandated to protect the public health interest, is becoming an agency for the management of risk to profits by the pharmaceutical industry. Federal research granting councils report to the Ministry of Industry, with the predictable result that government industrial policy influences university research funding. Moreover, granting councils themselves accept donations from private corporations, further compounding private sector influence over public funding of university research. Private corporations not only get a 100% tax deduction for such contributions, they also direct the specific research purposes which their donations, together with the requisite public moneys, will fund.[8]

Scholars and scientists are not entrepreneurs. They live out Aristotle's observation that the desire to know is one of the most basic human drives—more even than sex—whereas the desire to sell is contingent upon certain economic relationships. The scholar and the scientist pursue knowledge, faithful to the drive of their discipline; and they must preserve academic freedom and scholarly/scientific integrity. The entrepreneur knows no equivalent freedom. His integrity is paying his bills and abiding by the laws; his "freedom" is a mere license to sell; his (wholly contingent) drive is to market goods and services, to develop products, and to maximize profits. Scholarship and entrepreneurship are two different cultures, two different kinds of life: the life of the mind as opposed to the life of the bottom line. Some individuals manage to balance two such lives, but it is never easy: they risk turning a silk ear into a pig's purse.

The Expert Panel on the Commercialization of University Research was set up at the behest of the Prime Minister's Advisory Council on Science and Technology. How did it come to be that governments are now less interested in science policy than innovation policy? Why are they demanding partnerships, commercialization, and control of intellectual property? For decades the standard answer has been because post-secondary education is underfunded by governments financially strapped because of rising debt and deficits. They were forced to make program cuts, curtail spending on universities and basic research, and make up the difference by raising tuition fees and urging partnerships between universities and the private sector. A simple matter of cause and effect: lack of funding necessitates higher fees, commercialization, and private sector involvement in higher education.

But what if the *reverse* is true? What if the *cause* is actually the desire to link universities more closely to industry; to privatize public higher education and subject it to market forces; to harness and manage university research as an engine for economic growth in the so-called knowledge economy; to prioritize and promote the creation of knowledge for private profit? What if underfunding is the *effect*? Underfund in order to drive our public institutions into the clutches of private industry? Underfund to force commercialization and privatization of knowledge? Promote deliberate underfunding to cause distress? Deliberately raise tuition fees while holding back on student loans and refusing grants? Deliberate touting of the importance of the knowledge economy while cutting back on core support for education? Deliberate channelling of public funds to private sector partnerships, deliberate gridlock between federal and provincial levels to ensure that post-secondary education cannot be fixed? If this sounds like a plot—maybe it is.

In September of 1995, an Ottawa symposium was sponsored by Industry Canada, the three federal research granting councils (NSERC, MRC, and SSHRC), Statscan, and corporations such as Alcan and Nortel's R & D subsidiary BNR. The bible that was thumped was Michael Gibbons' book *The New Production of Knowledge*, its message that knowledge is produced in the context of its applications. It is outcome and product driven, not discipline driven, not knowledge for its own sake. Universities are old-fashioned, discipline-based iron cages. It is only the applications, outcomes, and products of knowledge which matter.[9]

At the same symposium, Tom Brzustowski, the newly appointed head of the Natural Sciences and Engineering Research Council (NSERC), argued there were new expectations for universities: namely, government expects the research community to stimulate economic growth through innovation. He defined innovation as "bringing new goods and services to market value added," almost exactly the same words used by the Expert Panel some three-and-a-half years later. Canada, he asserted, was good at basic science and education but poor at turning knowledge into value added products. University researchers were not responding to the needs of industry. But, asserted a director of the U.S. National Science Foundation, the charmed life led by university researchers since the 1950s was now over. Goals and outcomes of research must be known beforehand; get used to the new agenda.[10]

Seven years earlier, in April 1988, the Science Council of Canada concluded a comprehensive three-year investigation of university-industry linkages with a report entitled *Winning in a World Economy: University-Industry Interaction and Economic Renewal in Canada*. Here is what it said:

> A new economic order based on global competition in knowledge-intensive industries is emerging.

Canada's deteriorating competitive position in knowledge-intensive industries poses a clear threat to its economic future.

Universities need to engage more actively in the economic renewal of Canada. They must reorient some of their activities to provide the teaching and research required by the private sector.

Fundamental questions are being hotly debated: the pursuit of knowledge for its own sake versus knowledge developed to serve economic or social purposes; autonomy versus accountability; and academic freedom versus institutional planning and management.

A reassessment of the university's mission is necessary. Priority is now given to liberal education and fundamental research. Universities must contribute more effectively to economic renewal.

Hiring, tenure and promotion systems should increasingly recognize, support, and reward the transfer of knowledge and technology (to the private sector).

The concern that industry might use its financial clout to threaten academic values seems unwarranted. Universities are, in fact, far more at risk from the lack of participation by industry than from too much collaboration.

Canadian universities as a whole have little choice. If universities do not reach out to meet the needs of society, these needs will be satisfied elsewhere and universities will diminish in importance.[11]

In October of 1999, yet another flawed U of T donor agreement emerged, this time a $13.5 million agreement with Bell Emergis, a division of Bell Canada, to create four matching-fund chairs and four junior tenure-track positions in the Bell Emergis University Labs. Bell Emergis will fund the positions, the labs, and research projects approved by a committee composed of eight members, four each from Bell and the University. This arrangement gives Bell significant control and veto power over which research will be funded for commercial purposes.

Echoing the Report of the Expert Panel on the Commercialization of University Research, the University claims full ownership of the intellectual property generated by faculty researchers under this program. The University then

> grants an exclusive option to Bell Emergis to obtain from the University an exclusive, perpetual, world-wide license to make, use, reproduce, sell, modify, and sub-license, with a right to further sub-license, any intellectual property on commercially reasonable terms and conditions....[12]

The agreement contradicts the University's own policies on intellectual property, according to which both the individual researcher and the University share in such property. Never mind. The University has assured Bell that in order to be considered for research funding under this agreement, faculty researchers must sign over intellectual property rights to the University for transfer to Bell. No signature, no funding! If Bell takes up the option on a piece of intellectual property owned by the University, faculty researchers lose all rights to modify the invention or to capitalize on it themselves. Moreover, they are bound by strict confidentiality rules and lose moral rights to the intellectual property. (A moral right is the right to maintain the integrity of the work in relation to its uses. For example, atomic energy researchers may have a moral right which prevents their invention being used for purposes of mass destruction.) It is as if the university researchers have been rented out to a private corporation. There is in fact so little difference between university researchers and Bell researchers working in the same lab that the contract actually contains a section on how to distinguish them. You can tell a university professor from a Bell employee, it says, by their different medical benefit and pension plans!

As public institutions, universities pledge to protect academic freedom, not trade it off for commercial license to private corporations. Yet, in the most celebrated academic freedom case in our era—the case of Professor Nancy Olivieri at the University of Toronto—the University utterly failed to protect a faculty member's academic freedom and utterly failed to deal fairly with continued harassment against her and her colleagues. Indeed, the president of the University went so far as to lobby the Prime Minister of Canada on behalf of the very private corporation which had threatened the professor.

Attacks on academic freedom in the face of commercial license will intensify unless consistent and countervailing forces are brought to bear by university faculty members and their faculty associations, and unless the public-at-large is fully informed and armed with determination not to allow the public interest to be corrupted by private sector special interests and governmental compliance.

Mobilize. Organize. Act.

Commercialization and Resistance

WAYNE N. RENKE[1]

I shall pursue my topic from the perspective of a staff association politico whose research specialization is neither the history nor the sociology of the university. The matter being taken over is clear enough: post-secondary education includes our teaching, our research, and our self-governance, what we might call our peer-review form of governmentality. But it raises six main questions:

What do we mean by commercial take-over?

Is post-secondary education being taken over, and, if so, is the take-over of sufficient scope to warrant our concern?

If post-secondary education is being taken over, how is the take-over occurring—what is its mechanism?

Can we stop the take-over?

Should we stop the take-over, either in whole or in part?

How should we stop the take-over?[2]

COMMERCIAL TAKE-OVER

Talk of a commercial take-over resonates on five levels:

an observational level;

a level of concern with risks associated with economic relationships;

a level of concern with institutional directions and priorities;

a level of concern with the quality of post-secondary education; and

a level of analysis respecting the conceptual framework within which post-secondary education is coming to be understood.

Observational Level

In one sense, what is meant by the commercial take-over of post-secondary education is obvious. It is the common subject of common room chat, and the subject of empirical analysis. In this sense, post-secondary education is claimed to be subject to a commercial take-over in that many elements of post-secondary activity have been drawn into relationships with external business or are being treated as if they were business activities, and, judged from a prior, better publicly-funded time, the number of commercial relationships has increased and is increasing. Research is, allegedly, more and more often funded by private businesses. Public funders are favouring research projects with commercial applications or commercial links. Teaching is, allegedly, more and more often packaged and sold to consumers, particularly in distance education programs. Even institutional space seems increasingly to be for sale to external business interests, as named classrooms and facilities and on-campus advertising proliferate. Post-secondary education is, allegedly, more and more often treated as if it were a business by administrations, which adopt business-like management styles; by provincial governments, which impose performance indicators appropriate to corporate divisions; and by students, who, like sophisticated consumers, want good value for their ever-increasing tuition dollars. Academics are, allegedly, more and more often urged to be entrepreneurial, or to keep the customers satisfied, or both.[3]

Risks (and Benefits, Too)

In this sense, the commercial take-over of post-secondary education concerns not merely the economic relationships of post-secondary institutions, but the risks or potential influences supported by those relationships. He who pays the piper calls the tune: if external businesses are funding research or have decisive influence on the availability of research funding, there is a risk that, directly or indirectly, external businesses will dictate to researchers. Insofar as researchers are seeking external business dollars, there is a risk that they will constrain their selection of research topics, the type of research they perform, and the publication of results, to favour current or potential business clients.[4] Influence need not be confined to relations between particular researchers and their particular business sponsors. Large commercial sponsors may exert pressures on institutions. Representatives of large commercial sponsors may be granted political authority within institutions.

Talk of risk presupposes that the threatened events would cause damage to the matter subject to the risk. The skewing of research by private interest is a risk, given that research done at post-secondary institutions should not be affected by private interest, given that this research should be objective and impartial. It has been suggested that one of the main reasons academic researchers are provided with their privileged tenured positions, giving them freedom from the market, is just so that they are able to produce objective and impartial research. Our research, as the conference title has it, should be in the public interest, not in the private sponsors interests.

The concern with risks of economic entanglements should not be dismissed as the product of excessive sensitivity. Consider, by way of analogy, the position of judges. We expect judges to render impartial decisions, based on the law and the evidence. We would doubt the impartiality of a judge paid by one litigant. To preserve judges from improper influences, we guarantee judges independence, including their financial independence. Judges are paid from the public purse, with minimal governmental involvement in the setting of the compensation. Similarly, we expect academic researchers, researchers at public institutions, to render impartial, objective decisions on the evidence, according to the rules of their discipline. Academic impartiality appears threatened if research is funded by a party interested in research results.

While the commercial take-over of post-secondary education is accompanied by risks of skewing the post-secondary enterprise, risks and actual events should be distinguished. The existence of risk does not entail that any particular researcher or research has been tainted. Whether risks have become realities requires investigation of particular circumstances.

The concern with risks is real, but it should not be exaggerated. We cannot assume that just because a researcher is paid by a particular sponsor, the researcher will abandon his or her scholarly integrity to favour that sponsor. Some researchers, no doubt, are willing to abandon principles for dollars. It would be insulting to the research community to think that all researchers would. Even if we do not consider researchers' natures to be of stern enough stuff to resist economic enticements, we should keep in mind that peer review, publication, informal peer scrutiny, and institutional policies may deter malfeasance. Bent researchers are sometimes caught, and their careers irreparably damaged. Even a hint of impropriety may be damaging, so maintaining good research ethics is prudent. Self-interest motivates ethical work. Furthermore, while some sponsors may desire research to bolster particular products or interests, other sponsors may not expect their research funding dollars to have any direct connection to any product they are currently marketing or planning to market.[6] It would be insulting to the business community to think that *all* donations or *all* research funding must be expressly or by implication a payment for donor-favouring research.

If we choose to speak of the risks of business investments in post-secondary education, it would be churlish at least not to mention the benefits of business investments. Business provides money that post-secondary education would not otherwise get (in current circumstances). Some staff would not be working, and some research could not be done, without external business funding. We should also take care not to make unwarranted assumptions about persons in the private sector. They may truly have the interests of the post-secondary education at heart. The University of Alberta provides an excellent example. The chair of our Board of Governors is Eric Newell, the C.E.O. of Syncrude, a very large player in the Canadian oil industry. Mr. Newell, at a time when university staff seemed to be receiving very little public support, took our case to the Alberta Tory convention. He argued that deficiencies in post-secondary funding were harming our universities' abilities to recruit and retain staff. We at the University of Alberta were grateful for his intervention. Mr. Newell has consistently been a champion of the University's interests. Admittedly, other business leaders with influence over post-secondary education may not have the same good record.

Priorities and Directions

In this sense, the commercial take-over of post-secondary education concerns differential allocations of resources within institutions. Because private dollars may be available for some units on campus, and not others; because significant public funding may be available for those same units, and not those same others; because those same units may be in the enviable position to run more successful fund-raising campaigns than those same others; and because base grants to institutions are not large enough to permit administrations to correct economic disparities, some units on campus may be better off economically than others. They have greater resources, and are in a position to obtain still further resources. Success breeds success. Some diversion of institutional resources to these units (e.g. to pay for various overheads not otherwise paid for by external funds) is inevitable, as is the diversion of institutional or administrative attention to these areas.[8] The have areas of campus tend to be units whose output (research and students) has great market relevance—such as the Faculties of Business, Engineering, Medicine and Oral Health Sciences, or Pharmacy and Pharmaceutical Sciences, or the Department of Computer Science. Have areas may be in a position to hire new staff and erect new buildings. Have-not areas may find it difficult to find funds to hire instructors to ensure that basic course offerings remain available. Have-not areas may feel starved out or ghettoized.

Commercialization issues of this type are particularly difficult for institutional communities, since units that are successful are frequently justly successful. They deserve the funding they have won—judged, at least, by the prevailing funding criteria. Those funding criteria, moreover, are not set by particular institutions but by external bodies. Institutions and staff may have some influence over those criteria, but not necessarily decisive influence. The members of successful units are members of the academic community, and it would ill behoove staff associations and administrations to advocate measures that would specially prejudice those members. Other areas of the institution should be improved through strategies that increase resources for the whole, without tearing down parts.

Concern for Quality

To claim that post-secondary education is suffering a commercial take-over may be to claim, implicitly, that the quality of post-secondary education has declined, and is at risk of declining further. In ordinary parlance, to say that an activity has been commercialized is to suggest that its quality is not what it once was. What was formerly creative and inspiring has become standardized and diluted so it may appeal to the greatest number of consumers. In the post-secondary context, this sort of claim entails that we can identify some past academic benchmark, when education had higher quality than it does now; that, according to specified criteria, the quality of post-secondary education is measurably less than it was at the benchmark time; and that, if a measurable decline has occurred, its cause is commercialization. Each of these points, of course, is debatable. (Some no doubt would argue that none of the points can be established, and that commercialization has enhanced post-secondary education by making it more responsive to the concerns of students and the external community.) We should avoid the implicit allegation of decline in quality inherent in this sense of commercial take-over, unless we have evidence to justify it.

Conceptual Change

Least obviously, but perhaps most significantly, talk of a commercial take-over brings us to the contrasting ways in which we have traditionally understood and differentiated educational activities and marketplace activities, and to the colonization of educational activities by commercial categories. Working out the full nature of traditional educational and commercial categories would exceed my appointed space. In lieu of a proper discussion, please accept the following abbreviated phenomenological reflections.

Talk of a commercial take-over or the commercialization of post-secondary education assumes that the thing being taken over was, and to a degree still is, non-commercial. Non-commercial activities, in contrast to commercial activities, are pursued more or less for the sake of the activities themselves and for any intellectual, spiritual, or physical benefits that might accrue. Non-commercial activities are not pursued, or not primarily pursued, for profit. Non-commercial activities are not designed to fit into the market. Some forms of education have been openly and happily commercial, such as courses of study designed to transmit defined sets of information or skills. Education has always had a financial aspect: it costs money to operate a facility, recruit and retain instructors, and acquire teaching and learning materials. Courses come for a fee called tuition. Staff are paid salaries. One might say that a Vice-President (Academic) can never exist without a complementary Vice-President (Finance). Moreover, many do not pursue education just for the sake of education. Many students hope that their education will get them good jobs in the external community. Those who are academically inclined may hope that their jobs secure academic appointments. Post-secondary education is ringed round about and shot through with markets.

Post-secondary education, though, while *in* the market, has not been *of* the market. Post-secondary educational activities, at least in our recent history, have not been regarded as commercial activities. Post-secondary education does require, as a practical condition of its institutional possibility, the satisfaction of adequate economic or financial conditions. With those conditions satisfied, a space is created that is precisely free from the market, so that researchers can research, teachers can teach, and students can learn; so all can pursue, in various ways, the true, the good, and the beautiful, without any direct or immediate need to fit their activities into the market. Post-secondary education should transmit skills (e.g., the ability to read, analyze, comment critically, and communicate) and discipline-relevant information. Yet more importantly, it should spur the transformation of the student, through the student's participation in learning. Through the work of scholars, post-secondary education should develop knowledge and forms of creative expression. Both students' transformations and scholars' research take the form of public dialogues, discussions, or conversations (and sometimes arguments). The parties to the academic conversation vary, yet the conversation, which bridges time and space, is open to any who make the effort to understand and participate.

The commercial take-over of post-secondary education may be understood as a re-conceptualizing of activities formerly understood as non-commercial. Commercialization, the application of market concepts to education, occurs in many forms, in many areas, in relations between the university and the external community, in relations between members of the university community, and even within ourselves, insofar as we are constituted as educational vendors or purchasers/consumers.

We might take a page from Foucault's description of power, and describe commercialization as a multiform instrumentation: it is not univocal; it takes no single invariant form.[9] Commercialization (as, one might add, a form of power) cannot be localized in a particular type of institution or state apparatus; its relations go right down into the depths of society.[10] We might, nonetheless, point to three main features of the commercial: the commercial requires vendors, purchasers, and need.

To begin with, an individual or set of individuals is constituted as a vendor or seller. The constitution of the vendor has three moments: motivation, commodification, and translation. First, the motivation of the vendor is no longer the pursuit of an activity for its own sake, but the making of money. The second moment, commodification, is complex. The vendor transforms his or her activity into units or commodities, becomes a producer of commodities. That is, his or her activity becomes bounded, limited in form and content. Activity producing goods or services for profitable sale must be limited to a reproducible length and the activity must be sorted into units that are manageable and can fit into an accounting scheme. In contrast, activity carried on for its own sake can drift on in any length, in any direction. Commodities must also have or be recognized to retain their integrity for more or less lengthy periods of time. The paradigm commodity is a physical object, the product of manufacture. Intellectual productions can be conceptualized as analogous to physical objects, and can be individuated, held as property, and sold. Commodities are limited not only in form but in content. Commodities must be units of the type that will likely sell. This feature of commodities requires that the vendor anticipate the needs of prospect purchasers, and design the units of his or her goods or services to satisfy those needs. Third, the vendor must translate his or her perception of need into a dollar value for the commodities.

Complementing vendors are purchasers. Purchasers are individuals characterized by need, by a feeling of lack or incompleteness, which they are not competent to satisfy themselves. Need requires for its satisfaction the goods or services of vendors.[11] In substitution for the non-commercial relationship of community, the basis for the relationship of vendor and purchaser is this abstract perception of need. Purchasers too translate their needs into a dollar value.

Purchasers and vendors meet in the market, where they communicate through prices. In the marketplace, money talks. People need not. Since need and its dollar translation are the media of communication, the vendor and purchaser need not share any other common orientation. Purchasers are fungible; they may be completely anonymous. Purchasers, moreover, have a passive character. They do not participate in the creation of goods and services, but await their supply, then consume them. This does not mean that purchasers are powerless. They have their dollar votes. They may also express a lack of satisfaction through a satisfaction survey. Such surveys, though, reiterate passivity. Their point is that the vendor should have done a better job of satisfying the purchasers.

The key role of need in the constitution of vendor and purchaser is manifest. Need is anticipated by the vendor, experienced by the purchaser, and translated into a dollar amount. Furthermore, vendors may seek to create needs that do not have a natural base, may shape needs, and may attempt to convince purchasers that they cannot satisfy their needs without vendors' products.

In view of the foregoing, in the last sense, the commercial take-over of post-secondary education is the transformation of teachers and researchers into vendors, the transformation of teaching and research into commodities, the transformation of students and recipients of research into purchasers, and the transformation of conversation into market transactions.

THE SCOPE OF THE COMMERCIAL TAKE-OVER

What evidence do we have of a commercial take-over of post-secondary education, in any of the various senses? I can only speak, in a not very scientific way, of the situation at the University of Alberta.

On the level of commercialization as the proliferation of relationships between post-secondary education and business interests, I can report that some departments are virtually untouched by commercialization. Other departments have enjoyed long-standing relationships with the business community.[12] Certainly University of Alberta researchers have significant connections to industry and to the commercial development of intellectual property. The University of Alberta participates in all 14 Networks of Centres of Excellence.[13] In 1997–1998, the University had licensing revenue in excess of $4.3 million, the highest of any Canadian university, and the 25th highest of North American universities.[14] The University is ranked at or very near the top rank for spin-off companies from university research.[15] The University and its spin-offs hold more than 230 patents.[16]

Do these relationships import risks of academic impropriety? Risks have doubtless been imported, but, to my knowledge, no risks have crystallized into academic malfeasance for economic reasons, nor have funders attempted to influence research improperly. We have not had an Olivieri case. I freely concede that my ignorance is not determinative of the facts. Our community is aware of the risks, and has established policies to reduce them. The University of Alberta has a Conflict of Commitment and Conflict of Interest Policy.[17] This policy defines conflicts, provides for disclosure of conflicts, and creates a Research Overview Committee, which may permit, permit with conditions, or prohibit research projects respecting which a staff member has a conflict. Violations of the policy are disciplinable. We also have a University-Community Relations Policy,[18] which again deals with conflicts of interests, and forbids publication delays in excess of 18 months. We have a Research and Scholarly Integrity Policy, which prohibits dishonesty and fabrication in research. This policy requires that researchers apply

> stringent standards of honesty and of scholarly and scientific practice
> in the collection, recording and analysis of data . . . and other
> information, and in the dissemination of information . . . .; and avoid
> conflicts of interest and commitment, and the real or perceived bias
> that may arise from such conflicts; reveal to sponsors, universities,
> journals or funding agencies, any material conflicts of interest and
> commitment . . . . Our collective agreements contain provisions
> governing supplemental professional activities.[20]

The agreements confirm that staff members have primary responsibilities to fulfil University responsibilities, but recognize the importance of professional development achieved through professional activity, supplementary to those primary responsibilities. The agreements distinguish between major and minor SPA, with special rules applying to major SPA, and require that Faculty Councils develop regulations respecting SPA.[21]

Does the University of Alberta suffer from differential resource allocations? We do. Faculties such as Engineering and Medicine and Oral Health Sciences bring in large quantities of external funding. Our Faculty of Arts, in contrast, is in fairly dire financial straits. The 1997/98 budgeted operating expenditures for the Faculty of Medicine and Oral Health Sciences totalled $25,766,000; for the Faculty of Engineering, $17,131,000; and, by way of comparison, for the Faculty of Law, $2,708,000.[22]

Have areas of academic life been commercialized? At the risk of reading more into what might appear trivial than is warranted, one might detect commodification creeping into our day-to-day lives on campus.

We see the manipulation of need through advertising spread across increasing expanses of public space. For example, an arrangement has been made with Coke to be our single-source soft-drink provider. We therefore find Coke dispensers littering our hallways, and, for a time, a large dispenser marred even an historical site (it was promptly removed following complaints). One might object at this point: what is wrong with the Coke deal? The Coke deal does bring benefits to our students: over 10 years, Coke shall provide approximately $5 million for student bursaries and scholarships, with some additional funding for student services. The arrangement was not a unilateral administration initiative. It was approved by an undergraduate student referendum (graduate students, academic staff, and non-academic staff were not given the vote). Admittedly, the benefits of the Coke deal may justify it.[23] Moreover, no one objects to the availability of Coke on campus. Coke was available before the deal was struck, as were other soft drinks. The worry is this: Before the Coke deal, we happened to be soft-drink consumers. The deal, however, expressly constitutes us as a discreet target market, as a community of consumers. We are transformed from a community that happened to purchase certain goods, into a precise target of the vendors of those goods; we become conceived as consumers by virtue of our place on campus. By itself, this imputed labelling is harmless enough. In conjunction with the more extensive commercialization of university life, the labelling becomes one more strand in a smothering blanket of commercial conceptualization.

Some units on campus have been explicit vendors of services for fees, such as design of Web-based courses. Budgetary constraints do make fee-for-service approaches necessary for some units. Again, the worry is that this budgetary tactic contributes to the propagation of self-understanding in terms of the vendor/purchaser relationship.

Commercialized instruction is a growth area. I do not speak of our Faculty of Extension, which has offered informational and skills courses to the public on a commercial basis for many years, but of our new enthusiasm for distance education and continuing education for businesspeople. Distance education need not be commodified. It may be, simply, education delivered through distance-spanning technology. It becomes commodified when education becomes conceptualized as a product or service which must be modularized or carved up into purchasable segments, offered so that the institution may make a profit, and marketed on the basis of manufactured purchaser needs.

I must confess to a fear that at least some regular course instruction has taken on a distinct vendor/consumer appearance. Consider law school instruction: For all of its faults, the old Socratic method of instruction could not be thought of as commodified education. It demands, through the questioning of the student by the teacher, active participation by the student in the educational process. To the extent that the Socratic method is abandoned, to the extent that law students do not participate in class room analysis and discussion, to the extent that they are treated as (and adopt the attitude of) passive consumers of pre-packaged professorial words—to that extent law school classrooms replicate the vendor/consumer relationship. Regrettably, the Socratic method is in definite decline, and no equivalent pedagogical alternative is immediately obvious. We play a role in the consumerization of our own students.

Some less tangible influences of commercialization may bear on staff-administration relations. Particularly troubling is the widespread passivity of staff respecting important issues, such as the Reviews for the President of the University and the Vice-President (Academic) and Provost of the University; a proposed intellectual property policy that would have taken important rights from staff and brought new types of work under the policy; and the interference by the Premier of Alberta in our institutional autonomy, through his complaint to our President about a symposium held on campus (which allegedly cast Albertans as greedy and insufficiently concerned with the poor). Staff remain active, engaged, and highly productive in their professional areas. Within those areas, they are certainly keen to any perceived interference with their own academic freedom. Their passivity concerns institutional issues. This is doubtless the result of many factors, including sheer overwork and exhaustion of staff doing their jobs the best they know how in an under-resourced environment. Staff are too busy to worry overmuch about institutional issues. Insofar as commercialization drains resources away from the institution as a whole to select parts of the campus, under-resourcing, resulting staff overwork, and the loss of the opportunity to engage in collegial institutional governance may be laid at the feet of commercialization.

Commercialization could also impair the morale of staff who may be doing excellent work, but are simply not in a position to compete for market-oriented funding opportunities. Some staff may be disenchanted by watching dollars flow to other units, dollars that lie outside their grasp. Commercialization in its broad cultural aspect may be at work as well. Staff might be perceived to be acting as consumers, outside of their professional lives. They have been conditioned to a passive role because of the role of the market in their lives outside (and inside) the university, so they adopt that role even when it is not appropriate. Staff as consumers might be understood to be relying on the expertise of the administration (or even, to put a good face on things, on the expertise of their staff association). Consumer passivity could reinforce any administration tendencies towards autonomy. We are reminded of John Ralston Saul's remark that if citizens do not exercise the powers conferred by their legitimacy, others will do so.

In view of the foregoing, one could conclude that the University of Alberta has become commercialized to a significant degree. Other universities and colleges, we might predict, are in more or less similar states of commercialization.

THE TAKE-OVER MECHANISM

If it is conceded that a commercial take-over of post-secondary education is occurring, one issue that arises is the nature of the cause of the take-over: who or what is responsible? The answer is complex. Different species of commercialization are not the effects of a single cause. Rather, at least six main sets of interacting and overlapping causal factors may be identified.

The first causal factor is negative: the decline in and the lack of provincial and federal public funding for post-secondary education. Had post-secondary education adequate public funding, it would not need to court external business dollars and be subjected to the influence and direction that increased business involvement may entail. Commercialization may well have occurred even if post-secondary education had been adequately funded, but lack of funding has at least eased the commercialization process.

External businesses may exert commercialization pressure. They do so, despite their good faith, when they provide funding to institutions, if the funding is restricted in any market-related way. Members of business organizations who sit on boards of public funding agencies, who have the ear of government, or who hold seats in institutional governance organizations may also exert commercial influence, if only inadvertently.

Government may exert commercialization pressure. The Alberta Department of Advanced Education and Career Development (as it then was), signalled that university research should be oriented toward the commercialization of new knowledge and technology. It favoured partnerships and strategic alliances with, among others, the Alberta Research Council, business, and community groups. Significant new funding opportunities made available through the federal and provincial governments are market oriented or require matching dollars from external, typically business, sources. Alberta's Intellectual Infrastructure Partnership Program provides funding for university research, to the tune of about 40% of project costs. I2P2 requires a significant (about 20%) private sector contribution to each project. Alberta's Science and Research Fund provides funding for, inter alia, infrastructure developments, strengthening R & D partnerships, and intellectual property transfers. While Arts and Culture are a selective focus of the funding program, the strong focus is on such areas as agriculture, biotechnology, engineering, forestry, and health and medicine. The provincial government's use of key performance indicators as a basis for funding (even if the real effect of the indicators is only rhetorical) treats post-secondary institutions as if they were part of a business. The federal government's Canada Foundation for Innovation has a similar market orientation. It provides funding for the acquisition, modernization, or development of research infrastructure. It encourages partnerships with businesses, provincial organizations, and voluntary organizations. CFI will fund up to 40% of project costs. Remaining costs must be funded from other sources.

Institutional administrations may exert commercialization pressure. Post-secondary educational institutions need money. Administrators are under compulsion to look for it where it might be found. It might be found in the hands of external businesses alone, or it might be found by combining business dollars with government programs, such as the CFI or I2P2 programs. It might be found by doing a better job in-house of commercializing inventions of staff and by creating spinoff companies. If administrators are under pressure to maximize revenues and minimize costs, they can hardly be blamed for thinking in a business-like way, and for bringing a business-like approach to their part of institutional governance.

At the intersection of business, government, and administration lie creatures like the Expert Panel on the Commercialization of University Research. This Panel is funded by Industry Canada and reports to the Advisory Council on Science and Technology, which in turn reports to the federal Cabinet. The Panel's nine members include the President of NSERC, two administrators charged with intellectual property commercialization, and employees of private businesses. The Panel's recommendations strongly urge post-secondary education in a commercial direction. The main purpose of the recommendations is to increase wealth creation in Canada, and, expressly, not to produce new revenue streams for universities. The Panel recommends that universities add as their fourth mission, in addition to teaching, research, and service, innovation (or identify innovation as an element of the three other missions). By innovation, the Panel means the process of bringing new goods and services to market, or the result of that process. The Panel encourages the participation of small- and medium-sized enterprises, and supports the creation of spin-off companies to commercialize publicly funded research. The Panel wants universities to make reasonable efforts to commercialize home-grown intellectual property. If the Panel's recommendations are accepted by the federal Cabinet (and a decision has not been made to date), post-secondary institutions will be propelled toward the market.

We should not forget that commercialization is not always imposed, whether by business, government, or our own administrations. Sometimes it is the result of our own actions. We may freely choose commercialization, or choose to work in areas that are directly relevant to the marketplace. Some academics take on consulting jobs. More importantly, the type of research an academic wishes to pursue may have commercial applications. He or she is able to do good work, generate some revenue, and benefit not only himself and his or her institution, but consumers of the research product.[24] Staff who advance commercialization are not passive victims or unwitting dupes of external forces of commercialization.[25]

The last and most powerful set of causal factors directing us to commercialization is cultural. We live in an ever-more commercialized world. We are consumers of vast arrays of goods and services outside our academic lives. Coming to think of education in commercial terms may be inevitable, as we are coming to think of health care and other public goods in commercial terms. Adopting marketplace solutions to issues outside the market may seem natural. If the rest of our lives are turning into fragments of the market, why should post-secondary education be immune? We might consider student evaluations of teaching. These evaluations were introduced as a defensible component of a multifaceted, formative teaching evaluation process.[26] They have become, in at least some parts of the University of Alberta, the *sole* means of teaching evaluation. In the eyes of many staff, they have ceased to serve their original purposes, and have become mere consumer satisfaction surveys, telling more about professorial popularity and the emptying of challenge from courses than about instructional expertise. How did this transformation occur? Perhaps we might better ask, How could the transformation *not* occur?

CAN WE STOP THE TAKE-OVER?

Before asking whether we should try to stop at least some aspects of the commercial take-over of post-secondary education, we must ask whether we have the ability to do so; *ought* implies *can*. If we cannot stop the take-over, we might be inclined to go down with some grand gesture, like Horatio on the bridge, but we might not be inclined to recognize an obligation to oppose commercialization or commend others to follow our example.

Are we helpless? Is commercialization just too broad and too deep to permit us any significant chance of turning it back? No, we are not helpless. Power is always accompanied by resistance.[27] We maintain the possibility of inverting even dominant relations. We should remember as well that the organizations we confront, particularly institutional administrations, tend not to be unified or coherent. They are not monolithic power blocs (the same can be said of our own organizations). Persons in organizations may pursue a variety of ends, strategies, and tactics. Various elements in organizations we confront may seek to control us, but may do so in diverse ways and may have differing motives.[28] Various elements in administrations, such as our Board Chair, may even be entirely sympathetic to our position, and may be able to sway policy our way. If resistance is possible, though, it is not necessarily easy.

SHOULD WE STOP THE TAKE-OVER?

One might again turn to Foucault, and suggest that not all commercialization is bad, but that it is dangerous. It does import risks. In particular cases, however, it may bring great benefits to post-secondary institutions. Individual commercialization projects or adventures must be assessed on their merits, and neither swooningly embraced nor obstinately rejected. We must look and see.

Which commercial take-overs should be stopped? In light of what I'll say in a moment about how we go about stopping commercial take-overs, I cannot, on my own, purport to identify particular targets and strategies for even my own campus, let alone others. I can offer only some general considerations:

The starting point must be the mission of the institution, assuming that the mission statement is accepted as correct by staff. The mission tells us what the institution should do. Institutions should perform their missions to the best of their abilities, and not perform their duties in a substandard way or engage in actions that prevent them from performing their duties. Generally, institutions will be committed to excellence in undergraduate and graduate instruction, and to excellence in research. There must be a shared understanding of the nature of excellent teaching and research—otherwise, a standard for judging benefits and harms is lacking.

The degree of harm caused or risk of harm to an aspect of the mission raised by a particular commercialization effort must be assessed in all of the circumstances. Both direct and indirect risks must be addressed (direct risks might include interference with the types of issues researched and the types of questions asked and solutions offered; indirect risks might include (e.g.) diversion of staff from the normal distribution of their duties to focus on lucrative duties; increased institution overheads caused by taking on externally-funded projects; unfair revenue returns to particular Faculties or Departments, given service teaching or other relevant instruction by other Faculties or Departments; or potential effects on the morale of staff not in the unit achieving the benefits).[29] An important aspect in a harm analysis is the effect of the project on the assessment of the institution by the public. Will the project tend to bring the administration of post-secondary education into disrepute? Will taking on the project contribute to a political climate that supports reducing public support for universities? (For example, if the project brings the institution significant revenues for assisting a private corporation, the public might reason that if the institution wants to play in the private market, it ought to be treated like a private corporation, and should not be subsidized by taxpayers).[30]

The benefits sought by the project must be assessed. Generally, to justify any harm caused to the performance of the institution's mission, the benefits must promote some other significant aspect of the institution's mission. For example, a project might harm one department, but enhance another; it might advance research but impair teaching. If the project promotes a legitimate objective, benefits and harms must be balanced. In balancing benefits and harms, it should be determined whether any of the (particularly) financial benefits could be redistributed and used to repair or mitigate any damage caused. It should also be determined whether any processes or procedures could be instituted that would reduce or control risks of harm —for example, institutions should have in place conflict of interest policies respecting external research similar to the University of Alberta policy.[31] It should be determined whether any reasonably available alternative courses of action are available that would allow the institution to achieve the benefits sought, without causing harm or risk of harm to its performance of its mission.

The process leading to the decision to undertake the project and the process of balancing harms and benefits must be appropriate. The chain of approvals of internal governance bodies should be followed and not subverted. Even if the decision to undertake a project falls to the administration under its management rights, unilateral non-consultative administrative action must be resisted. All interested parties must have adequate notice of the project, and should have the opportunity to respond thoughtfully.

HOW DO WE STOP TAKE-OVERS?

I am embarrassed at the obviousness, simplicity, and probable lack of helpful-
ness of what I have to say about stopping the take-overs that *should* be
stopped. We should do what we've been doing, but better. Here's what I mean
(and I will refer to the university context):

Outside the university, other communities are struggling to find institutions
that will give voice to their concerns and considered judgments and that will
permit them to work together to develop solutions to the challenges they face.
They are seeking to reclaim what Michael Sandel refers to as their republican
freedom, their freedom to govern themselves. They are seeking a space that
lies between two great functionings—on the one hand, the market, with its
vast anonymous individualism; and on the other, municipal, provincial, and
federal government. Between the market and government, they are seeking to
find the ground of civil society, of local politics, of democratic community
interest; in Benjamin Barber's words, the third sector that mediates between
our specific individuality as economic producers and consumers and our
abstract collectivity as members of a sovereign people.[32]

We are remarkably privileged. In our relatively autonomous enclave of the
university, within our academic communities, republican freedom is not
merely our aspiration, it is our right. It is the third aspect of our academic
freedom, in addition to our freedoms to teach and do research. It is our right
to self-governance, our right to subject policies, programs, and proposed
courses of action to peer review. We are fortunate again that our common
interest, the set of objectives which we share, is defined for us (if only
vaguely) the promotion and protection of teaching, research, and self-governance. We are not forced to work out among ourselves the ultimate objectives
of our community. Furthermore—to the probable envy of other communities—the institutional foundation requisite for the exercise of our self-
governance has already been, to a large measure, constructed for us through
our university policies and regulations and our collective agreements. We have
departmental and faculty councils, linked to the overarching senate or general
faculties council. We have committees internal to faculties and departments.
We have university committees, reporting to vice-presidents and presidents.
We have members on our boards of governors. We have members who
become, for a time, chairs or deans, before returning to the ranks. In some
cases, members of our administration remain our members (and remain
practicing academics) while in office. We have, of course, our staff
associations, and their wide range of committees and opportunities for
insertion in university politics. We have members involved with virtually
every decision-making body on campus. We have seats at every table. We

have the institutional foundation for confronting commercialization on campus.

What of the fact that commercialization cuts across and beyond particular campuses? To quote Barber again: We live in a world of multinational corporations, global environmental and communication ecosystems, and transnational economic and cultural forces. We cannot solve, one by one and locally, the big infrastructural social problems created over half a century by national and transnational power.[33] We have, however, established coalitions that can trace the seams of commercial power. On the vertical axis, many staff associations belong to provincial associations of staff associations. Many belong to this national association, the Canadian Association of University Teachers (CAUT), which has international links. On the horizontal axis, back at our campuses, we have working relationships with the non-academic staff associations, with the graduate students associations, and (while these relationships may sometimes be more rocky) undergraduate students associations. We can reach out to other local labour organizations. We do not, of course, have the financial resources of even a good-sized corporate exploiter of university intellectual property, let alone a multi-national pharmaceuticals company or the World Bank. We are, though, rich in people, rich in networks.

So why is there a problem of commercialization? If we already have the structures we need, why has the problem not been better contained? What have we not been doing? To a degree, we have been doing what we should be doing. We have been acting in our local, provincial, and national communities, sometimes with small success, sometimes with none.

On the issue of our success, we should not be too hard on ourselves. The job of containing commercialization is huge. It must be approached with the humble understanding that we, as individuals, at some particular time in some particular forum, are not likely to be able to reverse tendencies that have the momentum of centuries and that have tendrils reaching into the most public and most private aspects of our lives.

But neither should we be complacent. We can do better. We have not used our best asset to our best advantage: our people. I referred before to our members' passivity. Our great challenge is to take steps to overcome that passivity. We must begin, to use the old expression, by raising consciousness, so our members gain a clearer understanding of what is to be lost and what is to be gained through commercialization on campus; and we must then motivate our members to exercise their rights to self-governance. We want them to deliberate about the issues, work out solutions, and execute those solutions in the various arenas of university politics. We cannot impose any views or courses of action on them. Opinions will differ. Our job is to encourage our members to work out local solutions they can live with.

But who is this *we*? Who has this great challenge? The *we* that faces the great challenge is that group of people who, through ambition, fate, or absent-mindedness, have become leaders in their communities. At least in its beginnings, the commercialization campaign calls on good leadership. Leaders have the responsibility to start to make things happen.

What is to be done? Here again, I cannot dictate to local circumstances, and I do not for a moment minimize the difficulties we face. I can only offer some suggestions for local association presidents (do as I say, not as I did.). The president needs time to work with the members. The staff association should therefore pay for release time for the president—the job of president is, for at least many people, a full-time job. If the president is given the time, then the president can do the job the president should do. And that job is pretty simple. The president should lead from in front. The president should ensure that he or she speaks to commercialization issues whenever the matter arises. Not just in homilies to the converted at staff association meetings, but at senate or general faculties council, in meetings of university committees. Speaking out will not make the president a one-trick pony. To speak out on commercialization is to speak out about academic freedom, which covers the expanse of our professional lives, and which we are obligated to defend.

The president and executive should attempt to involve as many members as possible in staff association committees and functions. Staff associations all have their troopers, familiar faces that have often provided decades of service, and their commitment must be maintained. But we also need to engage new people, get them working with us.

We must continue to do what academics do best: communicate, through our media, at our meetings. Staff associations might also consider doing what academics do second-best: create committees. An association might constitute a commercialization watchdog or oversight committee, or give a commercialization oversight mandate to an existing committee (such as a research and scholarly activity committee). Problems can be identified and tactics discussed at this level, and advice may be given to the association's greater assemblies.

We must ensure that our members who sit on various committees across the institution are in contact with the staff association executive. Information and assessments must flow in both directions.

As one small matter, we must ensure that we have seats on selection committees for senior academic and even non-academic staff—or at least that we have guaranteed input. The power and influence of individuals in local contexts cannot be discounted.

We must organize, plan, and prepare our local political activities at least as well as our student unions.

We must engage, as is appropriate, in provincial and federal politics, in lobbying, in standing committee hearings, and in elections.

We have all of the institutional structure we need to address the commercialization of post-secondary education. How we exercise our rights to self-government, what we do with our privilege of peer review, is our responsibility.

PART 2

Privatizing Knowledge

When Money and Truth Collide

NANCY OLIVIERI

Four years ago, I found myself at the centre of events which Professor Arthur Schafer, Director of the Centre for Professional and Applied Ethics at the University of Manitoba, later described as "the greatest academic scandal of our time." Those events show that for-profit companies have infested and infected Canadian public institutions. In this particular instance, a profit-oriented company worked in its own interest at an institution, Toronto's Hospital for Sick Children that claimed to be dedicated to protecting children's health. The scandal shows the effects of federal government promotion of inappropriate industry/university partnerships, and is a symptom, to paraphrase Bill Graham, of the sickness inside health care and research funding in Canada.

The story has been termed, but is not, "a scientific controversy." It is about a company which, with two respected institutions, the University of Toronto and the Hospital for Sick Children, sought to suppress scientific debate. These events were not "caused by a band of troublemakers" but rather brought to public view by a few people who stood up for patient protection and scientific integrity, and to whom this talk is dedicated.

In the early 1990s, Dr. Gary Brittenham (now of Columbia University, New York) and I began to study the effects of a new drug, an iron-chelating agent called Deferiprone or "L1," in Canadian children with a fatal blood disease, thalassemia major. I was the Principal Investigator of a trial supported by an operating grant from the Medical Research Council of Canada from 1989-1992. In 1993, to ensure the progress of these trials we signed a legal contract including a confidentiality clause that is, we are now advised, illegal under Canadian law with a Canadian generic drug company, Apotex Inc. That clause was intended to prevent me from disclosing scientific findings without permission of the company.

The company agreed partially to support the work in exchange for the opportunity to commercialize the drug, should trials go well. We at first thought the drug to be promising and published our data in the *New England Journal of Medicine* in 1995. We later observed that the drug was not only working inadequately in patients, thereby exposing them to complications of iron overload, but directly caused liver and heart damage.

We sent revised consent forms to the Research Ethics Board of the Hospital for Sick Children, and also to Apotex, aiming to inform patients of our new and worrisome findings. Within seventy-two hours, the company acted, abruptly and prematurely stopping the trials, sweeping all Deferiprone from the shelves of the hospital pharmacy, and on the basis of the confidentiality clause, threatening me with "all legal remedies" should I inform patients, parents, regulatory agencies, or the scientific community about the potentially life-threatening toxicity we had discovered.

Note that Dr. Brittenham and I were the only medical experts Apotex ever consulted in this matter, up to the moment Apotex began to make its threats. Together, we designed and implemented the only three trials (two in Toronto, another one-year short-term toxicity trial mainly in Italy) from which Apotex submitted data to regulatory agencies for permission to sell the drug. I was the Principal Investigator in two of these trials. Dr. Brittenham, a world leader in the evaluation and management of iron overload, and I were Co-Chairs of the Scientific Committee of the third trial conducted in Italy. The two Toronto trials were not only terminated prematurely by Apotex, when we raised objections to the drug, but Apotex them removed me as Co-Chair of the Italian trial. Dr. Brittenham voluntarily resigned his chairmanship because of the actions of Apotex. Other less experienced and less principled investigators in Italy and the US continued the year-long study, not designed in the first place to examine efficacy.

Apotex promptly began a campaign to vilify me personally and professionally. It has since pursued efforts to license the drug in Europe and Canada. Apotex has not yet tried to obtain licensing in the United States, although many more patients in the United States than in Canada are affected by thalassemia. Why?

The answer lies in the radically de-regulated system of drug approvals at Health Canada, the drug companies' awareness of this fact, and a similar arrangement in Europe. The United States would insist upon at least minimal evidence of safety and efficacy, not available for this drug.

Many have sought to claim that the drug's safety is a "complex issue" and a "scientific controversy." Here, a simple review of the literature is pertinent. Data from the only other trials (outside of Toronto's) to obtain precise evaluation of the drug's effectiveness support my original objections. No expert will deny that while receiving Deferiprone, 40-60% of patients increase their body iron burden to levels associated with premature death. Put another way, the drug is ineffective, and hence unsafe, in more than 50% of patients. There is nothing "complex" or "controversial" about this observation, about which I was threatened with legal action in 1996 and 1997.

In short, the severe health risks to patients using this drug over longer terms, include heart and liver disease, endocrine dysfunction, and premature death in children and young adults, persons for whom proven, safe, and effective treatment already exists.

In 1996, after I informed the Administration of the Hospital for Sick Children, and the University of Toronto, of the possible effects of this drug's toxicity in their own patients, these institutions sided with Apotex. Unknown to us, the Hospital and the University were at that very time negotiating a donation of $25 million, to be matched at least in part by other sources. This was to be the largest donation ever made to a university in Canada. The President of the University of Toronto, Mr. Robert Prichard, was personally involved in the campaign, and lobbied Prime Minister Chrétien on behalf of Apotex in a letter written August 30, 1999, urging the government to relax its restrictions on generic drug firms, such as, yes, Apotex.

After his letter was unexpectedly leaked to the press, President Prichard was induced to apologize for taking a stand in favour of a drug company, inconveniently one from which he had hoped and angled for a large donation. As it turned out, the government did not relax restrictions on generic drug firms and two weeks ago, the President of Apotex reneged on the donation to the University of Toronto (withdrawing $20 million dollars of the promised support), citing lack of sufficient profits over the past five years.

Despite threats and absent institutional support, we did notify our patients, inform the regulatory agencies in Canada, and two years later in August 1998, publish our data in *The New England Journal of Medicine*. (One month before my paper was published, The Hospital for Sick Children hastily declined a donation from Apotex, rumoured at $10 million.)

Over the next six months, the administration of The Hospital for Sick Children (possibly still disappointed at the need to turn down such a large donation six months before) tried repeatedly to dismiss me. Over the last three years, they have sought no fewer than four times to remove me from my position on trumped-up charges.

I was rescued the last time through the efforts of family and friends who spent, and continue to spend much of their time in outspoken support of academic freedom and the protection of patients in clinical trials; through the intervention of prominent figures in the international research community alarmed by actions taken by a supposedly reputable University and Hospital and who campaigned to have the University reverse my January dismissal; and through the work of the University of Toronto Faculty Association, which has now brought on behalf of my colleagues and me the largest grievance ever launched at the University of Toronto.

After my reinstatement in January 1999, the University and Hospital agreed to pay my legal fees to date, return my job to me, indemnify me against all costs in the event Apotex went on to sue me, declare all allegations against me "without force and effect," and provide me with a paid year-long sabbatical. On the other hand, none of the concessions grudgingly agreed upon in January 1999 by the Hospital have come to fruition. Most importantly, that 1999 agreement did not resolve the central matter: the preservation of academic freedom, scientific integrity, and the protection of children in clinical trials.

As Dr. Howard Frumkin said in circumstances like mine, the case of Dr. David Kern, formerly of Brown University, the ethical implications of the case are "so straightforward as to be almost uninteresting." As physicians, we are morally and ethically, as much as legally, bound in all circumstances to act in the best interests of our patients. What can we as scientists and researchers learn about health care research, and about the pressures we experience because of decreased public funding, and increased funding from the private sector?

Are we, to begin with, truly under threat? Don't most responsible universities and teaching hospitals successfully fight corporate influences? Although there are several examples in which a university kept its public duty, I know of none where an academic institution stood up to challenge a drug company issuing threats against a lone investigator.

Let us consider the responsibilities of those involved in clinical trials, often with the goal of evaluation of a new drug.

None of us should, of course, sign restrictive contracts. My contract was, as has been little publicized, co-signed with the Associate Director of the Research Institute of the HSC, the Second-in-Command at the time. Was Apotex legally on solid ground when it threatened me throughout 1996 and 1997 with "all remedies" should I inform patients, parents, regulatory agencies, or the scientific community about my concerns? Dan Soberman, former Dean of Law at Queen's University, writes that

> Under common law, any contractual clause is void to the extent that
> it offends public policy. Accordingly, to the extent that such a clause
> prohibits disclosure of information about a medicine that might
> reasonably be believed by a researcher to cause harm to the health of
> a person taking that medicine, the clause is void. Period. (*Macleans*,
> 23 November 1998)

Clearly, among matters to be considered in drug development must be the precautionary principle, which states that where doubt exists, and where human lives and health may be at stake, individuals in authority do not proceed without a reasonable assurance that it is safe to do so. If safety is in doubt, ethics dictate that we err on the side of caution. Throughout history, this principle has been stated variously, the Nuremberg Code, the Declaration of

Helsinki, Canadian common law, and the Hippocratic Oath being among many adumbrations.

What of the conflict of interest of individual investigators? In June 1996, I observed that 36% of patients exposed to the drug I was testing would exceed thresholds of body iron that expose them to a heightened risk of heart disease and therefore early death, based upon guidelines in the medical literature. I believed that caution was in order. I was immediately defamed by another group of investigators, who then, one month later, reported that not 36%, but 50%, of the patients exposed to the same drug will exceed thresholds of body iron that expose them to a heightened risk of heart disease and therefore early death. Yet, this group offered an overwhelmingly favourable interpretation of these data, admittedly to the amazement of much of the scientific community. It is clear that many if not most medical researchers will take, literally, the "company line" on drugs if the said researchers have been paid and supported, or financed, by the company conducting the trials.

Arnold Relman, professor emeritus of medicine and social medicine at Harvard Medical School and editor-in-chief emeritus of the New England Journal of Medicine, has pointed out that as budgets for research money from governments shrink, biotechnology and pharmaceutical companies sense their opportunities. And medical schools look for money where they can. Pharmaceutical companies and venture capitalists therefore come to make deals. For a modest investment, companies use the resources of the medical schools– the brains, the laboratories, the people--to work on projects in which they are interested. They dangle research grants and contracts before faculty to entice them to work on problems the companies want to pursue, in the manner the company desires, with questions phrased as the company likes. Companies have the right of first refusal, and faculty in turn have equity interest in the companies.

These conflicts of interest are worsening. One is reminded of Professor Ursula Franklin's phrase, "The University as a production site."

What are the responsibilities of the regulatory agencies? We now know the Health Protection Branch, Health Canada, is a deregulated body. It is under investigation for its actions with respect to the blood scandal. Our government purchased blood products from Arkansas prisons at a time when other countries, including Burma and China, refused this product for safety reasons. As a result, our blood supply was widely infected with hepatitis C virus.

Is the regulator responsible for the patient in the clinical trial? Absolutely. But Health Canada stories are discouraging. I came to Health Canada in the summer of 1996 to report on the lack of effectiveness, with Dr. Brittenham, my legal counsel, and two representatives of Apotex who, after having threatened me with legal action should I inform regulatory agencies of my concerns, insisted on being present at that meeting. One can see why. After Dr.

Brittenham and I had reviewed the potential threat to patients, the Head of the Bureau of Biologics leaned over and winked at the Vice President of Apotex. Why? Perhaps to indicate, "Don't worry; these concerns will go the way of others." Chillingly, this story brings echoes of the statement by a senior administrator at Health Canada in the days of Thalidomide, when the company manufacturing this teratogen was denying "rumours" (actual reports from Australia and Europe) of limb deformities: "The drug companies are our friends."

A second, more recent Health Canada story: This June, I travelled to Ottawa to explain my objections to this drug. Representatives of Health Canada first declined to meet with me, saying the matter was "too controversial." My lawyers convinced them the meeting was necessary. The people with whom we met included several senior officials, one of whom asked me to relate to her all the evidence I had showing the drug was toxic. Dr. Michele Brill-Edwards, formerly senior physician in charge of drug approvals at Health Canada, and a strong supporter, cited a section of the *Food and Drug Act* stating that it is not only incumbent upon me, as a lone investigator, to prove to Health Canada that the drug is toxic, but that Health Canada was compelled, under the relevant section of the *Food and Drug Act*, to prove that the drug is safe. As Dr. Brill-Edwards spoke, the group became increasingly dismayed.

Finally, I come to the responsibilities of our public institutions. How should, and how do universities act when confronted by the academic/ corporate conflicts inevitable in times of shrinking budgets? Far from struggling to uphold and protect the principles of academic freedom and scientific integrity, to protect the lone investigator, scientist or doctor, in the face of for-profit companies, such as Apotex, in situations such as mine, most universities and hospitals do mostly...nothing. Many uphold the principles of profit perhaps with promises of 25 million dollar donations to sway them and thus disregard their duty. In doing so, these institutions abjure public health responsibility, as well as ethics, as shown by the examples below.

Some illustrative cases: Dr. David Kern was an occupational health physician at Brown University when he observed a pattern of increased frequency of development of interstitial lung disease in workers at a nearby industrial plant, Microfibers. He submitted an abstract to a scientific meeting detailing this finding and the observed relationship between the occupational exposure and the development of the lung disease. Dr. Kern was threatened with legal action by Microfibers because on one of his visits to the Rhode Island plant he had signed, on entry to the plant as do all visitors to this plant, a form stating he would not reveal "trade secrets" of the factory. Dr. Kern was dismissed and the occupational department at Brown closed, through the actions of hospital and university administrators who were financially beholden to Microfibers. He nonetheless published his findings in 1998, but has relocated to another state and Brown university is the poorer for it.

Dr. Betty Dong is a researcher at the University of California, San Francisco. She began a trial, for the company Knoll Pharmaceuticals (Boots) to demonstrate the relative effectiveness and safety as between the Knoll formation of Synthroid, a drug used for hypothyroidism, and a generic formation. When Dr. Dong found these two formations were equivalent in effectiveness and safety, she learned this was not the answer Knoll Pharmaceuticals had in mind. The opposite conclusion would have provided Knoll with millions of dollars of increased revenue. Knoll threatened Dr. Dong with legal action, forced her to withdraw her paper from *JAMA*, and began a campaign of intimidation and pressure, including the hiring of private investigators, to trail Dr. Dong. Dr. Dong eventually published her findings in 1997, in *JAMA*, after the company capitulated.

Professor Neil Tudiver's fine book *Universities for Sale* describes the case of Peter Desbarats, showing how corporate donations influenced his behaviour while Dean of Journalism at the University of Western Ontario.

And in 1996, when Apotex warned me not to disseminate my objections to the drug, the Hospital for Sick Children and the University of Toronto declined to provide me with legal support.

Universities and institutions generally behave in a manner characterized by "the 4 Ds":

Deny. The Hospital and University began by denying a problem by stating the existence, not of an institutional conflict of interest, but of a "scientific controversy," and the Hospital recruited non-experts, paid by Apotex and the University, to support this opinion. Having created this fiction, they were able to express the desirability of "not taking sides."

In my case, the University elected not to intervene when Apotex immediately, abruptly, and prematurely withdrew funding which would have allowed me to continue evaluating Deferiprone in clinical trials, 72 hours after I forwarded altered consent forms for patients requested by the Research Ethics Board of the Hospital for Sick Children, which Board had mandated a change in these forms to inform the parents of my concerns. Next, the same Dean and President stood by while Apotex transferred large sums of money to the research accounts of Professor Gideon Koren at the Hospital for Sick Children. As a non-expert in the field, Dr. Koren then co-authored inter-pretations of my data with Apotex employees, without my prior knowledge or consent or that of Dr. Gary Brittenham (Professor of Medicine at Columbia University, New York, who had generated all the primary endpoints of the trials). The support from Apotex and its subsidiaries to Dr. Koren are a matter of public record{3}. Finally, when a committee was launched to investigate a "re-interpretation" by non-experts of my data without her knowledge or consent, the same Dean and President declared that such behaviour was entirely appropriate at the University of Toronto, and did not constitute a breach of appropriate research conduct.

Professors at the University of Toronto should now note that any non-expert colleague may publish data they have generated without their prior knowledge, review, or consent.

What was the importance of the University and Hospital's claim of a scientific controversy? In fact, this fiction created a "defence" but did not change the fact that the precautionary principle states that where any doubt exists, and where human lives and health may be at stake, individuals in authority do not proceed without reasonable assurance that it is safe to do so. And if the safety of proceeding is in doubt, authorities err on the side of caution.

Delay. Administration at the Hospital and University quietly, and determinedly, said and did nothing becoming "dogs that didn't bark in the night." They hesitated, waffled, deferred, hid behind legal technicalities, and ensured their future in the hottest regions of the Inferno, reserved for those who, in times of great moral crisis, maintain their neutrality.

Divide. There were attempts made to alienate and divide our supporters at the Hospital through an aggressive Administration campaign combining fear (including written gag orders and threats of job security), private undermining, and the courting of prominent individuals. Many of our public supporters were deluged with letters from individuals in Senior Administration defaming me personally and professionally. The Hospital became and remains a divided institution.

Discredit. Institutions characteristically launch a campaign to discredit independent-minded researchers in cases like mine. The University of Toronto was perhaps emboldened by the promise of 25 million dollars from Apotex. Characteristically, institutions abandon and undermine individuals who deliver bad news. The HSC and the U of T sought to outdo each other, and Apotex, in vilifying me publicly. The Chairman of the Department of Pediatrics and senior members of Administration initiated a public campaign of retaliation in which e-mails were forwarded all over Canada by Dr. Hugh O'Brodovich, the University Chairman of Pediatrics, vilifying me personally and professionally. I and those in my innermost circle were quickly characterized as "difficult." Our honesty, moral character, and professional abilities were questioned. Demotion and firing followed in my case, triggering a profound deterioration in professional productivity. Our finances have become a huge problem. The defamatory statements about both my professional abilities (for which I had been formerly lauded by Apotex) and my personal character (aggressively attacked by Apotex and the Chairman of Pediatrics of the

University of Toronto in several communications obtained through the *Privacy Act*) make interesting, if horrifying, reading.

In August 1999, Apotex succeeded in having the drug licensed for sale in the European community, through a Commission that did not adequately consider safety and did not review in full the available data. In October 1999, we issued a judicial challenge to that decision, based upon errors of fact and of law.

How can this sorry situation be repaired? Currently, we hope to challenge the structure of the Hospital through the University Grievance Review Panel, an independent inquiry, and legal options, including our European challenge.

More important, how can we put in place safeguards so this does not happen again? First, universities must recognize that drug companies need them and the patients at the clinical institutions, much more than the other way around. University administration must level the playing field this present moment is time to bring in regulations with bite. Drug companies must be told the simple facts of life that they cannot isolate and threaten lone investigators. Companies must learn they, too, have to follow the rules.

The words of another person who lost everything for standing up for principle, David Kern of Brown University, should be considered. David spoke eloquently of this at a conference on "Ethical issues in the publication of medical information" in 1998. He observed at the end of the conference,

> Early on we were instructed that well, we all make mistakes, we all display lapses in ethical judgment, so let's not focus on these examples of rarity in human behaviour because they occur so infrequently. Well, I think that evil happens, and ethics is about choices. It is true that it is more difficult to detect the subtle deviations from acceptable behaviour, but this in no way negates the reality that if we fail to address harshly and quickly the egregious gross abuses we haven't a prayer of addressing effectively the subtleties.

As for the University of Toronto, it now appears too late to do entirely the right thing, even as the promise of the now thwarted Apotex donation passes into history. The University had within its grasp an opportunity to act in the public good. Its then Dean of Medicine and its President abjured that responsibility. It is important that by contrast to for-profit companies, our academic institutions do not fail as the University of Toronto and the Hospital for Sick Children did. It is essential that instead, they choose appropriately between the competing interests of finances and truth.

Related Reading

Schafer A. *Medicine, Morals and Money*. December 1998.

O'Brodovich H, Buchwald M. Letter, *Nature Medicine*. 1 January 1999
Olivieri NF. Letter, *Nature Medicine*. 1 January 1999
Weatherall DJ, Nathan DG. Lessons from the unfortunate events at the University of Toronto. Editorial, *The Lancet*, 6 March 1999.
"60 Minutes" CBS Transcripts. 19 December 1999.

Private Interest and Public Peril at the Health Protection Branch

MICHELLE BRILL-EDWARDS

The Health Protection Branch's overzealous regulation of natural products has produced a public reaction unparalleled in our history. Even at the worst of the AIDS crisis, even through the recent blood scandal, there have never been so many letters on a single issue. The Branch has moved from relaxed oversight of natural products to overzealous regulation. Why? And meanwhile the Branch takes a lax view of high-risk products—prescription drugs, blood, and so on. In *both* realms the pharmaceutical interest is being served, rather than the public interest.

I joined the Branch in 1980 as a physician in the prescription drug section. The Branch takes research information on drugs from the very earliest stages of development through to clinical trial and then to marketing, judging drugs' benefit or potential hazard, and using information responsibly to decide whether drugs may be marketed, all of this in the public interest.

I took unpaid leave to return to the University of Toronto in 1983–6 to do research, teaching, and clinical work to qualify as a pediatrician and a specialist in clinical pharmacology. I returned to the Branch with increased duties, and in 1988 became Assistant Director Medical, the senior post for a physician in the regulation of prescription drugs.

At that point I had a baptism by fire. Just as I took over my position, the crisis over AIDS drugs peaked. People burned the Minister in effigy, demonstrating on the lawns of provincial legislatures and Parliament Hill for access to drugs they believed could help them to stay alive. My response was to examine the medical basis for evaluating those drugs, to consider the law, and then to ask about potential availability.

My team and I decided that the enabling law *was* there, and that access *was* allowed. Medical safety considerations need not prevent patients from having access to drugs that may save their lives. Patients and ordinary citizens began to realize you can accommodate the rights of citizens, stay within the law, pay attention to the usual traditions of medicine and science, and yet still provide access to life-saving therapies.

My team was proud of these achievements and of our approach to regulation. Unfortunately, many drugs were still being held up in the approval process, some unnecessarily, while others were speeded along without adequate checks. Since my duties were broad, I turned to other drugs, and there found similar patterns. Some submissions would be held up and nit-picked, yet others would zip through, whatever health questions they might raise.

These facts led me eventually to seek legal council, as I thought I had a duty as the senior physician to bring some of these activities to a halt. If senior managers in the Branch were not going to adhere to the law and allow me to ensure my staff could adhere to the law, then I would have to speak up.

The duty of the Branch is not a matter of discretion, but is imposed by enabling legislation requiring the Minister of Health to enforce the Food and Drug Act. This Act requires that new drugs reaching the market must be subject to research procedures full of checks and balances, akin to a legal process. Anyone who tries to interfere in the process or to change the outcome, for reasons of self-interest, is operating illegally. Only evidence about a drug and experience with a drug should determine whether it may go to trial or later to market or once on the market, to stay there.

I saw these procedures under threat. A drug arrived that brought things to a head, a medication for migraine sufferers. This drug was supposed to have no coronary side effects, and would thus have been an extremely valuable market commodity. Unfortunately, when we examined the file we found distinct evidence of coronary effect. Meanwhile, the submission was rushed through to approval without adequate description of coronary effects. In my judgment as a physician, I believed inadequate description of those side effects would lead to deaths. Indeed, there have been deaths, and litigation is now proceeding in the United States on this matter.

At the time, I was overruled by managers not medically qualified and without appropriate scientific training. One manager was under challenge for an appointment, as not meeting requirements set out by the Department. I joined the ongoing challenge to this appointment in Federal Court. In effect, this was a challenge of the Department's policy of de-professionalization, of appointing senior managers who would manipulate the approval procedures illegally. We won our case: the individual was demonstrated to be unqualified. Even so, little changed in the Department, except that it agreed it no longer needed senior medical advice. The person removed by Federal court order was reappointed six months later, the qualifications for the position having been suitably reduced. I began to realize there would be no investigation of the safety abuses which triggered the original court case.

By then I had won an international competition for a post at the World Health Organization [WHO]. I thought I had done what I could. I was then called into the Deputy Minister's office, and it was put to me that official endorsement of the WHO post would require that I sign a written gag order, that I never speak of the case that had been to court, that I never take legal action, and that I never participate in any legal action that might ensue. This was unacceptable to me as a physician and as a Canadian citizen.

I told the Deputy that it was not for me to negotiate, for private gain, a matter of public safety. I left her office knowing that I would not do what she was asking, but unsure what I *would* do. I returned to another post as a medical advisor in the cardiovascular area of prescription drugs, and worked to make the wrong-doing in the branch public. With the help of public-spirited groups, including blood activists, I tried to remind citizens of their rights, and to show what should have been done to protect their rights under the Canadian *Food and Drug Act* during the blood scandal.

In the meantime, another controversy arose over calcium channel-blockers. This category of heart drugs is used for high blood pressure and angina, then thought to be break-through products. For that reason, the first of these products, Nifedipine (short-acting), was brought to market very quickly—in nine months flat, as compared to the usual three, four, or five years. We knew we did not have sufficient information to justify making the drug available. As new information became available showing this drug to be problematic, we ignored it, despite the *Food and Drug Act*.

Things came to a head in 1995 when the issue became public. I watched as the Department dragged its feet. People not competent to judge the situation buried themselves in paper. An advisory committee to the Department met in secret, and perfunctorily reviewed the drug, and in the private, not the public, interest. I reviewed the file, and found that our staff, as early as 1981-82, had found safety problems which the Department refused to show to the committee. As a seasoned bureaucrat, I wrote appropriate memos and made appropriate interventions, but all for naught. I decided that it was time to leave, to speak publicly, and to stop the travesty.

I resigned and spoke publicly on the CBC investigative programme *The Fifth Estate*. To my shock and dismay, there was total silence afterward. The pharmaceutical industry is very powerful. Then a very happy thing occurred. Senior federal civil servants came to me and said, "You know, we saw the programme, and what we saw matches with what we're seeing in our own departments. We're seeing the same government kowtowing to industries supposedly subject to Canadian law. We're seeing inattention to the public interest."

We subsequently formed a group called the Alliance for Public Accountability. We have a number of purposes, but with respect to health, we have done quite a bit of lobbying, if you want to call it that, although we're not a lobby group, we're citizens. But we've put forward to the government, in as many different ways as we can, the evidence showing the safety hazards represented by some of the above examples.

In response, the Department has repeatedly agreed to investigate, but we know there have been no investigations. The Minister has been questioned in the House, and has misled Parliament in his answers. In October, our press conference on the issue of calcium channel-blockers was reported widely and internationally. The Minister was under sufficient pressure that he agreed to an investigation, then never spoke of it again.

At Christmas of last year, we wrote to every member of the Standing Committee of Health, giving them complete documentation of wrong-doing in the assessment of Nifedipine. The Standing Committee on Health clerk wrote back a perfunctory letter, telling us the committee noted our interest in the matter, but that the agenda for the committee was, sadly, filled for the coming year.

We did not give up. We made a presentation to the Committee on Industry, then reviewing Bill C-91. They thought it sufficiently interesting to include our work in their report, but did not investigate. Again we refused to give up. We went to the Standing Committee of Health on a different issue and talked about drug safety. They were almost unable to believe us, and in any case they were dissolving as there was to be an election call.

One of the seasoned bureaucrats in our group suggested we take it to the Auditor General. The Auditor-General has finally agreed that Health Canada needs a look-in.

Lax regulation of prescription drugs serves the pharmaceutical industry by allowing it a wide and long-lasting market. Similarly, overzealous regulation of herbal products permits multinational pharmaceutical industries to move into this area of medicine. The Branch subjects those products to zealous regulation, and thus out of the market, clearing the way for the multinationals.

This pattern is visible in other countries, where regulatory agencies overzealously regulate natural products in order to "level the playing the field" or, as we might rather say, "clear the way for multinational firms to move in."

As a regulator, I think that you, as citizens, have rights. You have the right to expect any piece of legislation in Canada to be applied fairly and evenly. That is necessity under law, and policy as set out by the Treasury Board for any government activity but especially for regulation. Whenever the Department changes either a law or a regulation, or its interpretation of a regulation, it should do so in an open and consultative manner, and with careful and orderly transition from the old way of doing business to the new.

This has not happened in the case of herbals. The Department is removing herbal products from the market, saying that they are drugs because they are pharmacologically active. As a regulator, I say this is an unworkable interpretation of the *Food and Drug Act*. We have never, in the history of this country, taken the position that because something is pharmacologically active, it will be regulated as a drug. Alcohol, caffeine, and most of the things we use are pharmacologically active. Is the Department really going to require DIN numbers on red wine?

My reaction as a regulator is that this is not a fair interpretation. Will we now have to have to label tofu and oat bran, because they are "active"? There is information that ketchup slows the progression of atherosclerosis, and that suggests we shall have to put DINs on ketchup.

Once you adopt extreme new policies and interpretations, you invite disrespect for the law. You engender in the public disdain for the Department, and undermine public trust required to regulate in a fair and judicious way.

On the matter of claims, consider our attitude to herbal products. The "literature" says that such and such a product should be treated as a drug. Yet we rush through the adoption of short-acting Nifedipine, where we have medical research evidence in the *Journal of the Canadian Medical Association* that this product is causing deaths and "should be abandoned." The Department, the Minister, and his staff have said, "No, we're not going to do anything. Doctors are on their own. Too bad, the claim is not on the label."

Meanwhile, we have not declared nicotine a drug. By the Department's own count, 45,000 Canadians a year die of diseases linked to the consumption of tobacco. To say we are going to regulate herbals, but not call a pharmacologically active substance like nicotine a drug, and not consider 45,000 deaths to be a health hazard—this is truly a travesty. Our neighbours to the south, and their FDA, have declared nicotine a drug in order to be able to use the *Act* to protect the public interest in trying to deal with the hazards of nicotine.

We are Canadian citizens, and live in one of the finest democracies in the world, but we will keep our democracy only if we tend to it. We must understand that institutions operate in their own interest, and that this has led to a culture of deception, a business culture in which deception for the advantage of the institution is acceptable. The institution seeking to protect itself against bad press, against accusations, against any kind of opposition, will not tell the truth. We, on the other hand, *must* require the truth, and send clear signals that we shall accept nothing less.

The mess over herbals is not mere bureaucratic bumbling; rather, there is a business purpose here. The Department will not roll over and play dead just because what we say is sensible and in keeping with Canadian law. We see on the CBC's *Fifth Estate* program what goes on behind closed doors, and how the Department secretly serves the pharmaceutical industry. The panel set up by the Minister has already announced it will operate in secret.

The most important thing we can do is to sustain a vibrant activism through community and public interest groups. Remember that the mission of the Department, and of government more generally, is not to be sensitive to pharmaceutical interests. Its mission under law is to serve the public interest.

Academia in the Service of Industry:
the Ag Biotech model

E. ANN CLARK

Industry agendas, including those of the "life" science companies, have assumed increasing prominence in academic research as traditional government support for non-proprietary research has diminished. At the University of Guelph, for example, between 1987 and 1997, expressed in 1987 dollars:

NSERC funding declined by 27%, provincial funding decreased by 69%, Federal funding increased by 16% (primarily in Centres of Excellence, Research Chairs, etc.), while business/industry funding increased by 117%.

The percentage directly derived from industry has more than doubled in recent years, from 7% in 1987 to 15% in 1999, but it is still a small fraction of the total external grants and contracts, as research administrators are quick to point out. However, as discussed below, through a variety of "matching" fund initiatives, both federal and provincial levels of government are ensuring that industry priorities drive a much larger fraction of academic effort than is superficially apparent.

What are Canadian academics to do if they don't accept the values implicit in industry funding? The withdrawal of meaningful levels of unconstrained[1] public funding for agricultural research in Canada has left academics with few choices:

1. sit on their hands
2. reconfigure their appointment to emphasize teaching at the expense of research
3. learn to ask different and less financially-demanding questions
4. take early retirement
5. suppress ethical, ecological, and other concerns and accept industry funding

The foregoing is hardly a revelation to anyone who has worked in

Canadian universities for the last decade or two. But the time is now, if indeed we are not already too late, to seriously consider the implications of industry encroachment for the future relevance of academia to Canadian society.

GOVERNMENT FACILITATES INDUSTRY ENCROACHMENT

Because this notion may be hard to swallow, let us first consider the steps government has taken over the past 15 or so years to effectively channel Canadian researchers into the service of industry.

First, government diminished its own responsibility for conducting science in the public interest, by divesting itself of a significant number of agricultural researchers and even whole research stations.

In the last decade alone, Agriculture and Agri-Food Canada (AAFC) closed research stations and experimental farms in British Columbia and at L'Assomption and La Pocatière, Québec, and reduced staff to just 1 or 2 scientists at Nappan, Nova Scotia, Indian Head, Saskatchewan, and Beaverlodge, Alberta. Major cuts in both staff and funding were imposed at most other research stations. At Charlottetown, Prince Edward Island, for example, the complement of research scientists was reduced from 24 in 1989 to 17 in 1999. Production agriculture in general and forages in particular were decimated, in favor of industry-friendly disciplines such as biotechnology.

Next to go was the historic role of government as a source of competitive research funding for academics and others to engage in "non-proprietary research"—of the sort that benefits everyone, and hence, is of no interest to industry sponsors.

For example, Benbrook (1999) noted that essentially no progress has been made on IPM (integrated pest management) in the US since the 1993 goal/pledge "75% IPM by year 2000". As is acknowledged by the ERS (Economic Research Service), USDA (1999) in their new report entitled "Pest Management in U.S. Agriculture", the USDA has not even established criteria assessing the baseline level of IPM adoption in 1993, let alone monitored progress in the intervening years. Integrated pest management is a largely non-proprietary technology for pest control, and as such, is a direct competitor for new GE technologies with the same purpose. The 1993 IPM pledge coincided with the emergence of ag biotech issues which have effectively channelized the attention of USDA personnel ever since.

The final hitch in the knot tying academic researchers to the service of industry was the requirement for matching industry funds to even apply for those government funds that still remained (e.g., NSERC Research Chairs; NSERC New Faculty Support Program; NSERC Industrial Research

Fellowships; NSERC Undergraduate Student Research Awards; NSERC Strategic Grants; Industrial Research Assistance Program (NRC); Matching Industrial Initiative (AAFC)).

Industry partnerships are clearly "the way to go" for government to support university research in Canada. Anyone doubting the degree to which government, including the much beloved and respected NSERC, has bought into this notion should have a look at the NSERC website *(http://www.nserc.ca/indus_e.htm)*. For industry, NSERC promises:

> Our shared-cost programs are flexible and responsive and they make business sense. They:
>> stretch your research dollar
>>
>> link you with skilled and knowledgeable people
>>
>> deliver creative ideas and practical solutions
>>
>> promote long-term partnerships; and
>>
>> provide access to specialized facilities and equipment.

NSERC affords numerous avenues for industry to "access"—some might argue "direct"—research at Canadian universities from top to bottom. For the major players, there are *Industrial Research Chairs (IRCs)*, which are intended:

> to assist universities in building on existing strengths to achieve the critical mass required for a major research endeavour in science and engineering *of interest to industry* (emphasis added); and/or
>
> "to assist in the development of research efforts in fields that have not yet been developed in Canadian universities but for which *there is an important industrial need*" (emphasis added again) *(http://www.nserc.ca/programs/resguide/irc.htm)*

The goal is to attract outstanding senior scientists, whose positions are jointly funded by NSERC and industry for 5 years, and who then move into tenure-track positions at their host university. The intent is to fund research "that *presents unique industrial opportunities and responds to industrial needs*" (emphasis added, here and below). Outstanding scientists—who are also in harmony with industry-based research directions and values—are thus inserted into academia at the most senior levels. Three of the several Research Chairs thus funded at Guelph in the last 10 years have focussed on plant and animal biotechnology.

The faculty position assumed upon termination of NSERC funding for an IRC need not have been, and of course often isn't, in the same research area as that which industry saw fit to fund. Thus, to access one of these prestigious IRCs, departments must be willing to sacrifice an existing position and discipline. The sacrificial position may come internally or can be extracted— with the help of sympathetic administrators—from another department.

For those somewhat less well endowed, there is the NSERC *New Faculty Support* grant program, where NSERC will match industrial contributions for up to three years, to bring highly qualified persons into junior level, tenure-track faculty positions. Among the selection criteria, apart from the excellence of the individual, is the following:

> Candidates must demonstrate significant potential to make, or have a proven track record of, *important research contributions of industrial relevance.*

Again, the discipline which industry chooses to support, and which then occupies one of the increasingly scarce tenure track positions in Canadian academia, has no necessary relationship to that which formerly occupied the same position. Plant biotechnology, for example, could displace pasture management.

The decision to fundamentally alter the discipline complement of a given department, which has profound implications for future research service to society, is unquestionably influenced by the opportunity to access fresh funding from industry— and hence, government. But to whose benefit?

For the next level of industry involvement, there is the NSERC *Industrial Research Fellowship (IRF)* or *Industrial Postgraduate Scholarships (IPS)* program to "provide what you are looking for". Industrial seekers are advised "Do you need a qualified scientist or engineer to carry out research in an area important to your future? Talk to us". To qualify for the latter, students "must spend at least 20% of their time working with you at the company facilities". Or, do you "need a top-notch research assistant, but can't afford one?" Not a problem, NSERC will provide funding for up to four months through the *Undergraduate Student Research Awards (USRA)* Program *(http://www.nserc.ca/programs/industrial_e.htm)*. Selection of steady supply of young stock with the requisite sympathy for industrial goals and values is thus ensured.

The net effect of these inspired government and NSERC funding programs is that industry agendas are systematically inserted into permanent tenure-track and support positions at every level of Canadian academia. So, what is wrong with that? Are those accepting industry funding more sympathetic to industry goals and values than those who don't? Can one whose very position originated with a particular industry sponsor objectively address the risks as well as the benefits of the technology owned by the industry?

HOW DOES INDUSTRY BENEFIT?

Apart from the clear value of directly inserting industry-responsive personnel into the ranks of academia, industry receives a variety of other benefits from current government policies on research funding.

Access to academia

The first and most obvious industry benefit is easy access to a supply of talented academic researchers. Professors can offer not just the energy and enthusiasm of a suite of graduate students, post-docs, and technical staff but a well-maintained research infrastructure, much of which is paid for by society. The government funding policy-imposed "hunger" of this population of academics greases the slippery slope of industry encroachment into academia. As noted above, both those with industry-based appointments and conventionally hired academics have little choice but to compete for industry funding—and accept the values implicit in the funding—if they want to access government money to do research.

Leverage

What is arguably the single greatest benefit afforded to industry arises through leveraging. With so little alternative (e.g., unconstrained) funding available, even a little bit of operating money effectively mobilizes or leverages a sizeable amount of university infrastructure. University infra-structure—not just buildings and light bulbs but research capability—was established by and is maintained at public expense. Thus, the roughly $10 million (1998 figures) which industry invests annually to support proprietary research at Guelph allows it to leverage a healthy chunk of the much larger (roughly $250 million) taxpayer investment at the university.

As stated by Smith (1997):

> What corporations desire is a form of socialism in which an exceedingly small level of investment allows them to leverage a vast amount of public funds, thereby displacing the financial risks associated with basic research to the public. But this is a perverse form of socialism, combining the socialization of risks, the privatization of rewards, and the imposition of profound social costs. The more university research is integrated into this perverse socialism, the more pressure will be put on the university as a place of rational inquiry.

Consider the magnitude of what government funding policies have handed to industry: the ability to cherry-pick from a platter of willing academics trained and refined at public expense those individuals who meet your immediate purpose, but without the bother of employing them.

Ownership

Findings and outcomes are very often proprietary, meaning that a newly discovered protocol in genetic research cannot be used even by the lab which discovered and refined it under contract, let alone by colleagues in neighbouring labs, without the express permission of the contractor. Careful research administration can ensure that the results are publishable in a reasonable time-frame in at least some cases, although the hunger issue pertains to research administrators as well as to researchers. There is always another school that can be approached if one is too demanding of academic privilege. And the fact remains that the direction and flow of scientific knowledge are driven, as explicitly intended in the wording of NSERC and government funding policies, not by human imagination, the spark of collegial discourse, or even by perceived societal needs— e.g., what we in academia are paid to do—but by industry interests.

Control: disincentives for non-proprietary research

The vacuum of industry sponsorship for technologies that *reduce* dependence on industrial products is understandable. As a result, however, the requirement for matching industry funds has sharply reduced research into non-proprietary approaches to achieve the same ends (e.g., pest or weed control) which industry claims can best be accomplished through purchase of proprietary products (see IPM above). Compare the $700 million currently spent annually by the federal and provincial governments to support genetic engineering with the *virtually undetectable* amounts allocated to support

> *organic farming* as an alternative to capital- and resource-intensive production practices (including herbicide-tolerant crops)
> *management-intensive grazing* as an alternative to growing annual grains (e.g., corn and soybeans) to support confinement feeding systems, or
> the design of *small-scale production cooperatives* to supply local foodsheds as an alternative to dependence on long distance transport of imported foods in Canada.

Where is a researcher to look for matching funds to support these and other promising initiatives for producing food in ways that are healthy for both society and the environment? The absence of well studied and documented benefits for non-proprietary technologies—the absence of which is unavoidable due to the scarcity of research funding—obliges producers to continue along the path charted for them by industry, for the benefit of industry.

One contemporary example would be the superficially compelling rationale that genetically engineering crops to produce their own pesticide, e.g. Bt corn, cotton, and potatoes, is a superior alternative to the use of chemical insecticides which are known to be harmful to health. Such pronouncements—if factually correct—frame the issue as an "either/or" argument. Reducing the options to either pesticides or genetic engineering ignores the variety of IPM (integrated pest management) and organic approaches potentially available to the same thing. However, as noted in the ERS report referenced above, the commercial attractiveness of non-proprietary approaches is weakened by the paucity of both basic and applied research—because non-proprietary strategies are not attractive to industrial sponsors, and hence, to government funding sources.

Monsanto made just such a claim in a press release dated 21 May 1999, in response to recent research showing an adverse effect of Bt pollen on Monarch butterflies. To support the thesis that Bt crops were less harmful than insecticides, Monsanto stated:

> In 1998 use of Bt insect-protected corn reduced or eliminated the use of broad spectrum chemical insecticides on some 15 million acres of US farmland.

Now that, if true, would be a pretty impressive achievement. So, let's see—some 71 million acres of corn were grown in the US in 1998, and data from the USDA National Agricultural Statistics Service *(www.usda.gov/nass/pubs/rptscal.htm*, courtesy Chuck Benbrook, personal communication) shows only a tiny fraction of corn acreage was treated with insecticides at all. Furthermore, we see that most insecticides are used for rootworms and soil insects, not European cornborer—the target of Bt-corn. Thus, *at best*, Bt-corn could have reduced insecticide usage on **1–2%** of the acreage sown to corn in 1998 in the US—e.g., 0.7 to 1.4 million acres, not the 15 million acres trumpeted by Monsanto. It is therefore somewhat surprising to learn from a survey of 800 farmers by Mike Duffy and colleagues at Iowa State University that growers of Bt corn actually spent more on insecticide ($18/ac) than those choosing to grow non-Bt corn ($15/ac) in 1998 (Duffy and Ernst, 1999).

Thus, industry benefits in a variety of ways from societal investment in Canadian universities. The question is, does society also benefit?

DUBIOUS ASSUMPTIONS

Implicit in all of the various permutations of "industrial partnerships" is the very clear and unambiguous assumption that "what is good for industry is good for society," a premise that seems to have been accepted uncritically, at best, in agriculture. A corollary to the "good for business" assumption is the even more dubious presumption that the goods and services best suited to supporting contemporary agriculture in Canada are necessarily proprietary (e.g., industry-driven). This unvalidated assumption is, at least arguably, a key contributor to both the low returns routinely received by primary producers and the environmental degradation associated with some aspects of contemporary agriculture (e.g., surface and ground water contamination; loss of biodiversity; exposure to endocrine disruptors).

It may seem plausible that governments with a mandate to serve their citizenry, including their farmers, would be motivated to investigate production technologies that are both less damaging to the environment and less dependent upon costly proprietary inputs. In reality, production approaches which may be both more profitable and more environmentally benign—such as organic farming (Sholubi et al., 1998) and management-intensive grazing—are essentially untouchable in today's research environment.

One example will suffice to challenge the assumption that what is good for business is good for society. Recombinant bovine somatotropin (rBST) is the flagship product of the life science industry, and one which was expected to be sufficiently profitable as to warrant an enormous investment by both industry and government.

How might rBST be "good" for society?

Recombinant bovine somatotropin (rBST) is a genetically engineered peptide hormone[2] which purports to force yet more milk out of high producing dairy cows[3]. A variety of arguments have been proposed to rationalize the use of rBST.

Health and welfare?

Does use of rBST promote the health and welfare of cows and humans? On the contrary, use of rBST leaves dairy cows so stressed as to compromise rebreeding and create a whole range of related herd health problems (Kronfeld, 1993; CMVA Expert Panel on rBST, 1998). One of these—increased incidence of mastitis, an infection of the udder, that worsens with increasing milk yield—exacerbates overuse of antibiotics, and hence, risk of carryover of antibiotic resistance into the human food chain. Another risk to human health comes from elevated levels of Insulin-like Growth Factor-1 (IGF-1) in milk from rBST-treated cows. IGF-1 has been associated with increased risk of prostate cancer (Chan et al., 1998). Other risks were revealed in the course of the expert committee deliberations which ultimately led to the rejection of rBST in Canada early this year (CMVA Expert Panel on rBST, 1998). For example, a pivotal Monsanto-run 90-day rat feeding trial, which Monsanto had interpreted as indicating "no toxicologically significant responses," actually found that 20–30% of the rats exhibited immunological reactions. Some male rats exhibited cyst formation in the thyroid, a warning signal for cancer.

Therefore, evidence available to date suggests that use of rBST to stimulate milk production from dairy cows is not consistent with the health and welfare of either the cows or the humans.

Running out of milk?

Perhaps there is some compelling need to increase milk production? With North American milk production capacity well in excess of demand, how can a product which stimulates *yet more milk*—and with so many unacknowledged costs not simply to herd health and profitability (Butler, 1999) but to human health—be of *service* to society? Yet hundreds of industry-funded papers have been published on rBST—many by academics employed at universities with a mandate to "serve the public". The net effect is a product that no major industrialized country—with the exception of the US—will allow. From a societal perspective, the problem is not scarcity but getting rid of what we do produce.

The "cheap food" argument

This is widely used to justify a range of capital-intensive, power-concentrating approaches to increasing production, of which rBST and other GE technologies are just one example. Cheap food policies, including a variety of approaches that have served to drive down prices by increasing supply in an inelastic demand market, may have been a valid approach to freeing up labor for factories in town several decades ago. Today, however–with less than 2% of the population in farming and a populace which spends the second lowest percent of its disposable income on food of all nations in the world—this is a specious, disingenuous, and self-serving argument. Producers commonly receive less than 10% of the dollar value paid by consumers for foods. Thus, the premise that rBST in particular, or genetic engineering in general, is somehow essential to keep food cheap is a groundless but curiously compelling dogma. Everyone likes a bargain.

Environmental sustainability?

Is rBST, or genetic engineering, somehow needed to protect the environment? Indeed, much evidence is available to suggest just the opposite. Rayburn (1993) compared management-intensive grazing vs. rBST as vehicles for increasing milk production in New York state. He contrasted the acreage needed for "pasture" and "barn" feeding (rBST) systems, where each was designed to produce the same amount of milk. Each ration, whether pasture or barn-based, was balanced using NRC nutrient requirements (Rayburn, 1993).

He concluded that more acreage would be needed to support the pasture option, particularly at higher levels of per-cow output. However, the *type* of crop grown in the pasture option would also include a larger proportion of soil conserving (less erosive) crops. The net effect was that while pasture-based milk production required more total acres to produce the same amount of milk, *total potential soil loss would be about 30% less on pasture than on barn-feeding* (rBST). The greater proportion of concentrates needed to stimulate high per-cow production on rBST comes from row crops (corn and soybean) which are more vulnerable to both soil erosion and degradation. Thus, rBST and other GE offerings (largely corn and soybean) cannot be justified on the basis of environmental soundness, particularly if pasture and forages are included in the equation.

In sum, if rBST doesn't promote the health and welfare of either cows or humans, fill a compelling need for more milk, keep milk cheap, or enhance the environment, how can it be argued that rBST is "good" for society? While the premise that "what is good for industry is good for society" would have to be evaluated on a case by case basis, it would be difficult to make a convincing case that any of the current ag biotech offerings (herbicide-tolerant crops; plant pesticidal crops) are "good for society". And if they are not demonstrably "good for society", how can government justify expending hundreds of millions of taxpayer dollars each year to develop and promote them?

THE UNEASY MARRIAGE OF INDUSTRY AGENDAS AND ACADEMIA

The mutually beneficial and symbiotic relationship between universities and society is in jeopardy. The burgeoning presence of industry on campus, filling the vacuum created by short-sighted government funding policies and deregulation, has created an irreconcilable conflict. Academic freedom, to provide objective and independent insight bearing on societal issues, is in direct conflict with the demands of fueling proprietary technologies. The inherently unstable balance between fulfilling these two competing demands has already shifted in favor of the latter, with grave implications for society, and for the institution of the university as a whole.

The objectivity and credibility of academics is increasingly suspect, and not simply because of the "academics-for-hire" that seem to blossom in such circumstances. The perceived conflict of interest for publicly funded institutions and individual faculty in receipt of large amounts of industry funding (e.g., Novartis at Berkeley; Monsanto at Davis) is tainting public perceptions of our reliability and professionalism.

But does industry funding actually compromise researcher objectivity? One of the few studies specifically looking at this uncomfortable question was a survey reported by Stelfox et al. (1998), a group of Toronto medical researchers. In a paper in the prestigious *New England Journal of Medicine*, they explored the objectivity of sources of published information on the use of calcium-channel blockers, which are used to treat high blood pressure. The controversy over this particular treatment arose because the potential for increased risk of heart attack death from the use of one channel blocker was already known to and reported by the National Heart, Lung and Blood Institute in 1995.

In a study of 70 published articles on channel blockers, Stelfox et al. (1998) used a panel of independent reviewers to categorize the authors of each paper as "supporters", "neutral", or "critical" of channel blockers, and then sent the authors' questionnaires to answer questions relating to funding sources (Table 1).

TABLE I

Evidence of impact of funding source (from Stelfox et al., 1998)

Questions	Supporters	Neutral	Critical
	% with financial ties*		
What proportion of the authors in each category have financial ties to the manufacturers of Ca-channel blockers?	96	60	37
What proportion of the authors in each category have financial ties to the manufacturers of *other* competing products (e.g., beta-blockers?)	88	53	37
What proportion of the authors in each category have financial ties to ANY pharmaceutical manufacturers?	100	67	43

*Defined as travel expenses, honoraria, support for educational programs; research grants; employment/consulting fees

The evidence presented is consistent with the hypothesis that the outcome of the research can be influenced by the funding source. Authors having a history of financial ties to industry, including but not limited to this proprietary product, were most associated with research outcomes favorable to the proprietary product. Conversely, authors with a more limited history of financial support from industry for this or other products tended to reach conclusions critical of the proprietary product. Such a finding, if substantiated in other disciplines, would bode ill for the credibility and reputation of researchers with substantial industry funding, or who had the misfortune of working in an institution with strong industrial linkages.

What place have industry values in academia? Who will society turn to for objective and independent opinion, as we increasingly absorb industry values— such as those below— within academia?

1. *Bigger (and fewer) is better*; in other words, consolidation is power (Table 2). Ten companies, including the life science giants, now control 32% of the $23 billion seed trade and 85% of the $30.9 billion agrochemical market worldwide (RAFI, 1999). Not surprisingly, the same companies controlling the seed trade also control the proprietary chemicals required to employ many of the GE crops marketed by the same companies.

TABLE II

Recent trends in consolidation within the Life Science companies (adapted from RAFI, 1999)

Year	Companies Combining	New Company
1996-present	Monsanto spent >$8 billion to buy part or all of such companies as Calgene, DeKalb, Agrocetus, including $1 billion for just Holden Foundation Seeds (source of 35% of the parental lines used by independent corn breeders)	**Monsanto**
1991	Ciba Geigy and Sandoz (and Northrup King)	**Novartis**
1998	Hoechst (including AgrEvo) and Rhone-Poulenc	**Aventis (pending)**; combined annual sales of $20 billion; annual R and D budget will be $3 billion
1998	Zeneca Group PLC (formerly ICI) and Astra A.B.	**Astra Zeneca**; combined annual sales of $14.3 billion;
1999	DuPont, which had bought 20% of Pioneer Hi-Bred for $1.7 billion in 1997, bought out the remaining 80% for $7.7 billion in 1999, as well as the rest of Merck & Co. for $2.6 billion	**DuPont/Pioneer Hi-Bred Intl.**

The scaled-down academic version of consolidation is the forced merger of disparate departments and even colleges which has been underway for a number of years in many Canadian schools. And to whose benefit?

2. *"If brute force doesn't work, you aren't using enough of it"* (courtesy William McDonough, Dean of Architecture, Univ. of Virginia). A case in point is the sorry spectacle of Monsanto prosecuting a Saskatchewan farmer, Percy Schmeiser, for saving his own canola seed. Farmers purchasing Monsanto GE seed must sign a binding agreement which precludes, among other things, the right of the farmer to withhold some of his own seed for planting next year. Percy apparently never bought the proprietary, herbicide tolerant "Roundup Ready" (RR) seed, and claims that stray RR pollen from neighboring GE canola fields was responsible for conveying the trait to his crop— through what is known as genetic pollution. The science is clearly on Percy's side, but Monsanto says that no matter how the proprietary genes arrived at the farm, the farmer is still liable. A $10 million countersuit is pending.

Is this so very different from the intense pressures applied by colleagues and others to force research into acceptable disciplines, subject areas, and even....outcomes? Consider the appalling treatment of Dr. Arpad Pusztai, an imminent senior scientist and world authority on lectin with a reported 270 publications to his credit. His 35-year career ended shamefully at the hands of his own colleagues at the Rowett Institute in Scotland, which had recently received a grant worth 140,000 British pounds from Monsanto. His entire program was shut down, his research grants withheld (including those not related to the subject research), his long-standing research team disbanded, and he was ordered to remain silent for 7 months or risk losing his pension.

And what heinous crime warranted this punishment from his peers? Winning a $2.4 million grant over 28 other tenders to study health impacts of GE-lectin on rats, and then reaching—and even worse, publicly reporting (not once but twice, each time with his Director Philip James' permission)— conclusions that challenged the assumption of substantial equivalence in the food safety of GE foodstuffs.

His work, recently reported in the Lancet, suggested that feeding transgenic potatoes modified to express snowdrop lectin (GNA)[4] affected the immune response and reduced the size of the liver, heart, and brain of rats. In contrast, unmodified potatoes spiked with GNA had a much lesser effect. From this evidence, he tentatively attributed the adverse responses to the transgenes themselves—not the GNA—and was forced to retire ignominiously two days later.

According to Dr. Ronald Finn, past president of the British Society of Allergy and Environmental Medicine,

> Dr. Pusztai's results, at the very least, raise the suspicion that genetically modified food may damage the immune system (Lean, 1999).

So what are we seeing here? An incompetent bumbler or merely an objective scientist, trying to do his job, in a collegial environment that is genuinely hostile to objective enquiry? And what of academic integrity? When scientists have to put their jobs—their careers—at risk just to do their job, then academic integrity is already in question. As industry-driven stakes get higher and higher, financially and professionally, the pressure to conform, to ask the "right" questions, and to publish the "right" results can only increase—to the detriment of us all.

As Dr. Pusztai stated himself:

> I believe in the technology. But it is too new for us to be absolutely sure that what we are doing is right. But I can say from my experience if anyone dares to say anything even slightly contra-indicative, they are vilified and totally destroyed.

When asked about what could happen to those who might try to repeat his work elsewhere, he responded:

> It would have to be a very strong person. If I, with my international reputation, can be destroyed, who will stand up? (Lean, 1999).

3. *Progress means increasing technological complexity.* In essence, if it doesn't bring increased income to the company, it is not worthy of study. Technology costs money, which justifies extracting yet more "rent" from those adopting the technology.

Research supporting capital-intensive, power-concentrating technologies for agricultural production have facilitated consolidation at the farm level, depopulating the countryside and disenfranchising generations of farm families. Because the cost of the inputs needed to stimulate yield are rising much faster than the value of the commodities, Canadian farmers retained less than 15% of the farmgate value of their produce in 1992 (below 10% now). Roughly 75% of the farmgate value of produce goes to input suppliers. In effect, the benefits of higher yield have been diverted from the farm to the supplier of the inputs needed to produce the higher yields.

Little to no evidence exists that larger, high tech farms are inherently more efficient, environmentally sound, profitable, or capable of supplying the needs of society for safe and sufficient food. Indeed, the capability of the mega-farm approach to production which is now in vogue can and should be challenged on several grounds. But no, this is where the funding is, so we continue to pursue scale-dependent research of dubious benefit to society or the environment. This is one of the inevitable by-products of short-sighted government funding policies that force dependence on industry funding.

CONCLUSIONS

Universities are intentionally structured, through the vehicle of tenure, so that academics **will** pursue novel research directions and **will freely share** their findings for the good of society, irrespective of external forces. To a very real extent, academics are *expected* to challenge societal directions, including the status quo, to continue the quest for new knowledge, and to open up new avenues for enlightenment. That is our job. It follows that to the extent that we fail to perform this function for society— for whatever reason— then we are not doing the unique and privileged job for which we are paid.

The role of academia in informing public opinion is of paramount importance when the issue is a potentially very lucrative, proprietary technology. There can be no better example of this than genetic engineering, which is promoted with exceptional power and influence by the self-proclaimed life science companies.

The decline of government funding for research, coupled with the obligation to obtain matching funds from industry to access what remains of government funding, is reshaping Canadian academia. The focus on industry objectives has permeated even so respected an authority as NSERC, such that NSERC funding is now used to systematically insert industry agendas, and people comfortable with industry values, at every level of academia. Industry benefits handsomely from this gift which is given freely and intentionally, but with little apparent cognizance of the deleterious implications it is having— both on academia and on society, including farmers. The premise that what is good for industry is good for society is unvalidated, and indeed, should be critically analysed and challenged. The example of rBST illustrates some of the many harmful effects of a technology which was heavily supported not simply by industry, but by government via academic researchers.

Industry values, as reflected in actions taken by the life science and other agribusiness industries, are difficult to reconcile with the mandate to serve those who pay our salaries—the citizenry of Canada and the environment which supports them. Evidence that such values are already becoming commonplace is not hard to find. But it is not hard to see that the credibility and objectivity of academics is correspondingly compromised by the degree to which we accept— indeed welcome— industry on campus.

Is this to our benefit? To society's benefit? Who is minding the shop?

REFERENCES

Benbrook, C. 1999. Internet communication entitled *Important New USDA Report on IPM* dated 17 October 1999 on SANET-mg@ces.ncsu.edu (archived). Benbrook Consulting Services, Sandpoint, Idaho and former Chair of the Board on Agriculture, U.S. National Academy of Sciences.

Butler, L.J. 1999. The profitability of rBST on U.S. dairy farms. AgBioForum 2(2) Spring 1999
(http://www.agbioforum.missouri.edu/AgBioForum/vol2no2/butler.html)

Chan, J.M. et al. 1998. Plasma Insulin-Like Growth Factor-1 (IGF-1) and prostrate cancer risk: a prospective study. Science 279: (23 January 1998).

· CVMA (Canadian Veterinary Medical Association) Expert Panel on rBST. 1998. *Report of the Canadian Veterinary Medical Association Expert Panel on rBST.* Prepared for Health Canada, November 1998 *(http://www.hc-sc.gc.ca/english/archives/rbst/)*

Duffy, M. and M. Ernst. 1999. Does planting GMO seed boost farmers' profits? *(http://www.leopold.iastate.edu/99-3gmoduffy.html)*

Kronfeld, D.S. 1993. Ch. 2. Recombinant bovine growth hormone: cow responses delay drug approval and impact public health. pp. 65-112. In: W.C. Liebhardt (ed) *The Dairy Debate. Consequences of Bovine Growth Hormone and Rotational Grazing Technologies.* Univ. of California SAREP, Davis, CA.

Lean, G. 1999. How I told the truth and was sacked. *Independent* (8 March 1999).

RAFI (Rural Advancement Foundation International). 1999. *The Gene Giants. Masters of the Universe?* March/April 1999 *(www.rafi.org/communique/19992.html)*

Rayburn, E.B. 1993. Ch. 6 Potential ecological and environmental effects of pasture and BGH technology. In: W.C. Liebhardt (ed). 1993. *The Dairy Debate.* Univ. of California SAREP, Davis, CA.

Sholubi, O, D.P. Stonehouse, and E. Ann Clark. 1997 Profile of organic dairy farming in Ontario. *Amer. J. Altern. Agric.* 12(3):133-139.

Smith, T. 1997. Some remarks on university/business relations, technological development, and the public good.
(http://grad.admin.iastate.edu/bioethics/forum/forum/smith.html)

Stelfox, H.T. et al., 1998. Conflict of interest in the debate over calcium-channel antagonists. New England Journal of Medicine 338(2):101–106.

PART 3

Teaching as a Commodity

Introducing the Automatic Professor Machine

An illustrated lecture given 1998–2000

LANGDON WINNER

After many years of questioning and criticizing information technologies of various kinds, I've undergone a change of heart. Today I offer a positive vision of the prospects for networked computing and new media in the activities of teaching and learning—prospects I now think look very bright indeed. My hope is that you will share my enthusiasm about these developments and join with countless others imagining new possibilities for education in our time.

In the past I have derided the way that television, computers, and other electronic devices have been used in our classrooms. Today, who can fail to realize that the tides are shifting? Many friends and colleagues are completely enthralled by personal computers, the Internet, and proposals for virtual education. It now seems to me that what they are proposing is not so bad after all. The world of education is moving in new directions, away from the approaches and standards I had learned decades ago and toward new, more vital ways of presenting knowledge to young minds. I've come to see my career as a technology critic as reminiscent of the plight of those poor, isolated Japanese soldiers, stranded on Pacific islands years after World War II ended, unaware that their side had lost, who rush out of the jungle, bayonet in hand, to attack a group of tourists at a luau.

My new role is the only one that truly makes sense for the new millennium—founding a business firm and getting products into the hands of today's education consumers. In that light, I introduce myself to you in my new role, as:

L.C. Winner, C.E.O.
Educational Smart Hardware Alma Mater, Inc.

Our firm will soon be listed on the NASDAC stock exchange under our acronym— *Edu-Sham, Inc.* (which, by the way, we like to pronounce "Edu-Shawm"). Allow me to describe our exciting new line of products and

89

services, along with the basic rationale that we, at Edu-Sham, Inc., believe makes them so appealing.

Let's begin by looking at the underlying forces that will drive education in the decades to come:

Commodification: Anything not previously a conveniently packaged, marketable product will now become one.

Globalization: All products and services must be priced competitively at every point on the planet.

Privatization: All resources formerly held by public institutions must quickly devolve into private hands.

Digital Transformation: All entities previously in analog format must be reconfigured in digital format.

In a great many places in our society we already see the effects of these forces at work. Take the bank teller. During the past two decades, thousands of branch banks have closed to make way for the ATM, the automated teller machine, while thousands of human bank tellers were laid off or retrained. Highly educated professionals like to think that these forces will affect lower level personnel only. But as the waves of downsizing and outsourcing make clear, this is simply not true. Even those at the highest levels of education and professional ability are subject to the forces of global change.

The law is often thought to be a field where only well-trained professionals can provide what you need. But that wonderful new product, the "Quicken Family Lawyer," contains on one CD-ROM just about everything you would normally expect from a lawyer (except exorbitant bills): easy programs for drawing up wills, living trusts, estate plans, leases, bills of sale, eviction notices, and dozens of other documents—including prenuptial agreements—all for about twenty dollars. Users fill in the details, print them out, have them notarized by a notary public, and the task is done; no fuss, no muss.

Today questions of how things are done, where they are done and by whom are completely open for redefinition and entrepreneurial imagination. This of course includes education and educators. We teachers like to think that we won't go the way of the telephone operators and bank clerks. But is this confidence justified?

This is where the Educational Smart Hardware Alma Mater Corporation has decided to make its mark by making a market. In today's dynamic global economy, the world of education is as an enormous $600 billion a year industry, but one stuck with a great deal of cumbersome, costly, outmoded baggage. Atop a lengthy list of absurd encumbrances we find:

Rigid, expensive material infrastructure: classrooms, libraries, faculty offices, and the whole range of campus facilities.

Outmoded, inflexible practices and structures inherited from a bygone crafts era of education masters and apprentices.

High-cost but notoriously low-productivity personnel: teachers, professors, administrators, librarians, and the like—with salaries, benefits, pensions, and cushy lifestyles.

Of course, the existing system is also burdened by requirements that much business be done by hard-to-schedule, time consuming, and often annoying face-to-face meetings. The basic problem here, my friends, is perfectly clear: *Inflexibility.*

Responding to these widely acknowledged problems, embracing the global forces that are driving education and everything else these days, we at Edu-Sham, Inc., offer an innovative product line predicated on a few core educational principles.

First, the Idea of Education itself. What *is* education? Of course, the philosophy of education has been debated ever since Plato and Aristotle, a conversation revived in the writings of John Dewey, Robert Hutchins, Ivan Illich, and other modern thinkers. But these grand theories seem increasingly tired, overblown, not to say beside the point. We at Edu-Sham, Inc. believe the key idea can be defined quite succinctly:

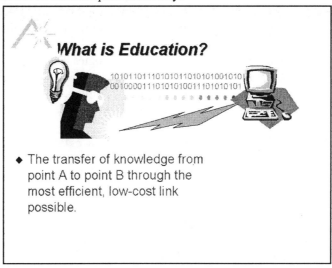

Education is the transfer of knowledge from point A to point B through the most efficient, lowest cost connection possible.

In today's world, what other definition makes any sense? I can't think of any. Obviously, the best means for effective knowledge transfer would be a

AUTOMATIC PROFESOR MACHINE

APM

direct link, perhaps a fibre optic cable, between the computers at Edu-Sham, Inc. and the brain of each student. Learners could then download course materials and other pieces of knowledge exactly as needed. Alas, this technology is not yet available, though my research staff tells me that it's probably just a matter of a decade or so. For the time being, we offer products of a more conventional sort, guided by innovative design criteria.

Today's students need educational technologies that are:

Low cost: Consumers will not accept high priced educational goods when they can get equivalents at lower prices.

Flexible: All education must change quickly to meet the needs of the moment.

User friendly: Customers must find our interfaces familiar, responsive and inviting.

Just-in-time: Exactly the right amount of education is shipped at precisely the right moment.

Let's move on to look at our first significant product, our APM: *The Automatic Professor Machine.*

[Music: Tape plays: Richard Strauss, "Also Sprach Zarathustra"]

This spring tens of thousands of these attractive consoles will be placed in schools, colleges, shopping malls, gas stations, fast food restaurants, video rental shops, and other places where people gather.

Available 24 hours a day, linked to Edu-Sham, Inc. computers by high-speed communications lines, the APM offers a complete line of educational services from pre-school to post-doc. Subscribers can:

Obtain lectures, quizzes, mid-terms, problem sets—all downloadable onto disks inserted into a slot near the video screen.

Upload completed work—exams, papers, requests for extensions and incompletes—into the same slot.

Obtain grades, evaluations, transcripts, hard copies of diplomas, and other credentials, along with Edu-Sham's frequently updated alumni newsletter.

Of course, the kiosk model is not the only way people can interact with the Automatic Professor Machine. Another model is available as the APM CD-ROM linking students to the World Wide Web via *edu-sham.com*. But regardless of hardware or software, all APM students will be connected to Edu-Sham's central institution, The Glow-Ball University, which dispenses knowledge and evaluates each student's progress.

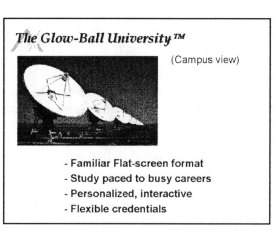

The Glow-Ball University ™

(Campus view)

- Familiar Flat-screen format
- Study paced to busy careers
- Personalized, interactive
- Flexible credentials

Unlike conventional universities and colleges, The Glow-Ball University has no campus, no faculty, and no actual physical location. It is composed entirely of bits and pieces of software strung around the planet, connected by satellite communications and other high-speed links. Unlike conventional, cumbersome educational institutions, the Global University is totally responsive to student demand. Today's students' pressing needs include:

Displays in familiar flat screen format (like with television and video games)

Study paced to busy work schedules

Personalized, interactive instruction (in which they are in direct contact with a computer that recognizes their name and has access to all the data ever collected on them)

Continual upgrading of skills

Flexible lifelong learning (essential for today's global marketplace)

Credentials matched to rapidly changing career objectives

Mentoring by IntelligentExperts™, an expert system offering comments, questions, and advice downloaded from Edu-Shawm's pre-recorded storehouse of standard professorial routines.

Let us say, for example, that a job seeker requires knowledge and skill in the use of Microsoft Excel. Why spend four years in college at $30,000 a year? At Edu-Sham, Inc. we offer thousands of downloadable, just-in-time courses a student can complete in anything from a few weeks to just a few minutes. Upon successful completion of the course, the APM issues a digitized certificate or mini-diploma, certifying that the student had passed.

We call this a Partner's Degree Quickly or PDQ. In this example, the student would receive a PDQ in Excel. After 32 of these, the APM would automatically issue the student a bachelor's degree, a cyber-event we like to call "commencement."

Of course, the life of scholarly inquiry need not end there. Students can continue collecting partner's degrees, eventually earning a master's or PhD or even several. The estimated average cost per course is only $500. Thus, the equivalent of a college education delivered through the APM would cost a mere $16,000, less than 1/5 of what most students spend on a bachelor's degree. I'm sure you can see that Edu-Sham's competitive advantage in delivering educational services will have enormous implications for your conventional, physically encumbered schools, colleges, and universities.

Now a question I'm sure many of you have been asking: What about the *quality* of an education delivered by APM?

First, let me assure you that we, at Edu-Sham, Inc., have an unswerving commitment to "total quality" through and through.

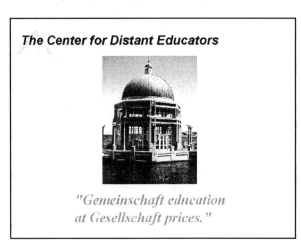

The Center for Distant Educators

"Gemeinschaft education at Gesellschaft prices."

Our research facility, The Center for Distant Educators, located in Tierra del Fuego, Patagonia, recently released a report emphasizing the following points:

Education via APM will use *only* state of the art electronics.

Our lectures and seminars will be given by the "Top Ten" stars in any given field.

We promise instantaneous delivery of all educational products.

There will be a 90-day limited warranty on all knowledge (students can purchase an extended warranty for a modest additional fee).

Students will be greeted by our customized "First Name Basis" software powered by our IntelligentExpert™ system.

As we move to computerized voice communication instead of today's keyboard and mouse approach, students will encounter skilled, knowledge-able, user friendly, virtual teachers able to listen to questions and comments and respond appropriately. We, at Edu-Sham, are fully committed to the highest industry standards for "interactivity" in learning: *only* computers, never people, will be involved in the communications process.

You're probably saying to yourself, "This is all well and good, but what about the *results* to be achieved by using the APM and the Glow-Ball University?" This is a serious question. We at Edu-Sham, Inc. are especially cognizant of an interesting finding in research on the effectiveness of using new technology in educational settings: namely, *no significant difference.* As summarized by Thomas Russell, director of instructional telecommunications at North Carolina State University,

> Technology will facilitate learning for some, but will probably inhibit learning for others, while the remainder experience no significant difference. .There is no longer any doubt that the technology used to deliver instruction will not impact learning for better or worse.

This may seem to be bad news for a start-up Info/Ed business like ours. If the technology makes no difference, why in the world would people buy it? But at Edu-Sham, Inc. we view this finding of "no significant difference" not as a setback to education, but as something entirely different—a challenge for marketing! For institutions intent on achieving quick, measurable, and positive results, we are pleased to offer the Automatic Professor Machine-Professional version, the APM-PRO. This model is similar to our plain vanilla APM except enhanced with the Hawthorne effect. Students of social science and organizational psychology will recognize this term immediately. The Hawthorne effect was discovered many decades ago by industrial psycho-logist Elton Mayo in his studies of worker/management relations at the Hawthorne Electric plant. Mayo's pilot studies of worker productivity showed that changing just about *any* variable would increase productivity. When the lights in the plant were turned up, productivity increased; when the lights were dimmed, productivity increased. Mayo and his colleagues concluded that workers *believed* something very important was happening and, because the spotlight was on them, put in extra effort.

When a school, college, organization, or individual consumer buys the enhanced APM-PRO model, our consultants come to the site to generate the Hawthorne effect. We'll make sure that there are plenty of stories about the machine and its use in local papers. We'll make sure that the mayor or governor or premier comes to visit the site for photo ops. In short, participants will feel that they are part of something new and exciting! That will achieve the positive results the customer wants.

Some who have observed the Automatic Professor Machine in operation have raised questions about how well the APM will handle a full range of learning experiences. It may be fine for vocational and technical subjects, but what about the humanities and the liberal arts?

Once again, I assure you these concerns are groundless. At Edu-Sham, Inc. we are on the cutting edge of new curriculum in The Liberal Arts™. Following our general approach to education, classes are closely matched to what students actually need in today's rapidly changing global economy. Here are just a few of the hundreds of useful and stimulating courses listed in our catalogue:

"Global Entrepreneurship"
"Resume Writing for the Web"
"Advanced Eudora"
"Re-engineering for Visionaries"
"Postmodernism as a Second Language"
"I Can't Believe It's Not Physics!"

Whether we're talking about the scientific and technical professions or The Liberal Arts™, there is an enormous change in the works. In the future we will be talking less about schools, classes, colleges, universities, and libraries as the focus of learning. Instead we'll be talking about the Educational Maintenance Organizations—EMOs—that will reshape the economics of the education industry in much the same way that HMOs have changed the practice of medicine. We've already seen what the advent of the ATM did in banking: it eliminated thousands of branch banks with costly buildings, staff, and maintenance. At Edu-Sham, Inc. we believe that the APM and its successor products will liquidate much of the costly, inflexible ballast that has come to be known as education during the past two centuries.

We recognize that some will still prefer the conventional, high-cost collegiate approach, just as there are those who collect old quilts and 19th century railroad time pieces. Today's educators may persist in thinking that they are still necessary, that education cannot take place without them. But they are simply mistaken. By the same token, many elevator operators probably rejoiced when the first automatic controls arrived in elevators, thinking that their jobs would now be easier and more fun: "Great! We can spend more time chatting with the passengers." Of course, we know what happened to the elevator operators.

At Edu-Sham, Inc. we view the elimination of old structures, methods, and personnel as good news. That's why, looking at the race to transform education today, we've adopted the motto: *Lighten Up! ......Or Perish...!*

On all sides we see a frantic but half-hearted scramble by those in old-fashioned institutions to catch up with the new technical and organizational dynamism. At Edu-Sham, Inc. we look on in amusement as teachers and administrators rush to sacrifice their previously held principles to the new era of global/digital communications. The winners here will be the new generation of educational maintenance organizations, business firms best prepared for the great showdown ahead: fierce economic and technical competition for the $600 billion dollars consumers spend on education each year.

By this point I'm sure you'll agree that the future looks bright for our little start-up company and for education itself. Here's what we see happening in the months ahead:

The Future of Education Looks Bright!

+ **Now**: Attract venture capital
+ **Fall 2000**: I.P.O.
+ Increase **APM** brand name identification
+ **Link** to other major players in education services industry: Disney, A.O.L/Time/Warner, Fox --
+ **Increase** market share in Info/Edu biz
+ **Merge-Acquire** Microsoft: 2001...???

Right now we are attracting venture capital on Wall Street and in Silicon Valley.

- This spring we'll be going public with our I.P.O.— Initial Public Offering. It would be a fine investment for your portfolios, especially if you get in early.
- As tens of thousands of APMs are purchased and put to use, we anticipate increasing brand name identification in the U.S., Canada and global marketplace.
- We expect to form partnerships with other major players in the Education Services Industry: Disney, A.O.L. Time/Warner, Fox, and perhaps a couple of universities that survive the great transition.
- We predict rapidly increasing market share in the INFO/ED business.
- While it is too early to tell, we of course look forward to an eventual merger with (or acquisition of) Microsoft sometime during the next decade.

But what, you may ask, are the longer term horizons? As it exists at present, the APM is a rather clunky device. Even the CD-ROM and Web connection will soon be rendered obsolete by technologies we can barely begin to imagine. In general, however, we anticipate a powerful momentum gathering behind one dominant trend. Education will move inevitably from the *COLLEGIATE* to the *CELLULAR*. In such a world, everyone will be able to buy speedy, low-cost educational services: Anywhere, Anytime!

[Edward Elgar's "Pomp and Circumstance" march begins playing softly in the background, as L.C. listens appreciatively.]

As you know, the boxes and chips we now call computers are becoming smaller and smaller, running faster and faster, and communicating with each other through efficient, wireless technology. Eventually, the experts tell us, we will wear computing and communication devices just as we now wear clothing.

[L.C. Winner holds up the world's first Wearable Glow-Ball University.]

Just as we now see students donning T-shirts and sweatshirts that announce the names of their Alma Mater, in the future the T-shirt will simply *be* your Alma Mater!

To conclude:

I realize that I have barely scratched the surface here, that there are a great many question about the future of education that remain to be addressed. For example questions about our price/earnings ratio, employee stock option plan, market volatility, intellectual property in the global economy, and the other great pedagogical issues of our time. But for now I must conclude by saying that my colleagues and I hope you've enjoyed this brief tour of an emerging growth industry and that you will decide to join us in the great adventure that lies ahead. As our potential customers and investors, we are certain you will agree that our product line deserves your lasting confidence. After all, in the last analysis, if we do not have that, what *do* we have?

That is why every minute of every day we, the folks at Edu-Sham, Inc., remind ourselves: *CONFIDENCE IS OUR BUSINESS!*

Thank you for your support!

Further information about the Automatic Professor Machine is available on-line at *http://www.rpi.edu/~winner/apm1.html.*

Digital Diploma Mills:
Rehearsal for the Revolution

DAVID F. NOBLE

"Those who cannot remember the past are condemned to repeat it"
George Santayana

All discussion of distance education these days invariably turns into a discussion of technology to political economy, and from fantasies about the future to the far more sobering lessons of the past.

Before proceeding with the historical analysis, it is important to spell out what is meant by both education and commodification, since these terms are often used with little precision. To begin with, education must be distinguished from training (which is arguably more suitable for distance delivery), because the two are so often conflated. In essence, training involves the honing of a person's mind so that that mind can be used for the purposes of someone other than that person. Training thus typically entails a radical divorce between knowledge and the self. Here knowledge is usually defined as a set of skills or a body of information designed to be put to use, to become operational, only in a context determined by someone other than the trained person; in this context the assertion of self is not only counter-productive, it is subversive to the enterprise. Education is the exact opposite of training in that it entails not the disassociation but the utter integration of knowledge and the self, in a word, self-knowledge. Here knowledge is defined by and, in turn, helps to define, the self. Knowledge and the knowledgeable person are basically inseparable.

Education is a process that necessarily entails an interpersonal (not merely interactive) relationship between people—student and teacher (and student and student) that aims at individual and collective self-knowledge. (Whenever people recall their educational experiences, they tend to remember, above all, not courses or subjects or the information imparted, but people, people who changed their minds or their lives, people who made a difference in their developing sense of themselves. It is a sign of our current confusion about education that we must be reminded of this obvious fact: that the relationship between people is central to the educational experience). Education is a process of becoming for all parties, based upon mutual recognition and validation and centering upon the formation and evolution of identity. The actual content of the educational experience is defined by this relationship between people and the chief determinant of quality education is the establishment and enrichment of this relationship.

Like education, the word commodification (or commoditization) is used rather loosely with regard to education and some precision might help the discussion. A commodity is something created, grown, produced, or manufactured for exchange on the market. There are, of course, some things which are bought and sold on the market which were not created for that purpose, such as "labour"and land—what the political economist Karl Polanyi referred to as "fictitious commodities." Most educational offerings, although divided into units of credit and exchanged for tuition, are fictitious commodities in that they are not created by the educator strictly with this purpose in mind. Here we will be using the term commodity, not in this fictitious, more expansive sense, but rather in its classical, restricted sense, to mean something expressly created for market exchange. The commoditization of higher education, then, refers to the deliberate transformation of the educational process into commodity form, for the purpose of commercial transaction.

The commodification of education requires the interruption of this fundamental educational process and the disintegration and distillation of the educational experience into discrete, reified, and ultimately saleable things or packages of things. In the first step toward commodification, attention is shifted from the experience of the people involved in the educational process to the production and inventorying of an assortment of fragmented "course materials": syllabi, lectures, lessons, exams (now referred to in the aggregate as "content"). As anyone familiar with higher education knows, these common instruments of instruction barely reflect what actually takes place in the educational experience, and lend an illusion of order and predictability to what is, at its best, an essentially unscripted and undetermined process. Second, these fragments are removed or "alienated" from their original context, the actual educational process itself, and from their producers, the teachers, and are assembled as "courses," which take on an existence independent of and apart from those who created and gave flesh to them. This is perhaps the most critical step in commodity formation. The alienation of ownership of and control over course material (through surrender of copyright) is crucial to this step. Finally, the assembled "courses" are exchanged for a profit on the market, which determines their value, by their "owners," who may or may not have any relationship to the original creators and participants in the educational process. At the expense of the original integrity of the educational process, instruction has here been transformed into a set of deliverable commodities, and the end of education has become not self-knowledge but the making of money. In the wake of this transformation, teachers become commodity producers and deliverers, subject to the familiar regime of commodity production in any other industry, and students become consumers of yet more commodities. The relationship between teacher and student is thus re-established, in an alienated mode, through the medium of the market, and the buying and selling of commodities take on the appearance of education. But it is, in reality, only a shadow of education, an assemblage of pieces without the whole.

Again, under this new regime, painfully familiar to skilled workers in every industry since the dawn of industrial capitalism, educators confront the harsh realities of commodity production: speed-up, routinization of work, greater work discipline and managerial supervision, reduced autonomy, job insecurity, employer appropriation of the fruits of their labour, and, above all, the insistent managerial pressures to reduce labour costs in order to turn a profit. Thus, the commoditization of instruction leads invariably to the "prole-tarianization" or, more politely, the "deprofessionalization" of the professoriate. (As investors shift their focus from health care to education, the deprofessionalization experienced by physicians is being extended to professors, who now face what some Wall Street spokesmen are already calling EMOs, the education counterpart to HMOs.)

But there is a paradox at the core of this transformation. Quality education is labour-intensive; it depends upon a low teacher-student ratio, and significant interaction between the two parties—the one utterly unambiguous result of a century of educational research. Any effort to offer quality in education must therefore presuppose a substantial and sustained investment in educational labour, whatever the medium of instruction. The requirements of commodity production, however, undermine the labour-intensive founda-tion of quality education, (and with it, quality products people will willingly pay for.) Pedagogical promise and economic efficiency are thus in contra-diction. Here is the Achilles heel of distance education. In the past as well as the present, distance educators have always insisted that they offer a kind of intimate and individualized instruction not possible in the crowded, competitive environment of the campus. Theirs is an improved, enhanced education. To make their enterprise profitable, however, they have been compelled to reduce their instructional costs to a minimum, thereby under-mining their pedagogical promise. The invariable result has been not only a degraded labour force but a degraded product as well. The history of correspondence education provides a cautionary tale in this regard, a lesson of a debacle hardly heeded by those today so frantically engaged in repeating it.

The rhetoric of the correspondence education movement a century ago was almost identical to that of the current distance education movement. Anytime, anywhere education (they didn't yet use the word "asynchronous") accessible to anyone from home or workplace, advance at your own pace, profit from personalized, one-on-one contact with your instructor, avoid the crowded classroom and boring lecture hall. In brief, correspondence instruction emerged in the last decade of the nineteenth century along two parallel paths, as a commercial, for-profit enterprise, and as an extension of university-based higher education. At the heart of both was the production and distribution of pre-packaged courses of instruction, educational commodities bought, sold, and serviced through the mail.

The commercial effort arose in the expectation of profiting from the growing demand for vocational and professional training, generated by increasingly mechanized and science-based industrial activity, and rapidly devolved into what became known as diploma mills. The university effort arose in response to the same demand for vocational training, as an attempt to protect traditional academic turf from commercial competition, to tap into a potent new source of revenues, and as a result of a genuinely progressive movement for democratic access to education, particularly adult education. While the universities tried initially to distinguish themselves in both form and content from their increasingly disreputable commercial rivals, in the end, having embarked down the same path of commodity production, they tended invariably to resemble them, becoming diploma mills in their own right.

The parallels with the present situation are striking. For-profit commercial firms are once again emerging to provide vocational training to working people via computer-based distance instruction. Universities are once again striving to meet the challenge of these commercial enterprises, generate new revenue streams, and extend the range and reach of their offerings. And although trying somehow to distinguish themselves from their commercial rivals—while collaborating ever more closely with them —they are once again coming to resemble them, this time as digital diploma mills. In the following pages we will examine in some detail the history of the correspondence education movement in the U.S., looking first at the commercial ventures and then at the parallel efforts of the universities. The account of the university experience is based upon heretofore unexamined archival records of four of the leading institutions engaged in correspondence instruction: the University of Chicago, Columbia University, the University of Wisconsin and the University of California, Berkeley. Following this historical review of the first episode in the commodification of higher education, we will return to the present to indicate some similarities with the current episode.

* * *

Thomas J. Foster established one of the earliest private, for-profit correspondence schools in Pennsylvania in the late 1880s to provide vocational training in mining, mine safety, drafting and metalworking. Spurred by the success of these efforts, he founded in 1892 the International Correspondence Schools, which became one of the largest and most enduring enterprises in this burgeoning new education industry. By 1926, there were over three hundred such schools in the U.S., with an annual income of over $70 million (one and a half times the income of all colleges and universities combined), with fifty new schools being started each year. In 1924, these commercial enterprises, which catered primarily to people who sought qualifications for job advancement in business and industry, boasted of an enrollment four times that of all colleges, universities, and professional schools combined. Copyrighted courses were developed for the firms in-house by their own staff or under contract with outside "experts," and were administered through the mail by in-house or contract instructors. Students were recruited through advertisements and myriad promotional schemes, peddled by a field sales force employed on a commission basis.

In their promotional activities and material, targeted to credulous and inexperienced youth, the commercial firms claimed that their courses would guarantee students' careers, security, wealth, status and self-respect. One firm pitched:

> If you want to be independent, if you want to make good in the world;
> if you want to get off somebody's payroll and head one of your own;
> if you want the many pleasures and luxuries that are in the world for
> you and your family; if you want to banish forever the fear of losing
> your job—then—sign the pay-raising enrollment blank! Get it to me!
> Right now!

The chief selling point of education by means of correspondence, the firms maintained, was personalized instruction for busy people. Another firm explained:

> The student has the individual attention of the teacher while he is
> reciting, though it is in writing. [The student] works at his own tempo
> set by himself and not fixed by the average capacities of a large
> number of students studying simultaneously. He can begin when he
> likes, study at any hours convenient to him, and finish as soon as he
> is able.

In all of the firms, a priority was placed upon securing enrollment and the lion's share of effort and revenues was expended in promotion and sales rather than in instruction. Typically between fifty and eighty percent of tuition fees went into direct mail campaigns, magazine and newspaper advertisements, and the training and support of a sales staff responsible for "cold canvassing," soliciting "prospects" and intensive follow-ups and paid by the number of enrollments they obtained. "The most intensive work of all the schools is, in fact, devoted to developing the sales force," John Noffsinger observed in his 1926 Carnegie Corporation—sponsored study of correspondence schools written when the correspondence movement was at its peak. "This is by far the most highly organized and carefully worked out department of the school."

"The whole emphasis on salesmanship is the most serious criticism to be made against the system of correspondence education as it now exists," Noffsinger noted. "Perhaps it cannot be avoided when schools are organized for profit," he added. Indeed, the pursuit of profit tended inescapably to subvert the noble intentions, or pretensions, of the enterprises, especially in what had become a highly competitive (and totally unregulated) field in which many firms came and went and some made handsome fortunes. In a burgeoning industry increasingly dominated by hucksters and swindlers who had little genuine knowledge of or interest in education per se, promotional claims were easily exaggerated to the point of fraud and the sales forces were encouraged to sign up any and all prospects, however ill-prepared for the course work, in order to fulfill their quotas and reap their commissions (which often amounted to as much as a third of the tuition). Enrollees were typically required to pay the full tuition or a substantial part of it up front and most of the firms had a no-refund policy for the ninety to ninety-five percent of the students who failed to complete their course of study. (In Noffsinger's survey of seventy five correspondence schools, only 2.6% of the enrolled students completed the courses they had begun.)

The remarkably high drop-out rate was not an accident. It reflected not only the shameless methods of recruitment but also the shoddy quality of what was being offered—the inevitable result of the profit-driven commodification of education. If the lion's share of revenues were expended on promotion—to recruit students and secure the up-front tuition payments—a mere pittance was expended on instruction. In the commercial firms the promotional staff was four to six times—and oftentimes twenty to thirty times—the size of the instructional staff and compensation of the former was typically many times that of the latter. In some firms, less than one cent of every tuition dollar went into instruction.

For the actual "delivery" of courses—the correction of lessons and grading exams—most firms relied upon a casualized workforce of "readers" who worked part-time and were paid on a piecework basis per lesson or exam (roughly twenty cents per lesson in the 1920s). Many firms preferred "sub-professional" personnel, particularly untrained older women, for routine grading. These people often worked under sweatshop conditions, having to deliver a high volume of lessons in order to make a living, and were unable therefore to manage more than a perfunctory pedagogical performance. Such conditions were of course not conducive to the kind of careful, individualized instruction promised in the company's promotional materials. (As Noffsinger pointed out in his Carnegie study, "the lack of personal contact between teacher and student" was the "chief weakness" of the instruction.) The central "pedagogical" concern of the firms was clearly to keep instructional costs to a bare minimum, a fact caricatured in vaudeville sketches of correspondence education in which all work was done by a lone mail-clerk and the instructors dropped out of sight altogether.

All of this made perfect economic sense, however, and was summed up in correspondence industry jargon in the phrase "drop-out money." Since students were required to pay their tuition up-front without the possibility of a refund, and instructors were paid on a piecework basis, once students dropped out there was no further instructional expense and what remained of the up-front payment was pure profit: "drop-out money." Given the economics of this cynical education system, there was no incentive whatsoever to try to retain students by upgrading the conditions of instruction and thereby improving the quality of course offerings. The economics in fact dictated the opposite, to concentrate all efforts upon recruitment and next to nothing on instruction.

Already by the mid-1920s—when the correspondence movement was at its peak—increasing criticism of the commercial correspondence firms had largely discredited the industry, which was coming to be seen as a haven for disreputable hustlers and diploma mills. In 1924, the New York Board of Regents condemned the schools for their false claims and for their no-refund policies. "There is nothing inherent in correspondence as a method of instruction to disqualify it as a way to education," wrote Noffsinger, an avid supporter of adult distance education (and later official of the National Home Study Council, established to try to regulate the industry.) However, he lamented:

> Unfortunately the majority of correspondence schools are not well
> equipped and still less conscientiously conducted. They are
> commercial enterprises designed to make quick and easy profits.
> Many of them are in the shady zone bordering on the criminal. A
> large proportion of those who enroll in correspondence courses are
> wasting time, money, and energy or even are being swindled.

Noffsinger condemned "the victimization of hundreds of thousands who now are virtually robbed of savings and whose enthusiasm for education is crushed." In the commercial schools, Noffsinger warned, "the making of profit is their first consideration, a dangerous situation at best in education."

The evolution of university-based correspondence instruction closely parallelled that of the commercial schools. Following some early stillborn experiments in academic correspondence instruction in the 1880s, the university-based movement began in earnest in the 1890s; by the teens and twenties of this century it had become a craze comparable to today's mania for on-line distance education. The first entrant into the field was the newly founded University of Chicago whose first president, William Rainey Harper, was an early enthusiast for distance education. By the time he moved to Chicago from Yale, Harper had already had considerable experience in teaching via correspondence through the Chautauqua organization in New York state, and he made the Home Study Department one of the founding pillars of the new university. Following the lead of Chicago, other institutions soon joined the ranks of the movement, notably the state universities of Wisconsin, Nebraska, Minnesota, Kansas, Oregon, Texas, Missouri, Colorado, Pennsylvania, Indiana, and California. By 1919, when Columbia University launched its home study program, there were already seventy-three colleges and universities offering instruction by correspondence. Emphasizing the democratization of education and hoping to tap into the lucrative market exploited by their commercial rivals, the universities echoed the sales pitch of the private schools.

Hervey F. Mallory, head of the University of Chicago Home Study Department, proclaimed the virtues of individualized instruction, insisting that education by correspondence was akin to a "tutorial relationship" which "may prove to be superior to the usual method of teaching."

> The student acts independently and for himself but at the same time, being in contact with the teacher, he is also enabled to secure special help for every difficulty.

Correspondence study, the department advertised, offered three "unique advantages": "you receive individual personal attention; you work as rapidly as you can, or as slowly as necessary, unhampered by others as in a regular class;" and your studies "may begin at any time and may be carried on according to any personal schedule and in any place where postal service is available." Mallory insisted that correspondence study offered an education better than anything possible in "the crowded classroom of the ordinary American University." "It is impossible in such a context to treat students as individuals, overcome peer pressure for conformity, encourage students who are shy, slow, intimidated by a class setting." Home study, by contrast, "takes into account individual differences in learning" and the students "may do course work at any time and any place, and at their own personal pace."

From the evangelical perspective of its proponents, then, correspondence education was more than just an extension of traditional education; it was an improvement, a means of instruction at once less costly and of higher quality, an advance, in short, which signalled a revolution in higher education. "What warrant is there for believing that the virility of the more ancient type of cloistered college and university could be maintained, except here and there, in our business civilization?" Mallory asked rhetorically. "The day is coming," President Harper prophesied, heralding that revolution, "when the work done by correspondence will be greater in amount than that done in the classroom of our academies and colleges, when the students who shall recite by correspondence will far outnumber those who make oral presentations."

As was the case with the commercial schools, here too the promises and expectations of enthusiasts were thwarted by the realities of commodity production. Although they were not for-profit organizations per se, the correspondence programs of the universities were nevertheless largely self-supporting and hence, de facto, profit-oriented; a correspondence program's expenses had to be covered "by profits from its own operations," as Carl Huth of the University of Chicago's Home Study Department put it. And while it was initially assumed that this new form of instruction would be more economically efficient than traditional classroom-based instruction, the pioneers quickly discovered that correspondence instruction was far more costly to operate than they had imagined, owing primarily to the overhead entailed in administration. Almost from the outset, therefore, they found themselves caught up in much the same game as their commercial rivals: devising promotional schemes to boost enrollment in order to offset growing administrative costs, reducing their course preparation and revision expenses by standardizing their inventory and relying on "canned courses," and, above all, keeping instructional compensation to a minimum through the use of casual employment and payment by piece rate. Before too long, with a degraded product and drop-out rates almost comparable to that of the commercial firms, they too had come to depend for their survival upon "drop-out money."

From the outset, the leaders of the university programs pointedly distinguished their work from that of their disreputable commercial counterparts. It was unfortunate that the universities had "stepped aside to leave large part of the field of adult education to commercial schools or even to confidence men and swindlers," Mallory noted, but the new university programs would correct for that failure.

> The most important fact about the university system of correspond-
> ence instruction in contrast to that of the commercial schools is the
> fact of institutional background, and that background is a great
> public-service institution—a modern university. . . . an organic whole

whose spiritual or immaterial aspects are far more important than the concrete parts.

The Home Study Department of the University of Chicago, he insisted, was "interwoven with the university" and thus reflected its exalted traditions and mission—what would today be called "brand-worthiness."

Accordingly, the Home Study Department initially emphasized that its courses would be taught by the same professors who taught courses on campus and, indeed, at the outset even President Harper himself offered a course by correspondence. But within a few years, most of the course delivery was being handled by an assortment of instructors, readers, associate readers, fellows, lecturers, associate lecturers, and assistants, their pay meagre and their status low. They were paid on a piece rate basis—roughly thirty cents per lesson and, under university statutes, received no benefits. Representatives from the regular faculty ranks were largely those at the lower rungs who took on correspondence work in order to supplement their own quite modest salaries. In order to make out, the Home Study instructors were compelled to take on a large volume of work which quickly devolved into uninspired drudgery, and it was understood that there was no future in it.

Initially, the Home Study Program was selective in its recruitment, requiring evidence of a prospective student's ability as a prerequisite for enrolling. Students had to have sufficient reason for not enrolling as a resident student and had to "give satisfactory evidence, by examination or otherwise, that he is able to do the work required." (The University of Chicago required at least partial resident matriculation for those seeking degrees and required examinations for credit given by correspondence.) Eventually, however, such entrance requirements were dropped in order to increase enrollments. According to the Home Study brochure some years later,

> You need not take an entrance examination, nor present a transcript
> of work done elsewhere. Your desire to enroll in a particular course
> will be taken as evidence that you are prepared to do the work of that
> course.

Although there were some early efforts at advertising and salesmanship, these were kept within what were considered proper bounds for a respectable institution of higher education—a university policy lamented by the Home Study Department, especially in the face of competition from other, more aggressive, institutions such as Columbia.

As in the case of the commercial schools, here too the reduced quality of the courses combined with the lack of preparation of those enrolled produced a very high drop-out rate. And—like the commercial schools—the University of Chicago adopted a no-refund policy; tuition was to be paid in full at the time of registration and, once registration was completed, fees were not refundable. As late as 1939, and despite the criticism of commercial schools on just this count, the University's president Robert Hutchins, the renowned champion of classical education, reaffirmed this policy. "The registration and tuition fee will not be refunded to a student whose application has been accepted and who has been duly enrolled in a course," Hutchins wrote to a correspondence student. "This statement reflects standard practice in correspondence schools everywhere."

Columbia University did not join the correspondence movement until 1919 but quickly became a leader in the field with revenues matched only by the University of Chicago. It owed its success to an unusually ambitious program aimed at a national and international market and an aggressive promotional effort that rivalled that of the commercial schools. A Home Study program was first proposed in 1915 by James Egbert, Columbia's head of extension, and the idea was enthusiastically endorsed by Columbia's president Nicholas Murray Butler, an avid supporter of adult education who had earlier in his career been the founding director of Columbia's summer session for part-time students. In full flower by the mid-twenties, the Columbia correspondence program was providing instruction to students in every state and fifty foreign countries.

Although Columbia never gave academic credit for its correspondence courses aside from a certificate of completion, the university nevertheless strove to distinguish its offerings from those of the commercial schools, emphasizing "personal contact and supervision," concentrating on recognized academic subjects, limiting the number of students in each course, and keeping standards high through regular review of material by the appropriate academic faculty. The two-fold aim of Home Study, according to Egbert, was to extend the enlightening reach of the university while at the same time generating additional revenue. He and his colleagues soon discovered, however, that the preparation of course materials and the administration of the program were more demanding, labour-intensive, and expensive than had been anticipated. To offset these costs, they moved to broaden the correspondence curriculum into more lucrative vocational areas of every sort and to expand their promotional activities in an effort to enlarge the enrollment.

In 1920, Home Study had 156 students; by 1926, there were nearly five thousand and that number was doubled by 1929. As Egbert undertook "to apply business methods" to his expanding operation, the program employed a national sales force of sixty "field representatives" (as compared to one hundred instructors) who were paid a commission according to the number of students they enrolled. In addition, Columbia mounted a full-scale national advertising campaign in the manner of the commercial firms, with such themes as "Profit By Your Capacity to Learn," "Will you Increase Your Fixed Assets?", "Turning Leisure to Profit," "Who Controls Your Future?" "Who is Too Old to Learn?" and "Of What Can You Be Certain?" In 1929, Egbert proudly unveiled plans for a vastly expanded enterprise which would be housed in a new twelve-story building.

Compared to the lavish expenditure on promotion, the Home Study program kept its instructional expenses to a minimum. Here too all payment for instruction was on a piece rate, per lesson basis. As at Chicago, while some faculty engaged in Home Study in order to supplement their salaries, they were likely to be "academic lame ducks," as one Home Study official described them, and the bulk of instruction was performed by a casualized low-status workforce of instructors, lecturers, and assistants. Overworked and undervalued, they were not quite able or inclined to provide the "personal contact" that was promised. While the Home Study Department continued to boast that all of their courses were "prepared so as to enable the instructor to adjust all study to the individual needs of each student," that "direct contact is maintained between the student and the instructor *personally* (emphasis in original) throughout the course,"and that correspondence students "can attain the many advantages of instruction of University grade, under the constant guidance, suggestion, and help of regular members of the University teaching staff," the reality was otherwise. Together with fraudulent advertising and an indiscriminate enrollment policy, inescapably perfunctory instruction produced a drop-out rate of eighty percent, a rate comparable to that of the for-profit commercial schools.

The experience of two of the largest state university correspondence programs, Wisconsin and California (Berkeley) was similar to that of the private Chicago and Columbia, even though their institutions could draw upon public funds, because here too the departments were required to be largely self-supporting (public subsidy might be available for overhead but not instruction, which had to be borne by student fees).

The Regents authorized correspondence courses at Wisconsin as early as 1891, a year before the University of Chicago, but it was not until 1906 that an actual correspondence department was established as part of Wisconsin's famous Extension Program. From the very beginning, it was made explicit that correspondence courses "shall not involve the university in any expense." Originally correspondence instruction was conducted under the auspices of the regular faculty although the actual instructional duties were performed by "fellows" and "advanced students." Because of the onerous workload, faculty participation was minimal and enrollment remained small. The effort was revived under President Charles R. van Hise and his new director of extension Louis E. Reber, two engineers attuned especially to the training needs of industry.

Van Hise had recognized the economic potential of correspondence instruction, judging from the experience of the commercial schools, and he commissioned a study of the for-profit firms. "The enormous success of the commercial correspondence schools suggested that here was an educational opportunity which had been neglected by the Universities," van Hise wrote in 1906.

> There are tens of thousands of students in the State of Wisconsin who are already taking correspondence work in private correspondence schools, probably more than thirty thousand, and they are paying for this work outside of the State more than three-quarters of a million dollars per annum.

Up to this point, Wisconsin's correspondence courses had offered primarily academic and cultural fare under the auspices of the academic departments, but van Hise, at the behest of businessmen who offered to make donations to the University if it reactivated correspondence study, pushed the enterprise in a decidedly vocational and industrial direction. Reber, formerly the Dean of Engineering at Pennsylvania State University, had the same industrial orientation, viewing correspondence study primarily as a way of providing a trained workforce for industry. He observed:

> It would be difficult under present conditions to provide a better means for meeting the persistent and growing demand for industrial training than the methods of correspondence study adopted by the University. This fact has been cordially recognized and the work encouraged and aided by employers of men wherever it has been established.

Before coming to Wisconsin, Reber visited the International Correspondence Schools in Scranton and undertook to refashion the Wisconsin correspondence program along the same lines as that leading commercial enterprise.

Reber succeeded in having the correspondence department established independent of the regular faculty, with its own non-academic staff of instructors and with its courses removed from faculty control. Under Reber's direction, the Wisconsin correspondence program grew enormously, drawing one of the largest enrollments in the country. The drop-out rate was roughly fifty-five percent and "drop-out money" was the name of the game.

Berkeley's program was modelled on Wisconsin's. Initially, Berkeley's correspondence courses were meant to be the academic equivalent of resident courses, taught by university faculty and supervised by academic departments, and the university pledged to "place each student in direct personal contact with his instructor." But here too, the program administrators discovered that, as director Baldwin Woods later explained, "correspondence instruction is expensive." Thus, for economic reasons, the program moved to expand enrollment by catering to the greatest demand, which was for vocational courses for people in business and industry, by engaging in "continuous promotion," employing "field representatives," and relaxing admissions standards ("there is no requirement for admission to a class save the ability to pursue the work with profit.") Enrollment increased four-fold and fees were later increased to whatever the market would bear. Most of the instructional work was done by low-status, part-time "readers" described by one director as "overworked" who were paid on a piece-rate basis of twenty-five to thirty-five cents per lesson. Not surprisingly, the drop-out rate averaged seventy to eighty percent. Students were required to pay full tuition up-front and a partial refund was allowed only if no more than two lessons had been completed. In 1926, the President's Report declared that "the fee for a course must be set to bring in income. Expansion must be largely profitable."

At the end of the twenties, after nearly four decades in the business of correspondence instruction, the university-based programs began to come under the kind of scrutiny and scathing criticism heretofore reserved for the commercial schools. The first and most damning salvo came from Abraham Flexner, one of the nation's most distinguished and influential observers of higher education. Best known for his earlier indictment of medical education on behalf of the Carnegie Foundation, Flexner had served for fifteen years as general secretary of the Rockefeller-funded General Education Board and later became the founding director of the Institute for Advanced Study at Princeton. After his retirement from the General Education Board in 1928, Flexner delivered his Rhodes Lectures on the state of higher education in England, Germany, and the United States, which were published in 1930 under the simple title *Universities*. In his lectures on the situation in the United States, Flexner excoriated the American universities for their commercial preoccupations, for having compromised their defining independence and integrity, and for having thereby abandoned their unique and essential social function of disinterested critical and creative inquiry. At the heart of his indictment was a scornful assessment of university-based correspondence education, focussing in detail upon the academically unseemly activities of the University of Chicago and Columbia University.

Flexner acknowledged the social importance of correspondence and vocational education but questioned whether they belonged in a university, where they distracted the institution from its special intellectual mission, compromised its core values, and reoriented its priorities in a distinctly commercial direction. The rush to cash in on marketable courses and the enthusiasm for correspondence instruction, Flexner argued, "show the confusion in our colleges of education with training." The universities, he insisted, "have thoughtlessly and excessively catered to fleeting, transient, and immediate demands" and have "needlessly cheapened, vulgarized, and mechanized themselves," reducing themselves to "the level of the vendors of patent medicines."

He lampooned the intellectually trivial kinds of courses offered by the correspondence programs of Columbia, the University of Chicago, and the University of Wisconsin, and wondered about what would make "a great university descend to such humbug." What sort of contribution is Columbia making towards a clearer apprehension of what education really is?" Flexner asked. He particularly decried Columbia's indiscriminate enrollment practices and especially its elaborate and deceptive promotional effort which, he argued, "befuddles the public" and generates a "spurious demand." If Columbia's correspondence courses were genuinely of "college grade" and taught by "regular members of the staff," as Columbia advertised, then why was no academic credit given for them?

If correspondence instruction was superior to that of the traditional classroom, then why did not Columbia sell off its expensive campus and teach all of its courses by mail? "The whole thing is business, not education," Flexner concluded. "Columbia, untaxed because it is an educational institution, is in business: it has education to sell [and] plays the purely commercial game of the merchant whose sole concern is profit." Likewise, he bemoaned as "scandalous" the fact that "the prestige of the University of Chicago should be used to bamboozle well-meaning but untrained persons .. by means of extravagant and misleading advertisements." Finally, pointing out that regular faculty in most institutions remained justifiably skeptical of correspondence and vocational instruction, he assailed the "administrative usurpation of professorial functions" and the casualization of the professoriate. "The American professoriate," Flexner declared, "is a proletariat."

Flexner's critique of correspondence education, which gained widespread media attention, sent shockwaves through academia, prompting internal efforts to raise standards and curtail excessive and misleading advertising. At Columbia, the blow was eventually fatal to the correspondence program. A year after the publication of Flexner's book—and the unveiling of Columbia's ambitious plans for a vastly expanded program with its own grand headquarters—President Butler wrote to his Extension director Egbert that "a good many people are impressed unfavourably with our Home Study advertising and continually call my attention to it. I should like to have you oversee this advertising very carefully from the viewpoint of those who criticize it as 'salesmanship,' etc." The result of this belated concern was a severe restriction of advertising (which lasted at Columbia until the late 1960s). The continued unwillingness of Columbia's Administrative Board to grant academic credit for correspondence courses—largely because of the low regard in which these courses were held by the regular faculty—coupled with the restrictions on general advertising which the Board had now come to deem "inappropriate and unwise", effectively undermined the effort to maintain enrollments sufficient to sustain the Department (especially in the midst of the Depression) and it was finally officially discontinued in 1937.

A year after Flexner's critique, and partly in response to it, the American Association for Adult Education launched a Carnegie Corporation-funded survey of university-based correspondence courses under the direction of Hervey Mallory, longtime head of the Home Study Department at the University of Chicago. Published in 1933 as *University Teaching By Mail*, the study, which generally endorsed and called for the improvement of the correspondence method, acknowledged the validity of much of criticism.

Referring explicitly to Flexner, the study noted that "many believe that correspondence instruction is not a function of college or university" and wonder "how does it come that literature and art have fallen to the absurd estate of commodities requiring advertisement and postal shipment?" The study argued, however, that while "there is something fine and entirely right in the demand for independence, integrity, and disinterestedness," on the part of universities, the "ideals of practical service, of experiment in educational method, and of participation in the life of the community", are not incompatible with it and insisting that many, especially mature, students had benefited from correspondence instruction. The study conceded, on the other hand, that

> it may be that schoolmen and businessmen have . created the demand by a false propaganda of success through education, of promise of additions to the pay envelopes proportional to the number of courses, certificates, credits, and degrees, and other rewards displayed in correspondence study advertising.

In surveying the weaknesses of the method, the study acknowledged the narrowly utilitarian motive and also the "very real isolation" of most correspondence students, owing not only to the intrinsic limitations of the correspondence method of instruction but also to the pressures on instructors which further undermined its promise. "One of the charges against the correspondence study system is that it tends to exploit the student by inducing him to enroll and pay fees, and then fails to give adequate service in return," the study observed; students routinely complained about "insufficient corrections and comments by the instructor" and the "lack of 'personal' contacts with instructors" which contributed to the excessively high drop-out rates. In the light of such apparently inescapable weaknesses of correspondence instruction, the authors of the study abandoned altogether earlier evangelical expectations about this new method some day supplanting traditional education and insisted instead, much more modestly, that cor-

116

respondence instruction should be employed only as a supplement to, rather than a substitute for, classroom instruction. "No reputable proponent of home study seriously suggests that correspondence teaching should replace classroom instruction," the authors declared.

> Correspondence study is not advocated as a substitute for campus study, but is established as a supplement with peculiar merits and demerits. Correspondence courses are of the most value to the individual when taken in conjunction with a residence program. They are not a substitute for education. They should not be taken merely in conjunction with one's job or avocation, nor are they to be used simply as a hobby or as an exercise of will power by itself. They serve individual purposes best when they fit into a long-time, socialized program of education.

Earlier claims about the alleged superiority of correspondence over classroom instruction were likewise abandoned and various attempts to "experimentally" compare the two were dismissed as scientifically spurious and inconclusive.

The study devoted considerable attention to the unsatisfactory working conditions of instructors—notably that they were overworked and under-paid—in accounting for the failings of the method, which depended ultimately upon "the willingness of the instructor to give a generous amount of attention to the student." "When that fails, the authors noted, "the special merit of the correspondence method, individual instruction, remains individual chiefly on the students' side alone—this is the chief weakness in method—perfunctory reading of reports, lack of helpful suggestions, and delay and neglect by over-burdened" instructors. Instructors excused their perfunctory performance on the grounds that the pay was too small to merit the effort and the authors of the survey confirmed that the workload of instructors was typically excessive and that "the compensation in nearly all the institutions is very small."

> The excuse of instructors that pay is too little has some merit. The merit of the excuse lies in the fact that in most cases in the present system the pay is small by the piece, and piecework may be irksome to the teachers both when it is light and when it is heavy, in the first place perhaps because the tangible reward is slight, in the second because the work piles up beyond one's schedule.

Most instructors, the study also found, worked on a part-time, fee-for-service basis, with little supervision which meant both that they suffered from job insecurity and that there was a noticeable "difficulty of maintaining standards."

> The employment of readers or graders or fee instructors, as they are variously called, has been severely criticized on the assumption that such readers are not qualified teachers or are doing a merely perfunctory job of paper criticism.

"Nearly all university correspondence teachers might be designated as fee instructors," the study found, "since few are on a salary basis."

While the authors of the Carnegie study criticized such pedagogically counterproductive employment practices—and also the "usual policy of the universities not to refund fees" to students who drop out—they placed the blame not so much on the university correspondence programs per se but rather on the commercial pressures with which they were unfairly burdened. "Most university correspondence courses are underfunded and understaffed," they noted, and each is forced to be self-supporting, leaving them no choice but to adopt the unseemly commercial practices of their for-profit cousins. "Correspondence instruction in the university should not be required to 'pay its way' in a business sense any more than classroom instruction," the authors insisted. "The business methods should not be those of a commercial concern whose prime motive is to dispose of commodities or services for a money profit." Yet the survey showed that such was clearly the case. Although the authors warned that no "university correspondence administration should not lay itself open even remotely to objection on grounds of dubious commercial practices, such as 'charging what the traffic will bear,' exacting from students fees that will yield a profit, or giving instructors poor compensation in order to keep costs low," they knew that, given the circumstances in which they were compelled to operate, the circumstances of commodity production, they had no other option.

The belatedly modest and critical tone of the Carnegie survey signalled that the heyday of correspondence education was over. The great expectations of this first foray into the commodification of higher education had been exploded and the movement was spent. Strong criticism of the private, for-profit correspondence schools was ritually repeated over the years, with little noticeable effect, particularly in a series of studies sponsored by the American Council on Education. Likewise, subsequent examinations of university-based correspondence education continued to confirm the findings of the 1933 survey. Thirty years later, the General Accounting Office was warning veterans on the G.I. Bill not to waste their federal funds on correspondence courses. In 1968, the Carnegie-funded Correspondence Education Research Project, which had been commissioned by the National Home Study Council (later renamed the Distance Education and Training Council) and the National University Extension Association, found that correspondence courses suffered from poor quality, perfunctory instructor performance, and a very high drop-out rate; that instructors endured low pay (on a piece-rate basis) and low status; that programs continued to rely upon "drop-out money" to survive; and that there was little prospect for improvement "as long as correspondence instruction is held in such low esteem."

All such investigations and attendant efforts at reform and regulation invariably failed to change the picture, even as correspondence programs adopted the latest media of delivery, including film, telephone, radio, audiotapes, and television. Universities continued to offer correspondence instruction, of course, but the efforts were much more modest in their claims and ambitions. Poor cousins of classroom instruction, they were for the most part confined to institutionally separate and self-supporting extension divisions and carefully cordoned off from the campus proper, presumably to spare the core institution the expense, the commercial contamination, and the criticism.

* * *

Like their now forgotten forebears, today's proponents of distance education believe they are leading a revolution which will transform the educational landscape. Fixated on technology and the future, they are unencumbered by the sober lessons of this cautionary tale or by any understanding of the history they are so busy repeating. If anything, the commercial element in distance education is this time even stronger, heralded anew as a bold departure from tradition. For, now, instead of trying to distinguish themselves from their commercial rivals, the universities are eagerly joining forces with them, lending their brand names to profit-making enterprise in exchange for a piece of the action.

The four institutions examined here as prominent players in the first episode of distance learning are, of course, at it again. The University of Wisconsin has a deal with Lotus/IBM and other private contractors to develop and deliver online distance education, especially under the auspices of its Learning Innovations Center while University of California has contracts with America Online and Onlinelearning.net for the same purposes. And the University of Chicago and Columbia are among the most enterprising participants in the new distance education gold rush. The University of Chicago signed a controversial deal with a start-up online education company called UNEXT.com, headed by Chicago trustee Andrew Rosenfield and bankrolled in part by junk bond felon Michael Milken. Principal investors in the company include the dean of the law school and two of Chicago's Nobel prize winning economists. The new game is less about generating revenues from student fees than about reaping a harvest from financial speculation in the education industry through stock options and initial public offerings.

The first university to sign up with UNEXT was Columbia, which has licensed UNEXT to use the school's logo in return for a share in the business.

"I was less interested in the income stream than in the capitalization. The huge upside essentially is the value of the equity in the IPO," Columbia's business school dean Meyer Feldberg, a friend of Milken's, told the *Wall Street Journal*. "I don't see a downside," he added, betraying an innocence of Columbia's history that would make Flexner roll over in his grave. "I guess our exposure would be if in some way our brand name is devalued by some problem with this experimental venture."

Columbia has also set up its own for-profit online distance education company, Morningside Ventures, headed by an executive formerly with the National Football League, satellite, and cable TV companies. Columbia's Executive Vice President Michael Crow explained the need for the company with hyperbole reminiscent of that of his prophesying predecessors in the correspondence movement. "After a thousand years, university-based education is undergoing a fundamental transformation," he declared; "multi-media learning initiatives" are taking us beyond the classroom and the textbook. And he acknowledged the essentially commercial nature of this transformation. "Because of the technologies required and the non-traditional revenue streams involved," he noted, "corporations will play a major role in these new forms of education. We felt the need for a for-profit company to compete effectively and productively."

Last but not least, Columbia has now become party to an agreement with yet another company which intends to peddle its core arts and science courses. Columbia will develop courses and lend its brand name to the company's product line in return for royalties and stock options. According to one source, the company has already been busy recruiting faculty to the enterprise as course developers and has suggested the possibility of using professional actors to deliver them.

For the time being, however, until the actors arrive, the bulk of university-based online distance education courses are being delivered in the same manner as correspondence courses of old: by poorly paid and over-worked low status instructors, working on a per-course basis without benefits or job security and under coercion to assign their rights to their course materials to their employer as a condition of employment. The imperatives of commodity production, in short, are again in full force, shaping the working conditions of instructors until they are replaced once and for all by machines, script writers, and actors.

Just as the promoters of correspondence instruction learned the hard way that the costs of their new method were much higher than anticipated and that they had to lower their labour costs to turn a profit, so the promoters of online instruction have belatedly discovered that the costs of this latest new method are prohibitive unless they likewise reduce their labour costs. As Gregory

Farrington, president of Lehigh University, observed recently, "unless the new technologies can be used to increase the average teaching productivity of faculty, there is virtually no chance that those technologies will improve the economics of traditional higher education." But increasing the "teaching productivity of faculty"—whether through job intensification, outsourcing, or the substitution of computers for people—essentially means increasing the number of students per teacher and this invariably results in an undermining of the pedagogical promise of the method, as the experience of correspondence instruction clearly demonstrates. And the degradation of the quality of the education invariably destroys the incentive and motivation of students. Already the drop-out rates of online distance education are much higher than those of classroom-based instruction.

So here we go again. We have indeed been here before. But there are differences between the current rage for online distance education and the earlier debacle of correspondence distance education. First, the firewalls separating distance education programs from the core campus are breaking down; although they first took hold on the beachheads of extension divisions, commercial online initiatives have already begun to penetrate deeply into the heart of the university. Second, while the overhead for correspondence courses was expensive, the infra structural expense for online courses exceeds it by an order of magnitude—a technological tapeworm in the guts of higher education. Finally, while correspondence programs were often aimed at a broad market, most efforts remained merely regional. The ambitious reach of today's distance educators, on the other hand, is determinedly global in scale, which is why the World Trade Organization is currently at work trying to remove any and all barriers to international trade in educational commodities.

In short, then, the dire implications of this second distance education craze far outstrip those of the first. Even if it fails to deliver on its economic or pedagogical promise, as it surely will, its promoters will push it forward nevertheless, given the investment entailed, leaving a legacy of corruption and ruin in its wake. In comparing Napoleon III with Napoleon I, Karl Marx formulated his famous dictum "first time tragedy, second time farce." A comparison of the past and present episodes of distance education suggests perhaps a different lesson, namely, that sometimes the tragedy follows the farce.

Trading Away the Public System: The *WTO* and Post-secondary Education

MARJORIE GRIFFIN COHEN

INTRODUCTION

Before the 1999 November meeting of the World Trade Organization (WTO) in Seattle, United States Trade Ambassador Charlene Barshefsky announced that the United States wanted to include free trade in education and health services in the new round of negotiations. She made her case strictly in economic terms by pointing out that "barriers" to trade in services hurt American corporations and "are barriers to American exports and jobs creation." She emphasized the importance to the United States of the trade in services:

> Our performance in a relatively closed world—$265 billion in services exports last year, supporting four million jobs—is simply an indicator of how much we can achieve in an open market.[1]

The U.S. position on trade in services created alarm among educators and health care professionals because it indicates that these areas, which are mainly in the public sector in Canada, are targets for increased privatization and competition from the private sector. The U.S. wants to liberalize a wide variety of services, but the specific focus for the round that was to have begun in Seattle was, in Barshefsky's words, "the professions, education and health." These are areas where the U.S. believes that it has a trade advantage because of new technologies. Barshefsky specifically mentioned "colleges which can teach, hold examinations and grant degrees via the Internet," as examples of institutions needing the support of liberalized trade agreements.[2] The U.S. is the world's leader in exports of educational and training services, generating in 1996 $7.5 billion in exports and producing a trade surplus in this area of $6.6 billion. Higher education is the fifth largest service sector export from the United States.[3]

One main point of this paper is to analyze the ways a liberalized trading regime in educational services will negatively affect public education. The focus will be on the post-secondary system because this is the level the WTO emphasizes as it promotes an agreement on trade in education. The WTO seems to recognize that achieving international rules on higher education would be easier to achieve than it would be in primary and secondary education, partly because the private sector is more strongly represented in higher education, and partly because there is world-wide support of public education at other levels.

In addition to dealing with the new areas of service negotiations, this paper will examine the position and options of the Canadian government as well as the strategies that can be considered by educators in attempts to influence the position of the government. Finally, this paper will discuss the trade-related problems that are created by the increased commercialization of universities. As certain aspects of universities in Canada are privatized and commercialized, universities are unwittingly brought under the long arm of international trade agreements.   Although the implications of new negotiations of the WTO for post-secondary education may be visible and thus closely monitored, the trade-related effects of commercialization of the universities are not at all transparent.

THE GENERAL AGREEMENT ON TRADE IN SERVICES

Until the WTO was created at the last round of the General Agreement on Tariffs and Trade (GATT) in 1994, there was no multilateral agreement on services. Trade agreements historically have mainly aimed to reduce tariffs and to eliminate other barriers to trade. Some services—transportation, communication, and financial services—have always been traded, but social services—education and health care, for example—have been too place-specific to be tradable. As service sectors have grown, and as trade in services has increased, in part because of technological changes, the rules that focussed only on trade in objects were considered inadequate to meet the needs of service providers. The usual ways of dealing with "barriers to trade" (including such barriers as tariffs and quotas), did not cover the problems service companies encountered when they tried to do business.

International corporations in the business of exporting services demanded and worked for new trading rules to foster international markets.[4] In the last round of international trade negotiations that established the WTO, an enormous first step was made toward a comprehensive agreement on international trade in services. That step was a document called the General Agreement on Trade in Services (GATS).[5] This agreement in principle covers *all* services, including health and education services.

WTO literature explaining the GATS emphasizes the enormous scope of this agreement. It is not only the first multilateral agreement to "provide legally enforceable rights to trade in all services," but even more significantly, it is also the world's first multilateral agreement on investment. As the WTO literature explains, "it covers not just cross-border trade but every possible means of supplying a service, including the right to set up a commercial presence in the export market."[6] The kinds of rights that corporations in general would have received through the Multilateral Agreement on Investment (MAI), had it not failed as a result of international public action, can be granted to investors in services through the existing GATS.

Only when a service is provided entirely by a government does it fall outside GATS rules. Since most education systems include private providers or permit some level of commercialization, nearly all education systems could be affected by the GATS in some way. Some analysts argue that any institution requiring payment of fees (even a public institution) would fall within the category of "commercial activity" and be covered by the GATS.[7]

The GATS applies to services like education in two distinct ways. First, there is a general framework of obligations for all countries in the WTO. This framework stipulates there should be no discrimination in favour of national providers (the national treatment principle) and that there should be no discrimination between other members of the agreement (the most-favoured-nation [MFN] principle.) The second part of the GATS identifies the specific commitments of member nations that indicate on a sector-by-sector basis, the extent foreigners may supply services in the country.

All countries must follow certain principles, although the extent to which some services, such as education, are fully liberalized has so far been a matter of national choice. In this sense, the GATS has been, in part, a voluntary agreement in which countries can decide, through "request-offer" negotiations, which service sectors they will agree to cover under GATS rules.

Canada so far has not committed itself to liberalized trade in education at any level. Neither has the United States (See Table I), although twenty-nine countries have a commitment to at least one sub-sector of education and training and twenty-one countries have agreed to accept free trade in at least some aspects of higher educational services.[8] Canada's position could change quickly despite the stalemate in agreement over negotiating priorities and principles that occurred in the Seattle meeting of the WTO. This is because the GATS initial agreement provided for continuing negotiations in services, or what is often referred to as a "built-in agenda" to liberalize services.[9] Sectoral agreements have already been reached on information technology (December 1996), telecommunications (February 1997), and financial services (December 1997). Deliberations over liberalized trade in these areas attracted little public scrutiny and proceeded without controversy. The new negotiations for services, through the Council for Trade in Services, began at the end of February 2000. These negotiations are expected to "achieve a progressively higher level of liberalization [which shall] be directed to the reduction or elimination of the adverse effects on trade in services... as a means of providing effective market access."[10]

CANADA'S POSITION

Several new developments indicate that Canada supports American efforts to liberalize social services, including education and health care services. In a discussion paper on education prepared for the new GATS negotiations, Canada's previous position—to make no commitment to free trade in educational services—was explained this way:

> Since many educational services in Canada are provided by or with the support of the government, this sector was viewed as being outside the competitive domain. In addition, educational services supplied for public purposes were specifically excluded from Canada's commitments under the North American Free Trade Agreement. GATS[11]

The government justifies changes in Canada's position since

> in the last few years the education and training industry has undergone dramatic changes and the Canadian market is facing increased competition both internally and from abroad. Therefore, the Canadian government is currently reviewing Canada's trade interests in the commercial education and training sector. GATS

The 'market' about which the document is concerned is not the entire education and training sector, but the private education and training market. The discussion document (which takes almost intact the approach and wording of the WTO's background paper on education) emphasizes promotion of Canadian exports in education. There is no analysis of the effect of trade liberalization in education on the public system. It maintains in one section that

> basic education, principally primary and secondary education, is often considered a social entitlement and, as a result, it is often provided by (or with the support from) public authorities. Such education services, provided by the State, are considered services supplied in the exercise of government authority and thus are not covered by the GATS. The GATS covers only primary, secondary, tertiary/higher, adult, and other educational services supplied on *a commercial basis where competition is allowed* (emphasis in original). GATS

The intent is to reassure people that *basic* education would not be subject to trade rules through the GATS.

The government recognizes that other forms of education, including higher education, would be subject to GATS rules. But in contradiction to the assertion that the GATS would not apply to basic education, the document later notes that "primary and secondary institutions are increasingly becoming involved in the international education markets. School boards are marketing their curriculum and specific programs in many new foreign markets." Under these circumstances, that is, by entering international markets, any educational institution that has a commercial presence could be subject to GATS rulings.

International Trade Minister Pierre Pettigrew supports including education and health care services in the GATS because he thinks Canada has a competitive advantage in these areas and needs trade liberalization to increase Canadian exports. When I asked him how Canada could gain access to other countries' education markets through GATS yet not expect reciprocal action, Pettigrew argued Canada "can have its cake and eat it too."[12] His position is that public education is fully protected from GATS rules, and the GATS in education will open export markets for Canadian educators without jeopardizing public education. At this stage, this is merely a ministerial assertion, since the federal government has undertaken no detailed analysis of the implications of free trade in education markets.

Canada's background paper deals particularly with access to foreign markets, asking Canadian educators and trainers who operate internationally to provide information about their activities. Industry Canada wants to know whether they have encountered any of the following impediments to doing business in foreign countries:

Problems in travelling abroad to supply services to foreign clients, problems in establishing offices abroad, and problems in seeking licenses to operate in a foreign country.

Problems related to a lack of recognition of certificates or degrees granted.

Difficulties of foreign clients entering Canada for training or educational purposes.

Increased competitive challenges as a result of internationalization.

Questions are also directed toward Canadians who have tried to obtain education and training services from foreign providers about the nature of the services offered and any difficulties Canadians encountered in accessing them. Included in this are questions about "domestic regulations or rules that make it unnecessarily difficult for you to obtain educational services from foreign suppliers," and difficulties in accessing "training services offered by foreign suppliers via new media (for example, the Internet)."[13]

Only one question under the section entitled *Should Commercial Education and Training Services be Included in Canada's Trade Commitments* asks if there are any items that should not be included in international agreements. No questions ask how the identification and removal of targeted "barriers" to trade in education could impinge on public education providers in Canada.

TRADE IN EDUCATION

In preparation for the ongoing negotiations in services, the WTO produced a background paper that explains trade in education services and begins to identify barriers to increased access to markets by private education companies.[14]

Education services are identified in five main categories based on the traditional structure of the sector. These are primary education, secondary education, higher education, adult education, and other educational services. *Primary education* includes the usual primary education and pre-school education services, but excludes child day-care services and adult literary programs. *Secondary education* services include high school education, as technical and vocational education, and school-type services for handicapped students. *Higher education* includes two distinct groups: one, the teaching of practical skills in post-secondary, sub-degree technical and vocational education institutions, and the other, more theoretical educational services provided by universities, colleges, and specialized professional schools. *Adult education* refers to all education services not in the regular school and university systems. This includes general and vocational subjects, literacy programs, and any education services delivered through correspondence or broadcast. It excludes any programs delivered through the regular education system. *Other* education services include anything not mentioned elsewhere, with the exception of recreational matters.[15]

The WTO has identified trade in education according to the four main types of trade that receive legal protection for foreign service providers through GATS. These activities are broken down into the cross-border supply of a service, consumption abroad, a commercial presence, and the presence of natural persons. The following are examples of educational activities that fit into these various categories:

Cross-border supply of a service includes any type of course that is provided through distance education or the internet, any type of testing service, and educational materials that can cross national boundaries.

Consumption abroad mainly involves the education of foreign students and is the most common form of trade in educational services.

Commercial presence refers to the actual presence of foreign investors in a host country. This would include foreign universities setting up courses or entire institutions in another country.

Presence of natural persons refers to the ability of people to move between countries to provide educational services.[16]

In each of these categories, barriers to trade have been identified. This activity has been part of the built-in agenda of the GATS and has been an ongoing exercise. The WTO was assisted in identifying barriers to trade by an organization called the Global Alliance for Transnational Education (GATE). GATE is primarily an organization of private, for-profit education providers dedicated to trade liberalization. Its vision statement identifies its purpose: "GATE is dedicated to fostering access to quality higher education resources on a global basis, focussing on transnational education."[17] GATE is conducting a cross-national survey in order to identify restrictive practices in cross-border educational services beyond those listed in the WTO background paper.

Restrictive practices already identified by the WTO suggest its future actions. The main point is that many of these practices that have been identified as barriers to trade are considered normal and necessary in order to maintain public systems of education.

Barriers to Commercial Presence:

• The inability to be recognized as a degree/certificate granting educational institution. [The background paper gives as an example the fact that in many countries foreign education providers are allowed in the market, but they are not legally recognized as universities. The granting of degrees is restricted to domestic institutions. The document notes that students enrolled in these foreign institutions, because of their differential status, often do not qualify for the kinds of subsidies that students in nationally-based institutions receive—that is, "student transportation passes and financial assistance."]

• Measures that limit direct investment by foreign education providers. [This includes equity ceilings that limit the size of foreign establishments.]

• National requirements. [This could include any national requirements for setting up an institution or courses, receiving government grants, or any other advantages granted to nationally based education service providers.]

• Needs tests. [This refers to restrictions on the type or quantity of services, or eligibility for services provided, according to governments' assessment of what is needed. If a government, for example, discovered that the increased education of a specific type of professional, such as doctors, put unnecessary financial pressure on the public system, any attempt to correlate education with public needs could interfere with the rights of foreign educators to gain a commercial presence.]

• Restrictions on recruiting foreign teachers. [The WTO specifically identifies as problematic national requirements for teachers and board members in Greece and the way in which France limits the inflow of foreign professors through regulations about length of stay, payments of taxes, and needs tests.]

• The existence of government monopolies. [This is the most intrusive of all the "barriers" identified by the WTO. Most forms of education in Canada are supplied through government monopolies that could be seen as barriers to the establishment of a commercial presence for foreign education providers.]

• High government subsidization of local institutions. [This "barrier" concerns government subsidies to domestic private education providers that are not available to foreign education providers. This "barrier" could apply to subsidies to public institutions in certain circumstances.]

Barriers inhibiting consumption abroad:

This list deals with barriers that restrict student mobility. As the background paper notes, at this stage the bulk of trade in education services takes place through the education of foreign students. The United States, France, Germany, and the United Kingdom are the leading "exporting" countries of this type of education service [See Tables II and III]. Barriers to student mobility include:

• Direct restrictions that limit the ability of students to study in other countries through immigration and visa requirements or currency controls.

• Indirect barriers, including the difficulties encountered in translating degrees into national equivalents

• Unequal access to resources for students

Some of these barriers to trade are unnecessary restrictions on the movement of persons and efforts to redress these issues of access are likely to receive sympathy from the higher education community in Canada. The matter of degree equivalencies, visa requirements and immigration controls are all issues that should be resolved in an international arena. The important point, however, is the way removal of these barriers to "consumption abroad" applies in distinct circumstances. For example, any country that highly subsidizes students (such as Canada) may find a requirement to provide equal access to these resources to students from another country (say, the United States) an intolerable strain on public finances. The result could be the elimination of public subsidies to all students.

Barriers related to cross-border supply of a service:
- Restrictive use of national satellites or receiving dishes
- Restrictions on certain types of educational materials
- Needs tests

In Canada, needs tests and restrictions on certain types of educational materials are closely related. Since the 1970s, the education system has consciously fostered Canadian research and education materials as a way of having students taught with information germane to Canada. The preference of educators for Canadian-produced education materials could be viewed as an inhibition in the cross-border supply of a service.

Barriers to the presence of "natural persons"
- Needs tests
- Different approval processes for national and foreign educational providers
- Difficulties in recognition of foreign educational credentials
- Visa difficulties
- National requirements

Some of the issues raised in this identification of barriers to the movement of natural persons deserve to be considered more thoroughly. For example, the difficulties foreign educators, particularly those from third-world countries, encounter in obtaining recognition of credentials should be addressed in Canada.

Other identified barriers are more intrusive and their elimination could undermine the public education system. The question of access to jobs and resources in the education field has, for example, been hotly debated in recent Canadian history. When the university system was growing rapidly in the 1960s and 1970s, the disproportional presence of professors from the UK and the United States crowded out those educated in Canada. As a result, entry requirements changed and Canadian universities must first advertise a position in Canada, and before hiring outside the country, they must demonstrate the inability to find a suitable Canadian or landed immigrant for the job. Accessibility to jobs in Canada for foreign educators will be especially important in private institutions and those areas of public institutions that are privately funded or have a commercial presence. Also, as more foreign education institutions establish a commercial presence in Canada, it is likely that they will want to import their own educators.

IMPLICATIONS FOR THE PUBLIC SYSTEM

WTO rules to include education services will affect Canada's higher education system in distinct ways, depending on the results of the trade negotiations and what the Government of Canada's position is in these negotiations. The following gives some examples of the restrictions that will be placed on the public system in two distinct cases. The first set of examples discusses the implications if Canada signs on to the existing GATS rules for higher education. The second set of examples examines the consequences of removing the barriers to trade in education services identified by the WTO.

Existing GATS Rules

If Canada agrees fully to cover educational services under the existing GATS rules, those rules would require foreign educational service providers be guaranteed access to the Canadian educational market. This would include the right to invest in Canada (establish a commercial presence), to provide services to Canadians from abroad (cross-border supply), to provide services to Canadians travelling abroad (consumption abroad), and to send educators and salespersons into Canada on a temporary basis (presence of natural persons). All the distinct "modes of supply" of educational services would be available to foreign education providers to provide education services to Canadians.

Governments will be required to give degree-granting authority to foreign educational services providers and to ensure non-governmental bodies that exercise delegated governmental authority, such as teachers colleges or professional associations, recognize degrees and diplomas granted by foreign educational service providers. Foreign higher educational institutions now operate in Canada on a relatively small scale. Phoenix University, a United States private education service operating in British Columbia, targets part-time and older students for United States undergraduate degrees. The University of South Australia operates in Nova Scotia and Newfoundland and provides Australian M.A. and Ph.D. degrees, degrees that require neither course work nor comprehensive examinations, in contrast to work for graduate degrees in Canadian universities. It is certainly conceivable there could be prejudice against these degrees thus devaluing them in Canada. This could lead to demands for the right of these institutions to grant Canadian degrees or the right for their students and graduates to receive the same treatment as graduates of Canadian universities.

Governments will also be required to provide foreign educational service providers with the same grants, financial assistance and other advantages that they provide to like Canadian educational service providers. In the same vein, any preferential tax treatment for like Canadian schools, universities, colleges and other educational institutions would either have to be eliminated, or also given to foreign educational service providers. These requirements that "like" institutions be treated the same would appear to protect the public system because governments would only need to support foreign educational providers to the extent that they support "like," that is, private educational providers in Canada.

The problem is that Canadian public institutions of higher education are becoming commercialized by entering into direct competition with the private sector in the financing and delivery of education services. This commercialization makes them look more "like" private institutions. The consequences are important for the interpretation of trade rules. As public institutions come into competition with private providers through their commercialized activities, "like" treatment can be claimed from their foreign competitors.[18] Public grants or tax incentives for research and development by Canadians at Canadian educational institutions would be questionable, as would any requirement that Canadians be given preferential access to the benefits of that publicly supported research and development.

Any residency requirements stipulating first preference for teaching positions be given to Canadians would have to be eliminated. Any governmental student loans, bursaries, and other financial aid to students attending foreign educational institutions or taking courses from such institutions, would have to be provided on the same basis as to students attending Canadian institutions.

Signing on to the existing GATS in higher education will substantially affect public higher education. Although some of these changes may meet the approval of the education community, these changes will not be made by education bodies themselves. Once codified in the GATS, any further changes will be managed through dispute settlement mechanisms at the international level, not by negotiations within Canada.

Eliminating "Barriers"

If the new round of negotiations succeeds in eliminating the barriers to trade and investment in education identified by the WTO, the private sector will receive enormous power to undermine the public delivery of educational services. One alarming "barrier" in the WTO background paper is the identification of *"government monopolies."* The underlying theory of trade liberalization in international trade agreements is that whenever something can be provided by the private sector, conditions should exist so that this provision can occur. These agreements are about creating and expanding private markets and, whenever possible, identifying and eliminating government actions which hinder the growth of the private sector. Clearly, whenever governments operate in what is, or potentially could be, a "market," their actions are "barriers" to the creation of private markets and, therefore, must be controlled.

How would the elimination of government monopolies in higher education be carried out? It is highly unlikely any countries would agree to direct attacks on public education systems, if only because of the political risk. Something more subtle than a direct attack will be required at the bargaining table to get governments to agree to the control of government monopolies.

The international corporate world has had considerable experience in honing effective, gradual steps to secure a firm base in undermining services in the public sector. The most striking examples in the U.S. are in the privatization of electricity, and, even more spectacularly, the private control of prisons and social welfare programs. It is a privatization process whose trajectory is familiar and successfully adopted in other countries throughout the industrialized world.

The first step is usually an overall attack on the funding of public institutions, accompanied by the claim that taxpayers can no longer afford to support overblown public institutions. As public institutions become weaker because of under-funding, they either no longer perform well and thus lose public support, or they pursue other funding sources. Our universities are doing this through high user fees in certain programs, appeals to private corporate financing for research and even whole programs, and by becoming more entrepreneurial in foreign markets. These public/private initiatives steer universities toward corporate-style education, and as a result bring the universities under the rules of private trading structures.[19]

The other method the private sector uses effectively, is to make sure it can tap into the money the government spends on education. As with the health care industry, private educators are acutely conscious of the vast sums of public money spent by governments on the public service. Private educators do not object to governments paying for education services. What they want, rather, is to have this government spending directed toward private sectors, much as private prison and welfare service providers in the United States rely on government funding to buy their services. The trade agreements are a crucial step in this direction since they allow the private sector to insist on a "level playing field" in the education market.

In Canada, where publicly funded university education is relatively inexpensive, students will not rush to enrol in expensive private universities. As the WTO's background paper notes, there are questions "whether higher education can be profitable for private investors without public subsidies."[20] The task for the private education industry is to organize things in such a way that governments are forced to provide subsidies for private education.[21]

Generally, when the private sector identifies for privatization an activity long in the public sector, it gets a toehold in the area through marginal activity in the industry. A good example is Phoenix University's targeting of older, part-time students, who are not particularly well served by universities. The strategy subsequently is to complain about government monopolies and the unfair competition they provide. The usual charge is that the public sector can provide the service cheaper than private providers can under normal commercial conditions because the public sector is subsidized by tax dollars.

Once it is established that government-funded institutions have an unfair advantage, trade agreements can support private sector claims for public money. The most obvious is to ensure the private sector is eligible for "like" treatment when it comes to government funding. As noted earlier, the GATS applies "national treatment" to subsidies and taxation, a feature of GATS that goes far beyond the NAFTA services agreement. We may see at the post-secondary level the kinds of funding arrangements made at the secondary level to support private education in some provinces. In other sectors of the economy (notably the electricity industry) wholesale restructuring of the industry occurs as governments accommodate private providers in what was once a public market.

Understanding the way the public sector is treated in trade agreements gives insight into the potential impact of removing "government monopolies" in education. The international trade agreement that has gone furthest in granting power to control public monopolies is the North American Free Trade Agreement (NAFTA). This document is important not just because it spells out in detail behaviour for government monopolies in goods and services, but also because it is a framework for negotiating services agreements in the wider international arena. The following are the rules required of governments in the regulation and supervision of private and public monopolies. They must ensure the monopoly does the following:

> provides non-discriminatory treatment to investment of investors, to
> goods and to service providers of another Party in its purchase or sale
> of the monopoly good or service in the relevant market; and
> does not use its monopoly position to engage, either directly or
> indirectly.in anti-competitive practices in a non-monopolized

market in its territory that adversely affect an investment of another Party, including through the discriminatory provision of the monopoly good or service, cross-subsidization or predatory conduct.[22]

These strong clauses greatly inhibit the ability of public institutions to provide educational services in educational markets now in the private sphere, as many universities and colleges wish to do. The clause on cross-subsidization is particularly significant since almost any commercial activity a university undertakes, independent of its main function of public education, could be identified as an unfair trade practice if it is in any way supported by the university. Even a common administrative structure could be identified as a cross-subsidy.

The most important requirement in the behaviour of monopolies, however, is that any monopoly, even if it is a government monopoly, behaves according to commercial objectives. NAFTA states that any monopoly must act "solely in accordance with commercial considerations in its purchase or sale of the monopoly good or service in the relevant market, including with regard to price, quality, availability, marketability, transportation and other terms and conditions of purchase or sale."[23] The text defines "in accordance with commercial considerations" to mean any action consistent with normal business practices of privately-held enterprises in the relevant business or industry.

The point is that Canadian post-secondary public education is not run mainly "in accordance with commercial considerations." The objectives of the post-secondary system are varied, but its very existence in the public sector means it is not primarily a profit-generating institution. The wording in the NAFTA text is present precisely because, in the absence of similar objectives, the cross-comparison between public and private education is difficult to make. However, with the requirement that the objectives of all monopolies be commercial, the justification for equal treatment seems more rational.

The requirement that public institutions behave as commercial enterprises and have profit-making as their primary objective, takes two forms. As the public sector becomes increasingly involved in commercial actions, the NAFTA rules can be invoked. Also, it is highly conceivable that NAFTA-type rules on monopolies could be negotiated through the GATS negotiations. The intention of this type of language is to encourage increased commercialization of the public sector in areas now relatively closed.

Another way that government monopoly in education can be undermined in the WTO is through the definition of an "investor." During negotiations for the MAI, there were attempts to define an "investor" broadly enough to include those operating for-profit and non-profit organizations, as well as government-owned entities. If educators in the post-secondary system are defined this way, all kinds of normal practices could be challenged as unfair competition. For example, SSHRC and NSERC require that recipients of research awards be citizens or have immigrant status in Canada. "Investors" in post-secondary education from a foreign country might claim that this discriminates against investment rights.

WHAT IS NEXT?

When United States Trade Representative Charlene Barshefsky attended the APEC conference recently, she identified what she called "the single greatest threat to the multilateral trading system" as "the absence of public support for that system and for those policies which have created that system."[24] She and other government officials around the world are determined the public must change its collective mind.

Public action on the MAI and at the WTO Seattle meeting show how public pressure can be effective in seeing that people are heard in the international arena. At the very least these actions slow down the pace of international deep integration and give supporters of the public domain time to analyze events and understand their own interests in complex negotiations.

For supporters of public education, the continued monitoring of negotiations and informing the public about their potential impact is extremely important. As a first step, the Canadian government should receive considerable pressure from educators to keep this country from signing on to the existing GATS in education. While this is an initial step to protect Canadian public education, it may not be sufficient as GATS negotiations proceed. This is because the voluntary nature of the GATS is a feature that business and the United States government have high on their priority list of things to change. The existing process of each nation deciding, on a detailed sector-by-sector basis which types of services will be governed by trade rules, is found to be a slow way to get education and health care services under the jurisdiction of trade laws. The United States government and private service organizations want a negotiating structure more "efficient" than the request-offer process, and are pursuing a comprehensive agreement binding on all members.

Some analysts, such as Scott Sinclair of the Canadian Centre for Policy Alternatives (CCPA), anticipate early results from the built-in negotiations on services that began at the end of 2000 February.[25] He maintains there is high consensus on the need for liberalized services through the GATS. Even developing countries have not raised significant opposition to an expanded services agenda. In part, this is because developing countries have fewer domestic industries to protect and often their public services have deteriorated so far that it is difficult to mobilize public support for them. Also, some developing countries (India, for instance) are beginning to export services like software programming.

Sinclair identifies the *Draft Ministerial Text* from Seattle as an indication of the degree of consensus on services negotiations. Although the draft text has no legal validity, it stipulates that "no service sector or mode of supply shall be excluded a priori" from negotiations and calls for "horizontal" approaches to the negotiations.[26] This indicates that all types of services will be under consideration for negotiation and that broad rules will be sought to apply across all sectors, making it harder to protect specific services like education and health.

In contrast to Sinclair's analysis, Canadian government representatives maintain that there is little consensus on services issues and that the new GATS negotiations would emphasize processes, rather than substantive matters. Generally the Canadian government argues that services will not be easily negotiated and, therefore, will not move ahead quickly.[27] Slower movement would be good news for those concerned about protecting public education. But if broad language is used to cover a wide band of services, specific discussions about free trade and education may not receive much attention.

The Canadian government well understands the scepticism of the public over new WTO negotiations and has promised to "protect" various sectors through specific agreements. Sheila Copps, for example, says culture can be protected if it is in the agreement. Educators should be wary of any approach that claims that we are worse off without specific language. It is true the WTO can affect education even in the absence of Canadian signature to an agreement, but it will be still worse off if education services, or some aspects of them, are specifically included.

Educators should guard against any "gradualism" that might be used to secure an agreement acceptable to all countries. The United States Coalition of Service Industries (the organization influential in getting the United States to initiate a services agreement in the Uruguay round) anticipated difficulties in securing open trade in all services in the new round of negotiations. It specifically advocates the "horizontal" approach across all sectors. Its President gave an example of how something simple, like "national treatment," if applied across all sectors, works to the benefit of private service providers. The usual practice now in trade agreements, which cover some aspect of public services, such as NAFTA, is for governments to specifically list the programs and practices they want exempted from the agreement.

These exceptions to agreements offer, at best, temporary protection for the public sector because they protect only existing measures and prevent new government programs. That is, current policy is frozen and all new measures must conform to the trade agreements. Worse, lists of exceptions to the trade agreements identify targets for subsequent rounds of negotiations. As the President of the United States Coalition of Service Industries noted, any minimal agreement in GATS would at least get countries to list the areas they wanted protected under each service. As he noted, this would be "useful as a transparency exercise, forcing countries to demonstrate explicitly their laws and practices that are trade restrictive."[28]

SUMMARY AND CONCLUSION

The failure of the Seattle meeting of the WTO to agree on an agenda for negotiating issues over the next few years was a victory for those who want to slow the process of globalization. This does not mean that negotiations for trade liberalization have ceased. Because negotiating on services was part of the "built-in agenda" of GATS, negotiations on trade in services have already begun and mostly without public scrutiny. In education services, negotiations will proceed for all levels of education, although the prime target for new rules is higher education services.

In education, so-called 'barriers" to trade identified by the WTO are all "subsidies" to the public system that restrict the ability of private providers to compete for students. These barriers include government monopolies, the inability to be recognized as a degree-granting institution, restrictions on recruiting foreign teachers, and high government subsidies to local institutions.

The Canadian government has indicated it supports trade liberalization in education and thinks it can open international markets for Canadian education exporters without having to compromise the public system. Its justification mentions only export possibilities and has not examined threats to the public system.

It would not be possible for an international agreement on free trade in education to leave the public system intact. Rather, those measures that provide market access for private educators will require substantial changes in the ways the public system operates.

Opportunities exist for those interested in the public delivery of education to affect the outcomes of the current negotiations. Canada did not sign the 1994 GATS agreement on education and although it has changed its position, there is still room for the public to exercise influence. If Canada, in response to public pressure, undertakes consultations with Canadians to arrive at a "Canadian consensus" for the GATS negotiations, there will be considerable opportunity for public discussions to raise national consciousness on this crucial issue. The rush to open all markets to liberalized international trade presents serious and substantial threats to the very existence of a vigorous public education system.

TABLE I

GATS
GATS Summary of Specific Commitments — Education Services

GATS

countries	Primary	Secondary	Higher	Adult	Other
Australia		X	X		X
Austria	X	X		X	
Bulgaria	X	X		X	
Congo RP			X		
Costa Rica	X	X	X		
Czech Republic	X	X	X	X	X
European Community	X	X	X	X	
Gambia	X			X	X
Ghana		X			X
Haiti				X	
Hungary	X	X	X	X	
Jamaica	X	X	X		
Japan	X	X	X	X	
Lesotho	X	X	X	X	X
Liechtenstein	X	X	X	X	
Mali				X	
Mexico	X	X	X		X
New Zealand	X	X	X		
Norway	X	X	X	X	X
Panama	X	X	X		
Poland	X	X	X	X	
Rwanda				X	
Sierra Leone	X	X	X	X	X
Slovak Republic	X	X	X	X	X
Slovenia		X	X	X	
Switzerland	X	X	X	X	
Thailand	X	X		X	
Trinidad and Tobago			X		X
Turkey	X	X	X		X
United States of America				X	X
Total Schedules	21	23	21	20	12

Source: WTO Secretariat, "Education Services: Background Note," Table 5.

TABLE II
**10 Leading Exporters of Education Services (Consumption Abroad)
in the World at the Tertiary Level**

Host Country	Year	Total number of students
United States	1995/96	453,787
France	1993/94	170,574
Germany	1993/94	146,126
United Kingdom	1993/94	128,550
Russian Federation	1994/95	73,172
Japan	1993/94	50,801
Australia	1993	42,415
Canada	1993/94	35,451
Belgium	1993/94	35,236
Switzerland	1993/94	25,307

Source: WTO, "Education Services," Table 3, citing UNESCO Statistical Yearbook (1997)GATS

TABLE III
**Origin of Students consuming Education Services
in the four main supplier countries**
GATS

Host Country	Year	Country of Origin Number of students				
United States	1995/96	China 72,315	Japan 45,531	Korea, Rep. of 36,231	India 31,743	Canada 23,005
France	1993/94	Morocco 20,277	Algeria 19,542	Tunisia 6,020	Germany 5,949	Cameroon 4,676
Germany	1993/94	Turkey 21,012	Iran 10,575	Greece 7,961	Austria 6,680	China 5,821
United Kingdom	1993/94	Malaysia 12,047	Hong Kong 9,879	Germany 9,407	Ireland 8,987	Greece 8,708

Source: WTO, "Education Services," Table 4, citing UNESCO Statistical Yearbook (1997) GATS

PART 4

Corporate Management and Its Consequences

Betrayal of the Public Trust: Corporate Governance of Canadian Universities

MICHAEL CONLON

"Board members are put on the board to give money or raise money. You either give, get, or get out."—David Bond, Chair, Board of Governors, Simon Fraser University

Corporate control of decision making in Canadian public institutions threatens to distort permanently our idea of the public interest. A particularly acute instance of this syndrome is the betrayal of public trust through corporate control of the university. How did corporate governance[1] install itself at the heart of an institution that should be publicly accountable? And how has corporate governance helped to transform the theory and practice of Canadian post-secondary education?[2]

During the expansive boom of the 1960s, the university embodied our national social ambitions of class mobility, universal access to education, and equal opportunity. Canadian post-secondary education was one of our great collectively-funded and publicly-administered institutions. Public funding of Canadian post-secondary education was the indispensable guarantee of genuinely autonomous thought and research. The Canada Student Loan Program (CSLP, 1964) was to ensure universal access through interest-free loans, supplemented in most provinces by student grants.

Today the 60s seem a mythical Golden Age. The goals and practice of that Age have been radically overhauled. Most provinces have eliminated grants, and federal funding for post-secondary education has been cut by over 50% since 1979.[3] The Canada Student Loan Program has been turned over to chartered banks. These changes were neither magical nor inevitable. They have a history and a politics. Erosion of the public mandate of Canada's post-secondary education system is intimately intertwined with corporate rule.

Tension between public and private/corporate interests in education creates a schizophrenic climate. Universities remain putative guardians of the public interest, but in truth are increasingly accountable to corporate interests.

The clash between commerce and social idealism is part of a larger neo-liberal struggle to eviscerate publicly-accountable institutions.[4] Simply put, the business community sees the principle of public or collective good as anathematic to profit. Civil society, in any form beyond its policing and incarceration functions, has become the enemy.

Although corporate control of boards of governors is ostensibly the product of historical and political coincidence, the erosion of federal and provincial funding provided unprecedented opportunities. Cuts have forced universities to rely on tax-deductible corporate "gifts" to fund core operations. Corporate Canada has thus been able to leverage a controlling interest in the governance of universities.

The transition to corporately-controlled boards of governors has not only changed the culture of institutions (all largely publicly funded), it has compelled Canadian universities to forge dubious links between industry and university researchers. The University of Toronto provides an instructive example of the hidden costs of corporate donations. The University of Toronto has raised a staggering amount of cash in private and corporate donations in just ten years. Success has its price in lost freedom to undertake free teaching and research.

Consider the case of Dr. Nancy Olivieri. A researcher at the University of Toronto and the Hospital for Sick Children, Olivieri was contracted by Apotex (Canada's largest drug manufacturer and one of the University's most important donors), to test a new drug treatment for the blood disorder thalassemia. In the course of her research, Olivieri discovered several disturbing side effects and recommended the trails be discontinued, or at least suspended, until the risk to patients could be assessed. When Olivieri sought to publish her results and to alert her patients, she was threatened with legal action. A smear campaign called into question both her competence and her sanity.[5]

The actions of the drug company are less disturbing and surprising than the behaviour of the University. Rather than support Olivieri in a matter of public safety, the University sought to fire her, all the while doing what it could to mollify Apotex. University of Toronto President Robert Prichard went so far as to write a letter to the federal government in support of Apotex's call for legislative changes favourable to the company. Though Pritchard was later criticized for lobbying on behalf of Apotex, the University of Toronto Board consistently refused to support Dr. Olivieri or to reconsider the University's research relationship with Apotex.

Thomas O'Neil, President of Price Waterhouse, candidly remarks that "Federal government funding cuts were a positive because it forced each institution to take a whack at its agenda." O'Neil, a member of the Board of

Trustees at Queen's University, said this in a year in which his company generated $22 million in revenue from privatization of public institutions. Canada's corporate elite is dismantling the university's public mandate and, in the process, reaping financial rewards from the weakened public system.

The slow-but-steady entrenchment of corporate values and practices was precipitated by several interrelated factors. Canada's shift from a resource-based economy to a technocratic economy made universities a prime target for profit-making intervention. In 1983, the establishment of the Corporate-Higher Education Forum (CHEF) and the findings of the Macdonald Commission signalled the corporate sector's demand for ready and cost-effective access to the knowledge produced by universities. CHEF boasted CEOs from companies including Shell, Xerox, the Royal Bank, and Nortel along with most university presidents.[6]

There was similarly a move among partisan think tanks and quasi-academic free market "consultants" to spread the message that publicly-administered institutions were inefficient, bleeding tax dollars through amateurish management.

This view was buttressed by the Macdonald Commission, which concluded that faculty, staff, and students were unable to properly run post-secondary education institutions. Greater corporate participation has been the enduring legacy of the Macdonald Commission Report, reaching an apogee with release of the Report of the Expert Panel on the Commercialization of Research in May of 1999. Commissioned by the Prime Minister's Advisory Council on Science and Technology, the Panel included leading figures from high-tech industry, a Canadian university administrator and an American counterpart with experience in the commercialization of research. Despite, or perhaps because of the absence of university researchers on the Panel, its report recommends sweeping changes in the way research is produced, funded, and regulated in Canada.

Arguing from the premise that Canadian research is under-capitalized and under-exploited, the Report suggests inducements and punitive measures to ensure commercial potential of research is always privileged over not-for-profit research in the public interest. The Report, finally, ties funding for research and core facilities to the ability of a university to commercialize its research.

The widespread attack on public institutions has produced a kind of corporate nationalism, changing the very vocabulary of public discourse: "efficiency" is now defined by profit. Commercialization is the measure of innovation. Democracy is equated with an unfettered free market. Greater corporate presence in post-secondary education is equated with the very future of our country.

It is hard to underestimate the power of this discourse. Merciless, consistent repetition of the message prepared the cultural and ideological ground for today's public/private partnerships and corporate dominance of the public sphere.

The business strategy foresees growth in two areas, first, the profit potential in intellectual property. As John Roth, President of Nortel put it,

> The university is the source of our continuous renewal. From primary to post-graduate levels science and technology [are the key to Nortel's success].

Second, business sees potential profits in private administration of post-secondary education itself. At the 1999 World Trade Organization (WTO) talks held in Seattle, Washington, Canada refused to rule out the possibility of negotiating greater trade liberalisation in private delivery of post-secondary education. The WTO refers to public education as a "state monopoly" and defines publicly funded and administered post-secondary education as a trade barrier. Hence, O'Neil's comment that a "whack" at the "agenda" of public education is a "good" thing. Canada's position is, of course, influenced by a well-funded and relentless lobby effort by private providers of post-secondary education.

What of corporate governance's effect on one of the defining elements of a public university—access to education without regard to income? Like most social goals, universality is made possible by economies of scale realized by pooling the contributions of all taxpayers. Until the 1980s, tuition costs remained relatively low and this arrangement, at least symbolically, promoted post-secondary education as a means of softening class division. Gradual withdrawal of government funding for post-secondary education in the 1990s led to a rise in the average student debt from $8,000 to $25,000, and a national average increase of 126% in tuition fees.[7] Corporate ideologues appointed to boards of governors helped make this painful transition, and corporate dollars ensured that university administrations would organize no effective opposition to federal cutbacks. As the case of Dr. Olivieri demonstrates, the need for increased institutional revenue nearly always takes precedence over political courage.

The second fundamental result of corporate governance has been privatization of student financial aid. Tuition fees have been de-regulated in many provinces; in some cases courses are now offered on a full cost-recovery or for-profit basis. This development goes to the heart of the second business opportunity I outlined earlier, the potential for profit in the administration of a completely deregulated, market driven post-secondary education sector. One area in which corporate Canada is already reaping the benefits of privatization is student financial aid.

In 1995, after then-Minister of Human Resources Development Lloyd Axworthy's infamous Social Policy Review, the government of Canada stopped guaranteeing student loans, and turned responsibility for collecting and administering them to the chartered banks. The banks took control of the program in exchange for a "risk premium" of 5%.[8] Since then, the banks have put the federal government under intense pressure to change eligibility criteria so as to lessen their "exposure" and to generate profit from the student loan portfolio. Banks now may carry out credit checks similar to those for consumer loans, and the bankruptcy law now prohibits bankruptcy on student loans for a period of ten years.

Even as senior bankers pressed for these changes, bank governors continued to sit on many of Canada's major university boards. Beyond control over the public loan program, the push for deregulated tuition and privatized student aid led to two further business opportunities: private lines of credit, and matching fund programs of student aid. The boon in private, secured lines of credit is a direct benefit of the deregulation sought by corporately-controlled boards of governors.

At the University of Western Ontario, tuition fees for dentistry school are $18,000. Since the Canada Student Loan Program and the Ontario Student Assistance Program cap at $9,200, the Bank of Nova Scotia (whose president, Peter Godsoe, happens to be the UWO chancellor) introduced a private line of credit, administered and disbursed with the blessing of the University administration.

The trend to find matching funds for everything from building maintenance to student financial aid has made a strong corporate presence an absolute necessity for any university.[9] The provincial governments' matching fund programs for student aid link corporate and private donations to a particular institution with public dollars—in other words, government favours institutions that are well-connected to corporate Canada. Such funding programs leave the university open to the academic and ethical peril illustrated by the Olivieri case. They have also quickly produced a two-tier system, in which universities committed to corporate governance reap public and private benefits.

This same policy development provides a ready alibi for market-driven tuition. Fee hikes of up to 300% can be justified because a portion of the revenue generated from tuition fees is set aside for student financial aid. In fact, such scholarships offer funds only to the top 3 to 5 percentiles, and aid packages are rarely increased by more than 20% of the tuition fee hike. Private administration of financial aid allows universities to target programs favoured by the private sector while squeezing out programs not so easily rationalized. In addition, such funds are generally needs-blind: they reward only the narrowest form of academic achievement. The outcome of this financial aid strategy must be the homogenization of university campuses along racial, gender, and class lines.[10]

More ground is to be recovered than defended when it comes to the autonomy of our universities. Boards of governors—the universities' highest decision making bodies, and guardians of the fiscal and democratic integrity of public institutions—remain unencumbered by those who might question their ethics and propriety. Minimal investments in the form of tax-deductible gifts allow corporations to hold universities to ransom. Secret and lucrative deals lead to the signing away of intellectual property rights. When there is a possible conflict with the public interest, legally binding contracts preclude disclosure of compromising research data.

David Noble summarizes why corporations find research deals with universities irresistible: "The risk and costs are socialized but the benefits and profits are privatized."[11] John Polanyi, Nobel Prize winner for Chemistry, cautions:

> At a certain point we don't have universities any more, but outlying branches of industry. Then all the things industry turns to universities for . breadth of knowledge, far time horizons and independent voice . are lost.[12]

It is hard to imagine a dollar figure large enough to compensate for loss of public space for academic debate. When knowledge and critical thought become private property, voices of dissent are marginalized. A self-interested tide of discourse has helped to demonize the notion of "public" institutions. Any challenge to this regime in the labs, classrooms, and boardrooms of public universities entails risks and rewards not measurable by Key Performance Indicators.

Impact of the Corporate Management Style

MAUREEN SHAW

BACKGROUND INFORMATION

The British Columbia college and institute system is unique in Canada in its level of comprehensive educational offerings—from remedial to degree completion. The following summary is provided for those unfamiliar with the BC college, university-college, institute, and agency system, and to introduce CIEA, the College Institute Educators' Association of BC, the largest union representing faculty and staff in that system. For twenty years, CIEA has worked to protect the integrity and quality of public post-secondary education in BC. CIEA's members have become increasingly concerned about the effects of the corporate agenda and commercialization within our institutions.

College Institute Educators' Association of BC
CIEA is a provincial union with a federated structure. Each local association within CIEA holds its own certification and has its own collective agreement, (although in 1998 we negotiated a common agreement, with common provisions on a number of issues and a common salary scale). Currently we comprise 10 college locals, five university-college locals, two First Nations institute locals, two provincial agency locals, and three private sector locals. Our membership is more than 7,000, including faculty—teaching and non-teaching—and staff in some locals. Our diversity is both our greatest challenge and our greatest strength.

CIEA protects its members' interests in three main areas: lobbying and working with governments; collective bargaining; and contract administration. Our vision is of a college and institute system which provides equitable access to a quality learning experience for students and fairness for educators and staff. We believe especially that quality working conditions and quality learning conditions must go hand in hand.

CIEA devotes significant resources to putting forward our policies to decision makers, the public and the media. Representatives meet regularly with federal and provincial government Ministers, Deputy Ministers, and other officials, and with opposition MLAs and MPs. Other representatives participate on a number of provincial government and other advisory committees and councils, dealing with education policy, pension fund investment, professional development, college and institute funding, and admissions and transfer issues. CIEA representatives also played a key role in the development of new legislation and new governance structures, including the creation of education councils, for the BC college and institute system.

With new co-ordinated employer bargaining structures in the college and institute sector and greater government involvement in collective bargaining, CIEA took part in two provincial bargaining rounds, most recently achieving a common agreement which expires in March 2001. CIEA has been successful in defending members' rights in grievances, arbitrations, courts and tribunals. CIEA has supported a number of legal proceedings furthering rights for temporary and contract faculty, and furthering the academic freedom of our members.

CIEA is a member of the Canadian Association of University Teachers and the BC Federation of Labour. We are members of the Coalition for Public Education, along with the BC Teachers' Federation, the Confederation of University Faculty Associations of BC, the Canadian Union of Public Employees, the BC Government and Service Employees' Union, and the Canadian Federation of Students. Through our involvement with other organizations, we are able to advocate for the protection of public post-secondary education and to oppose the increasing incursion of the private, for-profit sector.

BC's college, university-college, institute and agency system

British Columbia has over 100 campuses throughout the province, with programs offered in 93 communities. In 1999/2000, our system offers over 1,000 full and part-time post-secondary education and training programs to 83,842 full-time equivalent (FTE) students. It provides an additional five million hours of continuing education programs in communities throughout the province.

Each institution has a governing Board, which comprises government-appointed members and elected members representative of faculty, staff and students, and an education council, with 50% elected faculty representation and 50% made up of staff, student and administrative representatives.

The college system offers a complete range of programs. At the one end of the spectrum, we offer Adult Basic Education and English language training courses. We offer career, trades and technical programs for people seeking employment-related education and training. At the same time, the college system offers university level programs to nearly 40,000 people in BC communities. Our five university-colleges offer both the complete range of programs and services provided by community colleges and third and fourth year university-level studies leading to baccalaureate degrees, to 28,314 FTE students. Our colleges in other areas offer first and second year university transfer courses. Through a sophisticated system of credit transfer, students can move readily from institution to institution towards the completion of their program of studies.

In many areas of British Columbia, colleges and university-colleges eliminate the barrier of geography for people who would never otherwise be able to obtain access to post-secondary education. The BC college and institute system is comprehensive throughout the province, ensuring that post-secondary education is available and affordable for all.

CORPORATE MANAGEMENT

In post-secondary education, the corporate management style has become increasingly evident, as the corporate agenda itself has become more pervasive. This style means that faculty members are seen and treated not as autonomous professionals, but as subservient workers.

The impact of the corporate management style became most startlingly evident to me on a study tour of England and Wales in September 1998. We met with Dan Taubman of the National Association of Teachers in Further and Higher Education, who described recent changes in further education in England (the college sector): corporate agenda models had been imposed in 1993, union membership had declined, workload had increased, public funding had declined, and faculty was demoralized. He warned us about the increasing "macho managerialism" all too pervasive in the college sector.

We then met with the "macho" president of a college—dubbed one of the success stories in the drive for change. He was proud of the "turn around" at his college and most gleefully exultant over "smashing the union" which had tried to block his reform efforts. The faculty we met that day were subdued and fearful—with good reason. Only 17% were members of the union (Margaret Thatcher having done away with the closed shop). The college president revealed his *modus operandi* by announcing triumphantly in our final meeting that he had successfully fired one of the faculty "incompetents" only an hour before. There was probably little recourse for that fired faculty unfortunate, unless she happened still to be a member of the union.

That experience confirmed what I had intuitively concluded for some time: a strong union is the *only* response to the corporate management style.

The corporate agenda in our institutions has come about from a variety of well-known factors: decrease in public funding, increased reliance on private

153

dollars, and a drive towards an entrepreneurial model of education. But other factors must be acknowledged as having a profound impact on the way our institutions are managed and the way faculty must respond. These are the changes in the law which make the employer clearly responsible for the environment of the institution. Throughout the nineties, this fundamental legal shift has made our work in the union different, and our relationship with management very different.

Employers—that is, managers—now have legal responsibility and subsequent liability to maintain a workplace and a learning environment free of harassment and discrimination, and to accommodate a great diversity of students and employees. All our institutions are governed by the Charter of Rights, human rights legislation, Workers' Compensation, Employment Standards, and, if unionized, labour law.

This legal framework is essential. What we now need is a clear way of ensuring our rights are protected under these laws. It is management's responsibility and management's right to act if there is a perceived danger, threat, or alleged harassment, but management actions must be governed by clear rules and restrictions. Unfortunately, those in charge rarely have the range or quality of "management" skills needed to do the job. The union therefore faces greater pressure to ensure things work properly.

THE COLLEGIAL MODEL

We have noted increasing tension between the collegial model and the union model, and I would like to point out some of the factors leading to that tension and the inclination within CIEA to lean towards the union model.

The collegial model can be somewhat inadequate, and sometimes harmful to the course of natural justice. We only need to look at the Liam Donnelly sexual harassment case at Simon Fraser University for an example of what can go wrong when internal panels judge other members. In a collegial process, colleagues judge colleagues for purposes of hiring, promotion, merit pay, and even dismissal. Avenues of appeal can be slim for the hapless faculty member who may be so judged.

There are other problems with the collegial model. A 1990 United States Supreme Court decision said administrators at New York's Yeshiva University and other private universities were not obliged to negotiate with faculty unions because the professors were "an arm of management."

> In particular, faculty members were denied the right to organize since they were in effect substantially and pervasively operating the enterprise. (Hacker, Andrew. "Who's Sticking to the Union?" *The New York Review*. February 18, 1999: 45–48.)

Some 250,000 faculty at some 2,000 private colleges and universities in the U.S. now can organize only with administrative consent. I don't know how many have been successful in organizing. I suspect not many.

A number of cases from our own system illustrate what we're struggling with. One college has established a task force to look into collegiality and how to work with collegial models and union models. They have a "Mission and Values and Strategic Directions" document containing language with which you are probably all too familiar. This college has developed an entrepreneurial arm partly devoted to international education—another realm that requires some scrutiny. We are selling our programs, our curriculum, and, sometimes, our faculty, to international regimes and countries, yet we lack sufficient measures to safeguard standards and ensure quality. Institutions bring international students here in order to make a profit—potentially a very large profit— so international student programs are seen as "cash cows" for the institutions. As a consequence of this increase in entrepreneurial activity, the college has become divided between the old and the new, and the collegial model is found inadequate to deal with some of the ensuing tensions.

Another college had problems with management, problems with lack of respect, lack of collegiality, and so on. What did management do? They hired a management company to look at the problems. They now have a report: *Analysis of the existing organizational structure and business processes at Langara College*. Full of management-speak, it cost a total of $85,000 to produce. And its conclusion? "Appoint a task force to develop an action plan and implementation strategy." The Langara faculty association reports that little has changed and the problems continue.

THE NEW TAYLORISM: WHY WE NEED UNIONS

Taylorism means breaking down a job, an occupation, into component parts. This can then be accompanied by payment for the component activity on a piece-work basis. A prime example of Taylorism in an academic setting is the Open Learning Agency, a provincial institution supposed to be the centre of distance education in BC. It comprises the Open School for K–12, the Open College for the college system, the Open University, and some other arms. It sells curriculum internationally, and is responsible for the province's educational television, the Knowledge Network.

Support staff and program staff at the Agency were unionized in 1981 by the BC Government & Service Employees' Union. Individuals who developed, revised, and delivered the courses were, however, hired by personal service contracts. Approximately 10 years later, CIEA took an application for certification for the OLA tutors who delivered the course material.

The certification process was difficult, with the employer at first contending that the tutors were not employees but independent contractors. After more than 10 days of hearings at the Labour Relations Board, the Open Learning Agency Tutors' Association (OLATA) was certified in October of 1991.

The first round of bargaining was equally difficult. The employer tried to narrow the scope of the bargaining unit by claiming course development work and course revision were not part of the certificate. After a near strike and almost an entire year of bargaining, the union achieved a first collective agreement, but many of its provisions reflected the previous working conditions and pay arrangements. For example, the collective agreement contained a pay grid which required tutors to bill the Agency for each and every minute piece of work at different rates of pay, or not at all. Tutors are paid piecemeal at piecework rates—for example, payment for each assignment marked. When students drop out, the tutor receives lower pay.

Over the past 18 years the Agency has taken a consistent position that the tutors are not faculty. One of the strike issues in the first round of bargaining was the fact that the Agency refused either to refer to the tutors as faculty or allow the tutors to refer to themselves as faculty. Tutors were often not involved in course revision or curriculum discussions. When they were assigned course revision work of any kind, they were given a personal contract of service outside the collective agreement. Monies received for this work were not considered salary for the purposes of eligibility for benefits or pension contributions.

In 1996, the issue of including course development work in the collective agreement came up again at the bargaining table. The employer refused to include this work in the collective agreement and the union charged the employer with failure to bargain. The union's application failed, but was followed in 1998 by an application to vary the union certificate to include course development work in the collective agreement. After another 15 days of hearings and mediation at the Labour Relations Board, a settlement agreement was reached to include course development work.

In 1997, the Tutors' Association applied to the Labour Relations Board to change the name of the union local to the "Faculty Association of the Open Learning Agency" (FAOLA). The employer opposed this application as well. Currently, the Faculty Association of the Open Learning Agency is made up of over 150 members, many of whom have Ph.D.s or Master's degrees and hold faculty positions at other colleges and universities.

The Agency is firmly entrenched in the belief that these employers are tutors, not faculty. The philosophy of the Agency is that course material is self-instructive, and tutors mere human back-up.

The Tutor Wage Schedule, just one of many fee schedules appended to the collective agreement, goes on for pages, exhaustively detailing telephone tutors, group delivery, pay ranges, nursing tutors, clinical tutors, lab instructor rates, lab time per hour, student assessment per section. There is a whole schedule of how much you get paid for each course and each assessment in each course, how much you get paid if you come to a meeting, how much you get paid if you have an additional office hour, if you participate in employee evaluation, if you prepare a grade appeal, if you advise on course content, if you advise on transfer credits, and so on.

This is how our work could be structured if we're not careful. This is "Taylorism" in its worst form, and this could be your future. In order to get a collective agreement at OLA, we entrenched what we knew to be an unacceptable practice and we continue to try to change it. We do not intend to have this model apply to the rest of CIEA. We will fight so that these people are treated, on the whole, as faculty members.

THE UNION MODEL

How does the union model address all these concerns? I must acknowledge that this model does not fit readily into the academic culture. To quote from an article from *Canadian Dimension*, entitled "Academic Labourers: The New Proletariat":

> There's also the problem of elitism. Academics don't like to think of themselves as union material. I remember a meeting of English sessionals last September where one of my co-workers dared to mention unionization. He was blasted by a fellow sessional who launched into a harangue about how unions are too antagonistic for an academic environment. We are professionals, he said. We need to maintain a collegial atmosphere.
>
> For people who still believe that academic life is detached from the work that gets done out in the real world, talking about wages and job security is like talking to the taxman about poetry. You just can't do it. They never considered that the mystique of the detached ivory-tower life blinds them to the dismal labour practices they work under.

What the union model does ensure is protection through due process for all. The grievance procedure has many checks and balances within it to ensure fairness *and* resolution, and an outside decision-maker, if the internal processes don't work. The union model is based on concepts that we should hold dear: "an injury to one is an injury to all" and that those who work in the system deserve a say and a clear means to counter decisions that affect their futures.

LOBBYING ALLIANCES

In CIEA we have benefited from our alliances within the post-secondary education sector, and with labour and students. We have gone outside our institutions to find, develop and forge common cause. For example, we have worked closely with the Canadian Federation of Students on preserving the tuition freeze, preserving access, and ensuring spaces are available for students.

Most recently, CIEA members have attended public forums throughout the province arranged by the BC Business Summit, speaking out against this particular corporate agenda. Our experience with the BC Federation of Labour there has been a shared understanding of the corporate agenda and an intense concern about the effects of commercialism on our schools, colleges and universities.

We are also members of the Coalition for Public Education in BC, and we are working with our partners to try to preserve what we all value: accessible public education. We know that we need to improve our dialogue with the public and with our communities. We need the public involved in defending public education.

Another example from England typifies what *not* to do in a public campaign. Some professors in higher education protested wage inadequacies with signs that read "*Rectify the anomalies.*" That's just not a public winner. We need to remember that we are members of the public —we need the public, we need their support. We are workers—we need labour's support.

WORKS CITED

Babiak, Peter. "Academic Labourers: The New Proletariat." *Canadian Dimension.* January-February 1999: 41–44.

Capilano College. *Mission and Values & Strategic Directions.*

Faris, Ron, Ph.D. "From Elitism to Inclusive Education: Development of Outcomes-Based Learning and Post-Secondary Credit Accumulation and Transfer Systems in England and Wales. A report on observations and lessons learned by a study-visit team from the Centre for Curriculum, Transfer and Technology and the BC Council on Admissions & Transfer." 1999.

Hacker, Andrew. "Who's Sticking to the Union?" *The New York Review.* February 18, 1999: 45–48.

Leatherman, Courtney. "Report Laments Rise of 'Collegiality' as a Factor in Tenure Reviews." *The Chronicle of Higher Education: Today's News.* [On-line]. September 22, 1999.

McNaught, Kenneth. "The Letter on the Principal's Desk." *The Canadian Forum.* July 1999: 17–21.

Reed, J.H., and Associates. "Analysis of the existing organizational structure and business processes of Langara College." June 16, 1999.

Shall We Perform or Shall We Be Free?

WILLIAM BRUNEAU

In summer 1994, the Council of Ministers of Education, Canada [CMEC] met to continue work on a Pan-Canadian Education Indicators Programme. As usual in public events of this kind, much had been done in advance of the Ministers' arrival in Toronto. Unusually for Canada, this time chartered accountants worked closely with administrative colleagues and policy-minded bureaucrats to prepare the agenda and background papers.[1]

The presence of accountants, and repeated calls for "accountability" before, during, and after the 1994 meeting, hinted at a sea-change in Canadian education. For the first time in Canadian history, political leaders and, to a lesser degree their henchpersons, showed signs of being willing to give up a measure of discretion over students, curricula, and research in public schools and universities. Indeed, they looked as if they were ready to move some types of administrative control directly into the hands of the accountants, and to decide appropriate levels of public funding on the basis of purely statistical measures.

Among the accountants and statisticians of that meeting and many others like it in the mid-1990s, there were, of course, moderates. If those particular bean-counters had triumphed, the new statistics might have been mere guides to educational policy,[2] or perhaps soporific reading matter for obscure Treasury Board officials.

Alas, the moderates did not win.[3] In the end, the "true believers" and their ideological sponsors in the Business Council on National Issues, the Fraser Institute, and the C.D. Howe Institute acquired new and unexpectedly strong influence over public educational policy. Particularly in British Columbia, New Brunswick, Alberta, and Ontario, claims for performance measures took on a compulsory tone. The dominant theme of discussion from 1995 onward was that public spending on education must be held even, or decline. Furthermore, the entire public post-secondary system should—indeed *must* —become more "responsive" to private sectors of "the economy" (however the "economy" was defined by the ideologues of any particular day).[4]

New statistics would, so the accountants and their political masters claimed, provide reliable links between teaching and research on one hand, and "markets" on the other. The links they proposed are reminiscent of the many "ties" Gulliver experienced as he awoke from his famous shipwreck:

> ...[W]hen I awaked it was just day-light. I attempted to rise, but was not able to stir: for...I found my arms and legs were strongly fastened on each side to the ground; and my hair...tied down in the same manner. I likewise felt several slender ligatures across my body, from my arm-pits to my thighs. I could only look upwards.[5]

That is, no single measure would necessarily, by itself, interfere with university autonomy. Nor would any one measure necessarily undermine provincial government responsibility for higher education. But if universities and colleges and schools were directed (at least in part) by the *several* requirements of labour markets, of financial and service markets, and many more markets yet to come—the net effect, the sheer *accumulation* of market ties would have the effect of tying post-secondary education so tightly to business—national or trans-national—that institutional autonomy would be emptied of meaning.

Performance indicators [PIs] were already in the 1980s and 1990s a worrisome (and costly) distraction from the teaching and research work instructors and students in Canadian post-secondary education are supposed to do. Already they threatened to displace authority and responsibility, and to change (I would argue, to weaken) public accountability.

Then Ontario Premier Bob Rae's speech of 1994 October 25 made explicit the meanings and use of PIs:

> Our standards and our achievements should be truly international in scope. We should draw comparisons in our testing and assessment of how we're doing and we should use these comparisons to improve how we do things....In most businesses, it's called benchmarking. And it's something the public sector had better get used to.

Mr Rae's frustration with public education was palpable. He wanted performance benchmarks, and thought schools and universities "must be held accountable" if they do not meet or surpass those benchmarks. By accountability, Bob Rae meant *control*, control by government (through funding mechanisms) and control by clients (who will vote with their feet if an institution does not measure up). Mr Rae only hints at the final result of a system that works on a basis of accountability:

> If you were to come from Mars and watch TV, your assumption would be that lawyers and doctors and those involved in the criminal world are the three occupations....It's very important to realize the culture we are up against is a culture that doesn't recognize enough the importance of science and mathematics....we have to create wealth before we can share it.[6]

The way forward (according to Mr Rae, but also to the Ontario Council on University Affairs and a number of Ontario university presidents) is through benchmarks and inter-university rankings on PIs.

In 2000 as in 1990, proponents of PIs think that numbers should decide, or at the very least play a crucial role in deciding what should be taught, where and when, and even how (as, for example, by distance education techniques that lend themselves to measures of knowledge-acquisition speeds).

Now those same proponents go much, much further. They argue that statistics make it possible to decide "automatically" how much money universities and granting councils need be given for research in the natural sciences, the humanities, and the social sciences. The newest PIs take into account how many patents a department has registered, how many matching grants it has found, how many employable students it has graduated, whether those students are working in the exact fields for which they were trained (the word "educated" rarely appears), and of course, how many dollars per student were expended to produce all those results. Where the PIs of the 1980s and early 1990s were mildly interventionist, and occasionally helpful in the cause of broader access to liberal, post-secondary education, the new PIs of the *fin de siècle* are wildly interventionist, and pose a serious threat to academic freedom, university autonomy, and accessible, critically-minded, liberal education.

The reason for the shift is not hard to find. The PIs of the early- to mid-1990s had a controlling and sometimes punitive tone, but rarely mentioned the private sector. It is a crucial and revealing fact of educational politics in 2000 that PIs have made the move from public to private. Now they don't just mention the private sector: they tie the universities, as the Lilliputians tied Gulliver, to a world, and to a way of life that has little to do with education and everything to do with the private interests of companies and investors.

The tone began to shift in Alberta, where the provincial government set aside an "envelope" of "performance funding" available to institutions that do well in the PIs sweepstakes but may not otherwise merit additional funds. Ontario in 2000 announced its intention to do likewise. Across the country meanwhile, governments and business have argued (energetically) that the usual forms of academic governance should and must be set aside or profoundly "reformed." PIs and "modernization" do not welcome the careful and critical style of governance and decision making that scholars hold dear.

No longer need university Senates decide if Italian or Physics should be taught, nor should university administrations negotiate the funding of courses—for in place of *publicly accountable* (but "cumbersome") procedure, PIs would be rapidly decisive, thus making due process an unnecessary sideshow. Statistics on costs of instruction, student throughput, student satisfaction (read "customer satisfaction"), and employability would bring in a new system capable of nimble and resilient action—with rapid response to the latest news from the NASDAQ.[7]

Although provincial governments are not yet acting in this extreme way (they are mostly just talking about it), recent university history shows how quickly we are moving in the general direction. The idea of PIs, including commercially-driven PIs, took root in Canada in a brief space, but built on a lengthy tradition of so-called "neutral reporting devices." These "neutral" measures have, again and again, turned out not to be neutral at all, even in the early decades of the century. As early as World War I, "neutral" statistics were used to influence or even to replace informed academic discussion and judgement in senates and administrations—and to discourage students and their families from participating fully in Canadian liberal education.[8] Since 1983, when cuts to public funding of education began in earnest, the commercialization of post-secondary education, more than any other new factor, has encouraged the performance indicator movement on one hand, and continued declines in public funding on another.

Conjoined with ideological and political forces that have always encouraged indicators, the "new commercialization" has had unforeseen and worrisome effects on the content, the pedagogy, the funding, and the governance of Canadian post-secondary education. But it is not just Canada's universities and colleges that feel the pressure. In the 1980s and 1990s, the presidents of Canada's research granting councils came to agree that market "ties" made sense, and for the first time since the War, spoke of them without embarrassment. They had accepted by the late 1980s that it was a good idea to measure the economic effects of research, not merely seek to produce such effects.[9]

In a way, the councils were driven to it by the Mulroney and Chrétien governments. But those governments wanted to go much further, eventually hoping (or requiring) that the councils would accept public funding that depended not just on measurable economic pay-off (PIs), but also on finding "matching funds" from "industry." In the Natural Sciences and Engineering Research Council, this was widely agreed by 1992. By spring 1995, the president of the SSHRCC was pressing social scientists and humanists to start looking for corporate partners.

In 1996, Finance Minister Martin announced a new programme of funding for advanced "mission-oriented" research, the Canada Foundation for Innovation. Legislated in the 1997 spring session of Parliament,

> The Canada Foundation for Innovation (CFI) is an independent corporation established in 1997 by the federal government to strengthen Canadian capability for research. The CFI will achieve this

objective by investing in the development of research infrastructure in Canada. The CFI's mandate is to increase the capability of Canadian universities, colleges, hospitals, and other not-for-profit institutions to carry out important world-class scientific research and technology development. [T]he...Foundation, in co-operation with funding partners, provides infrastructure for research and development that will:

    •support economic growth and job creation;
    •lead to improvements in health, the environment, and quality
    of life;....[10]

The funding for CFI, nearly a billion dollars across five years, was the first infusion of new money for public post-secondary education in some time. Notice that, like the funding for many NSERC and SSHRC programmes, it required "co-operation with funding partners" (generally, 50% funding), and would support investment in "infrastructure," not basic, or "core" operating funds.

Without quite saying so, the Federal government's requirement that universities acquire matching funds from the private sector, in general equalling what they get from CFI, amounts to a performance indicator. In a sense, it is a *perfect* "performance indicator." Those universities most able to find matching funds in private industry will do better than those that cannot or will not. The result is"automatic" expenditure of public funds for post-secondary education based on "performance" in the private sector, but without the bother of having to gather statistics, or to take explicit and public decisions on funding!

Then in March 1999, the federal government's Expert Panel on the Commercialization of University Research produced a first version of "Public Investment in University Research — Reaping the Benefits." In its response to "Public Investment," the CAUT noted that the Panel had relied on inaccurate data from the OECD and elsewhere, purporting to show that Canada's productivity growth had been dismal over the past quarter-century. The CAUT was especially worried

that the report's recommendations would facilitate the expansion of corporate control over university research. This would happen because the report's recommendations encourage the steering of research toward the commercial interests of private corporations, undermine the tradition of open communication between scholars, and provide for the expropriation of the results of university research to the corporate sector.[11]

The Panel recommended that universities take commercialization to be a core function of higher education in Canada, either (again to quote the CAUT response) "adding it as a fourth mission alongside research, teaching, and community service or by incorporating it...."

The obvious effect of all this would be to infringe on academic freedom, tying (yet another tie) university research to the private sector, making a profoundly public service the obligated servant of corporate interest.

To make its position utterly clear, the Panel at one point recommended that universities incorporate professors' commercialization track records into decisions on promotion and tenure. As the CAUT commentary put it,

> This is good news for researchers developing highly marketable products, no matter how trivial they are. It spells career stagnation or worse for those who specialize in theoretical physics, child poverty or English literature.

The Panel announced that it was not aiming "primarily to produce new revenue streams for universities," for they thought "the revenues from commercializing research constitute a small addition to university budgets, *generally below 1 percent.*"

In recommending the hiring of administrators and new industrial liaison offices, at public expense, the Panel followed a well-developed international practice. In New Zealand, Australia, and the United Kingdom, the tremendous cost of developing and publishing and using PIs is never considered in arguments for or against PIs. It is as if PIs cost nothing, whether in time or money—and as if PIs really would result in more or better research.

***

Where does this kind of thinking come from? Certainly the 1980s were full of it, as for example, the 1988 Science Council of Canada report, *Winning in a World Economy*:

> A new economic order based on global competition in knowledge-intensive industries is emerging... In an age when international economic success increasingly depends on knowledge and techno-logical innovation, universities need to engage more actively in economic renewal in Canada ... ways must be found to strengthen the role universities play in the economy ... Universities must reorient some of their activities to provide the teaching and research required by the private sector ... Priority among university activities is now typically given to liberal education and fundamental research ... however, universities must contribute more effectively to economic renewal; they are the primary source of the people and knowledge so urgently needed for industrial revitalization ... hiring, tenure, and promotion systems should increasingly recognize, support, and reward the transfer of knowledge and technology to industry ... If universities do not reach out to meet the needs of society, these needs will be satisfied elsewhere and universities will diminish in importance.[12]

But even in the 1980s the proponents of PIs and of commercialization (by no means always the same people) built on much older practices and theories.

Beneath and behind was a long history of public interest in measures and devices of all kinds. The proponents of performance indicators, among them the Canadian Comprehensive Auditing Foundation, the Corporate Higher Education Forum, and the Canadian Small Business Association, shared an ancient dream. It was the dream of the statistically-minded social scientists of the 1920s, the behaviourist psychologists and social psychologists, the Taylorists and efficiency-cultists of the period after about 1910, and of social engineers in the late 1940s. It was the dream of education and society as machines, efficient devices for the attainment of high social objectives on one hand, and inculcation of measurable knowledge and skill on the other.

It is tempting to see the "new" PIs as outcomes of economic and social developments beginning with the Oil Price Crisis of 1973, rising public sentiment in the developed world that public expenditure had got out of hand, and the appearance of neo-liberal administrations in the United Kingdom (Margaret Thatcher, Prime Minister from 1979–1990) and in the United States (Ronald Reagan, President, 1981–1989). Besides, one might argue, the vast expenditures of the 1960s on public higher education and health had, for whatever reason, not been sufficiently tested for efficacy and efficiency. But even Thatcher and Reagan built on history. Thatcher's advocacy for greater independence of the individual from the state, an end to "excessive" government interference in the economy, and reductions in public expenditures (with tax cuts) and the printing of money (monetarism) itself had a long pedigree.

At the turn of the twentieth century, two forces came together to lead governments of the day to try out the first publicly-administered system of PIs. The first was Taylorism (after Frederick W. Taylor), or "scientific management." The application of industrial and physical principles to every department of life became a national passion among the capitalist class and among many civil servants. Because Taylorism (and Fordism) came at the end of a century-long fascination with social statistics and social physics, as Auguste Comte might have termed them, and at a time of rapid growth in the forms and extent of the State, its popularity was assured.

But President Webster of Clark University finally grew tired of it:

> I am tired of scientific management, so-called. I have heard of it from scientific managers, from university presidents, from casual acquaintances in railway trains; I have read of it in the daily papers, the weekly papers, the ten-cent magazines, the fifteen-cent magazines, the thirty-five cent magazine, and in the *Outlook*.... For fifteen years I have been a subscriber to a magazine dealing with engineering matters, feeling it incumbent on me to keep in touch with

167

the applications of physics to the convenience of life, but the touch has become a pressure, the pressure a crushing strain, until the mass of articles on shop practice and scientific management threatened to crush all thought out of my brain, and I stopped my subscription.[13]

Taylor believed above all in EFFICIENCY (he would have capitalized the word)—that is, the elimination of waste. Management and industrial work could be improved by giving up "rule of thumb" methods. There was always one, and only one best way of doing any particular job, and this method could be determined through "scientific" study. Once determined, the method should be applied through an "...an almost equal division of the work and the responsibility between the management and the workmen."[14]

The keys to the method were the stopwatch, detailed studies of movement (time-motion studies), standardization, functional foremanship (the hiring of foremen who could teach effectively the parts of a job), and forward planning ("global" planning). Almost immediately after its publication in 1911 and 1912, the Taylor message was carried with evangelical zeal into all areas of public life, not just industrial activity.

When it was applied to education, the results were predictably grim. The most famous educational applications were those of John Franklin Bobbitt. His 1915 article on "High School Costs"[15] still repays close study.

> Accurate cost-accounting lies at the foundations of all successful business management.... [S]atisfactory instruction in high school English can be had for fifty dollars per thousand student-hours...and those responsible for high-school management have a standard of judgment that can be used for measuring the efficiency of their practices....Fifty-nine dollars paid in Rockford is the median price paid for algebra and geometry. There is no reason to think that the results obtained in Rockford are in any degree inferior to those obtained in the dozen cities paying a higher price.

By the 1920s, superintendents in Baltimore and Boston were handing out merit pay to Latin teachers based on a formula that linked heating costs, salary charges, time-on-task (both teachers' and pupils'), administrative salaries, and examination results. If you lowered the heat to 60° F, gave merit pay for good examination results, and inspected the classroom every second day to be sure no one was wasting time, then....you had an efficient school. Never mind that it was a prison, that the administration was reminiscent of Genghis Khan, that inspection from the centre took no account of people's local circumstances, and that the main point of education—to give people some joy in learning, to give them the mental furniture they need to have permanently interesting lives, to make them into critically-minded researchers and citizens—was utterly lost.

Matters worsened in the 1950s with the temporary ascendancy in some social sciences of naive behaviourism. The idea that costs and detailed educational behaviours could sensibly be linked, was contemplated (and sometimes adopted) in university after university—most often, alas, in university faculties of education.[16]

The behaviourist edifice tottered and (some say) fell in the late 1960s, with the rise of a generation determined to pay attention to educational principles, and insistent on their presumed right to participate in educational decision making.

***

The rise of PIs may, then, be explained *partly* by considering the 19th century fondness for detailed statistics on social life, and by the appearance of Taylorism and behaviourism. But the sudden popularity of PIs since 1980—a kind of re-birth, if you like—also requires an ideological explanation.

That ideology has three faces. It has the Thatcherite face mentioned a little earlier. This is the face of Mr Klein's policies in Alberta, policies premised on the notion that the state is evil, and much too big. Elimination of public education may not be his final goal; but the appearance of Charter Schools, unilateral reductions of funding to universities and schools through most of the 1990s, and rewards to private educational providers suggest that the diminishing of public education would be the outcome of Mr Klein's policies.

The PI ideology has a second, anti-intellectual face. It considers consumption, and growth, and the manipulation of things we can *see* to be the primary business of life. The moral emotions, the possibility of intentional community, the political commitments that democrats must share —the unseen things that glue us together, and the things that distinguish us from the animals—are not the business of the public, and certainly not the business of public education. This view is worse than pernicious; it is vicious, and reminiscent of certain political theories of the 1930s.

Finally, the PI ideology has a still more unpleasant face, what some have called the "culture of envy." It is the unspoken belief that if X (*any* X) is complicated and hard to understand, then X is necessarily effete and probably immoral. Certainly it doesn't deserve public funding!

If we consider PIs that have attracted the most attention in the United States, the United Kingdom, New Zealand, Australia, Western Europe, and...Canada, then we see that all three of these ideological "faces" are plainly visible.

One of the most beloved PIs in Europe and Australasia is called "first destination" ($PI^{1st\ dest}$), that is, the first job (or underemployment, or unemployment) a graduate gets on leaving university. If $PI^{1st\ dest}$ shows that graduates of University X are 90% employed in secondary and tertiary industries immediately on completion, then University X's claim on certain funds (in Ontario, these would probably be called "Economic Renewal Funds") would be strengthened.[17] If University Y, whose programmes in Forestry, Education, Architecture, and Law had a *lower* PI[1st dest], University Y would be in financial trouble. The Ontario Council on University Affairs 1994 PIs *could* be used this way, although the Council has been at pains to say they *might* be used in some other, unspecified ways. PI[1st dest] could, nevertheless, be used to redirect funds in highly interventionist manner, around the post-secondary system, or away from it altogether.

PIs, oddly enough, help civil servants and politicians to hide these ugly facts from the public and from themselves. In the endless manipulation of numbers and ratios, the hard consequences of their actions are magically insulated, if not banished from sight and mind.

PIs, in most countries that have them, include measures ("bibliometric measures") to show whether a university or department is performing well in the publish-or-perish sweepstakes. (It's odd, for the reason I gave a moment ago, that PIs about scientific research and publication should help civil servants and politicians *not* to think about the negative consequences for R&D of expenditure reductions in the very institutions that *do* the R&D.) In the United Kingdom, "units" (that is, departments, institutes, and/or faculties) are rated and funded on a five-point (now six-point) grading scheme.[18] A unit's "grade" may be influenced markedly by the performance of a single "star" academic who publishes frequently in big-name journals. That unit may therefore have to make extraordinary salary offers to their potential "star," and may want to avoid larger curriculum reforms that might "marginalize" or distract from the star's research and publication. The spectre of unlimited inter-university competition thus takes on new meaning and corporeality.

In the UK, officials and public commentators alike have confused "competition" with "ranking" of universities from the earliest Thatcherite period. Competition has been an integral feature of the university life since the High Middle Ages, when Bologna, Montpellier, and Paris competed for medical students, and theologues from Paris and Oxford held dialectical show-downs in the streets. In a recent article, Ernst Benjamin of the American Association of University Professors, describes constructive forms of competition that have helped to shape the American system of higher education (and accreditation, by the way).[19] A kind of competition is implied in the groupings of universities in the American Association of Graduate Schools (Research Universities Groups 1 and 2, and so on), the Carnegie Foundation's groupings, and our own views of the tasks of universities as different as Brandon and UQAM and Dalhousie and UBC.

To "rank" universities in one long list, a list that necessarily compares apples and oranges, and that inevitably twists (and may even undermine) the universities' aims and missions, is to satisfy only those who like long lists—and these include amateur statisticians and politicians of the OK Corral variety. The excellence of Canada's smaller universities is a matter of record. In a long list ranking universities by the size of their laboratories or libraries, that excellence will be lost.[20]

Such a list can do permanent damage to the fabric of communities in every region of the country, and to the very fabric of learning in Canada. Some two years ago, Canadian university business schools were ranked in the business press. The statistical insignificance of differences between them were forgotten in the rush to put all those schools in one long, ranked list. Business deans who had rushed to embrace the survey when it began, recoiled in horror when they saw what it meant in practice. Although Canada's business journalists would love to sell a few more papers, no similar ranking has since appeared.

In Britain, meanwhile, rankings produced at huge expense by the State have had the unexpected effect of frightening off some international students altogether, or clustering them in a few, lucky institutions. As a result, the British are hastily modifying the reporting structure to eliminate (if they ever can) meaningless distinctions. They will not, of course, succeed. The British ranking of research universities is a wonderful example of a mountain labouring mightily to produce a mouse, since it has shown (to the surprise only of Zimbabwean rebels only just emerging from the bush) that Oxford, Cambridge, and London are the UK's major research universities.

It makes sense to group universities for purposes of careful description, as Carnegie sometimes does. The differences between institutions turn out, of course, to be statistically insignificant, especially as regards "quality." If one wanted to improve research, one might look for creative and promising departments where good science was being done and give them financial support; one would improve the budgets of the granting councils; one would assist in public education campaigns about the importance of science (broadly defined to include the humanities and social sciences); and so on and on.

Private-minded, anti-intellectual, and premised on a culture of envy: the three ideological faces of performance indication are all present in the move to league tables, rankings, and senseless commercialization.

PIs—Costs Without Benefits?

In a word, PIs have made British (and American and Canadian) university departments strongly conservative, the opposite of the effect they were supposed to produce. These departments must think twice before changing their curricula on merely "educational" grounds—that is, for the sake of critical thinking or liberal education—unless the numbers call for it. Nor can

171

departments plan their staffing in advance, for staffing is driven by employability PIs on one hand, and by the star system—and over these matters the department has no control. The president of Wolfson College, Oxford, once remarked:

> If you have a post open these days, you don't say: "Let's find someone who can build up a good research centre and hope he can teach well, too." Since research brings in the money, teaching is losing out.[21]

Frans van Vught, director of the Centre for Higher Education Policy Studies at Twente University of Technology in the Netherlands, is alarmed:

> One of the most negative developments is the coming into existence of a 'compliance culture,' especially in the U.K. Academics easily find out how to perform if performance is to be directly connected with funding. The whole thing becomes a costly show, with no effect whatsoever on quality.[22]

Returning to the point about research and teaching, PIs encourage universities and governments to strive for instant relevance and industrial utility—then punish universities that turn in that direction, saying their professors are not publishing enough or in the right places.

The use of PIs to reallocate public money is just the first phase. In a second phase (in some jurisdictions the first and second phases are contemporaneous, and in others there may be *only* a second phase), PIs reduce the range of choices in university senates and boards of governors. It's not that high civil servants and politicians arrive on campus with calculators and check-lists in hand, posing a direct threat to university autonomy. Rather, they arrange funding formulae so that some good academic programmes and choices may become unfundable and/or politically dicey for the university concerned. On the other hand, they may not. For PIs are not driven by academic considerations, and so may accidentally "reward" programmes academics themselves consider to be good and intellectually significant.

The universities' own decision making systems thus become irrelevant in a world dominated by numbers, numbers that come to have lives of their own. The people who best know the university—its programmes, its practices, its research, and its links to the wider community—are no longer a vital part of the picture. Teachers, staff members, and students under PIs find their input is reduced in importance and impact. This anti-worker bias goes against every management principle now in vogue, whether it be TQM (Total Quality Management), MBO (Management By Objectives), MBWA (Management by Walking Around), or Quality Circles.

PIs cost money, lots of money. CMEC staff tell tales of financial woe, and the burden of their lay is this: the CMEC's own offices just cannot afford to go on staffing such things as Statistics Councils, administering tests across the country, and hiring another bureaucracy. In the UK, the cost and inefficiency of centrally-administered PIs have led to important shifts in the PI bureaucracy. In 1994, the *Times Higher Education Supplement* described one such change:

> The Higher Education Funding Council for Wales is forging an agreement with the Higher Education Quality Council which could open the way for a single quality agency. It aims to sidestep complaints about the present system, under which funding councils go into individual departments and assess teaching and learning. Meanwhile, the HEQC audits the university procedures that are supposed to assure quality. Institutions argue that the whole system is costly and time-consuming.... From the beginning the Welsh have not been happy with the English system of grading departments ....and have aspired to a 'pure profile', a description of a university department that eschews grades in favour of an outline of strengths and weaknesses, and suggestions for improvement.[23]

The training of English and Welsh assessors itself became a major academic "growth industry" in the late 1990s in Britain.

This is just one example of a more general truth, which is that PIs have unexpected effects, and produce consequences the opposite of those intended (so far as anyone can figure out what *was* intended).

What Should Be Done?

Despite the volume of talk about PIs, most proponents are still unclear exactly what PIs are. They have forgotten about the constant re-invention throughout the twentieth century of PIs, and (on a generous interpretation of the facts) may not know they recommend a monster. They may be social mechanics, but naive. Really, this is altogether *too* generous a view. At a time of constant pressure to replace public funds with private money, to participate wholeheartedly in private-sector markets of all types, and to use PIs to judge how quickly universities are making these moves—the naive social mechanics of another era are gone, replaced by knowing neo-liberals.

The neo-liberal call is for accountability, accountability, accountability. Now, professors and instructors cannot oppose, and would not wish to oppose, either the theory or the practice of public accountability. The Canadian Association of University Teachers policy says Canadian universities should accept a form of accountability to government.

The Canadian professoriate has always said it is ready, willing, and even anxious to describe what professors and their universities do for the country, the society, and the culture—and to make claims on public funds based on those descriptions. Funding levels may rise or fall (although, after thirty years of cuts, one justifiably hopes for the former). But any shift should and must depend on political and social factors, and should occur only after open and fair public discussion of the matter in open meetings of our university senates, our boards of governors, and our legislatures. The automatic mechanism of PIs simply assures that universities and colleges will be less accountable in the true sense, and ultimately, less excellent.

And this touches on a crucial point. PIs simply do not do the job for which they are intended. *They do not encourage or enhance accountability.*

If accountability means that universities and colleges must possess the means, and the inclination (i) to say what they do, and (ii) to say why they do it, then they are accountable as never before. We would do better, all right, perhaps publishing our course outlines on the Web, our salaries on the Internet, and our CVs on media the public might care to consult.

But we already publish reams of statistics on ourselves, thanks to the ministrations of Statistics Canada and CMEC, and we are audited endlessly by insider CAs and outsider CAs.

From the president of the university to the president of the student society, Canadian universities already report exhaustively on their financial arrangements, their curricula, their research, their admissions and their graduates, the professorial life, student life, the work of professional and technical staff. All report in straightforward ways for those not wanting to be bothered by thousands of pages of data; on the other hand, for those who do, the data await. Finally, all these data are subjected to public scrutiny in university senates and boards of governors, institutions replete with government appointees and public representatives, not just the universities' professors, students, and administrators.

By these standards, universities are truly accountable. There is little justification for PIs, unless of course one seeks to make universities LESS accountable to public purposes. That may well be the objective of some who press for them.

On another hand, I wonder how accountable we *can* be. The mandates and missions of Canadian universities are, after all, a mass of vague and platitudinous generalization. If we are to be accountable for carrying out our historic and democratic obligations, then we must be crystal-clear what our mandates are. How accountable *can* we be when the meaning of accessibility is not spelled out at the University of X? How accountable can we be when we are unclear what we consider our economic and research tasks in our regions and provinces? How accountable can we be when we say we are "global" institutions? Where is the accountability in an institution that pretends to a global "mission" and answers to a global "clientele"? To whom, or to what, is it answerable?

Obviously, we have something like a vacuum at the top, in Canadian university and college mandates. There is every good reason to fill that vacuum, and to do so as quickly as we may. After all, the criteria and standards by which we wish to be judged are to be found in the local history, in local social and economic conditions (for these, we would wish to consult widely in the populations we serve), in the political structures (participatory democracy) that permitted the foundation—and the maintenance—of publicly-funded universities in this country, and in the deeper requirements of the fields of study for which we educate—the mandate to teach and to do research in the disciplines (or between them) as best we possibly can.

Our present legislated mandates are necessarily broad, encompassing, and culturally inclusive. The trouble, is they are not terribly precise. If we do nothing to revise them, then we are open to the imposition of commercially-driven PIs, and such PIs are very precise indeed. Appendix A lists PIs from several provinces and states, the UK, New Zealand, and Australia. The list is divided into popular categories (or "types"), and ends with examples of PIs actually in use.

The narrowness and partiality of these statistical "indicators" are instantly noticeable. They increase "system accountability" and "quality" —but only if we measure by simple-minded and irrelevant standards. They do tell politicians which universities to reward and which to punish at provincial budget time. But surely we have better ways of judging how to build publicly-funded, publicly-responsible post-secondary education in this country. (Besides, the idea of giving up so much control over public funding has made not a few Canadian politicians nervous. That nervousness has so far kept them from going to extremes, as for example, the State of South Carolina, which claims to base 100% of its public funding decisions on performance indication.[24])

Canadian universities aim to educate people. This means, first, that universities do their best to put students in a position to conduct various kinds of "research" about their society and about the physical world around them. This may mean anything from life-long, well-organized reading in our national literature and history—in aid of sound decision making in the community—or a systematic inquiry in one's professional field, whether it be law, or engineering, or education, or another of the many fields offered in Canada's universities. Second, universities do their best to ensure that students know and act on their citizenly rights.

Because of the importance of these two tasks, it is morally and politically essential that everyone have access to a university education. That is why in the past thirty years, Canadian universities have paid special attention to this matter of access, and to the related question of equity in the university itself.

Canadian university teachers and students have consistently invited the public—and not just its elected officials—to check whether we are indeed open to all sectors, classes, and groups, and whether we govern ourselves in a way that ensures all have the opportunity to learn once they are at university. The CAUT has called repeatedly for a system of university governance that would guarantee openness and due process in financial decision making, like the guarantees we have in curriculum decisions. Without openness about money, and this must include openness at the levels of Cabinet and Treasury Board, it will be hard to ensure openness in matters of access and equity. PIs do nothing to help in the achievement of ANY of these great goals.

In sum, the imposition of PIs, in conjunction with public funding cuts and intense commercialization, must surely reduce the quality of teaching and research, lessen the social and economic value of universities' "output," undermine public accountability, and do exactly what the Fraser Institute claims it does not want—produce a new and expensive government bureaucracy. If one sees "accountability" as *control,* rather than as *openness and honesty in a system characterized by due process*, PIs make good sense. Otherwise, they make no sense at all.

The CAUT's policy on PIs,[25] and its strategies for responding to the PIs "movement," would help reoccupy linguistic space occupied by PIs, would encourage a renewed public vision of accountability, would help to reinvigorate participatory university governance (not to mention provincial and federal governance), and would rest, ultimately, on the creation of clear university mandates rooted in democratic politics.

Because it would turn public post-secondary education away from its central purposes, the movement to install market-driven PIs is among the riskiest developments in the Canadian university since the 18th century. Because the movement is still young, and because it is not equally attractive or influential everywhere in Canada's federal state, it is possible this great change may yet be stopped. One can only hope that PIs, and the commercial impulse that makes them attractive in the year 2000, will have been long forgotten by the end of the 21st century.

Appendix A

TYPES AND INSTANCES OF INDICATORS

TYPES

1. System-wide / University-wide / by Unit
    Example: Ontario Universities Applications Centre keeps track of
        **[total applications by Ontario university] / and
            [total applications/ entire Ontario system]
        **[total number of admission offers, system wide] / and
            [# of offers accepted by university]
        **[average grades of students accepting, system wide] / and
            [average grades of students accepting by university]
        **[library holdings, expressed as volumes / student, by university and
            systemwide]
        **[computing facilities (for example, CPUs, terminals, modem lines / by
            university/ by student][1]
2. Internal / External / Operational (or "Inputs/Process/Outputs")
    Example: Jarratt [UK] Report.[2]
        Internal   market share (applications/university/by subject)
                graduation rates (number of students not completing)
                MA/PhD attraction rates/university
                higher degree success rates/university
                time taken/degree/unit/university
                acquisition of research funds/unit/university
                teaching quality (undefined)
        External   first destination of graduates/university
                general employment of graduates/university
                publications/citations/professor/unit/university
                patents & consultancies/unit/university
                memberships in learned societies/unit/university
                papers at conferences/professor/unit/university
        Operational   unit costs (less is better)
        (or "*Process*")   student/staff ratios (higher is better)
                class size (bigger is better)
                course options (unclear if more is better)
                staff workload (more is better, but with formula giving reductions to
                    publishing researchers)
                library size (bigger is better)

---

[1]Taken from Association of Universities and Colleges of Canada, *Measuring Up: Using Indicators to Manage Change* (Ottawa: The Association, 1994), vol. II, p. 22.

[2]Keith Jarratt, *Report, Steering Committee for Efficiency Studies in Universities* (London: Committee of Vice-Chancellors and Principals, 1985), p. 53.

computing availability (more is better)

INSTANCES
A more extensive version of the preceding
1. Outcome indicators (sometimes contrasted with "process" indicators)
    1.1 Test scores (national/international and standardized)
    1.2 Test scores (university and/or professor-administered, and ordinarily not standardized)
    1.3 Employment rates of graduates
    1.4 Income levels of graduates
    1.5 Goodness-of-fit between training/education received and employment
    1.6 Publication rates (refereed articles/professor, books/professor)
    1.7 Citation counts
    1.8 Copyrights acquired/size of professoriate
    1.9 Grants received by professors and instructors
    1.10   Industry funding received (by individual professor/instructor; by department and/or faculty; by institution)
2. Degree and diploma completion rates
    2.1 Time to completion
    2.2 Drop-out rates
3. 'Qualitative indicators'
    3.1 Educational "structures"
        Usually administrative. An example of such an indicator might be lists of institutions where Senates had significant influence on budget matters, or where Senates had [say] ≥25% members drawn from the professoriate; the degree to which a university or college administration was 'consultative'; how far lay people may participate in decisions
    3.2 Educational "practices" (number of classrooms considered to be magistrocentric *vs* student-centred, and so on)
    3.3 Behaviours of participants (amount of time students spend studying, doing salaried work, and so on)
    3.4 Climate and atmosphere (chilly or not-chilly; closed or open)
    3.5 Curriculum (liberal *vs* vocational; thematic *vs* fragmented; science *vis-à-vis* humanities, and so on)
    3.6 Professorial reward system (teaching *vs* research *vs* service)
        Includes **time** spent on direct instruction *vs* time spent otherwise
    3.7 Teaching space (this indicator is open to quantitative expression: number of students:number of m^2:subject of study; age of building; light and heat)
4. Contextual indicators
    4.1 Resource levels (public and private finance of universities and colleges; industrial support in kind)
    4.2 Government policies
        :on proportion of tax receipts to spend on public education
        :proportion to be spent on higher education
        :and the like
    4.3 Social structure (distribution of wealth, for example)

4.4 Economic system(s) that support universities/colleges

4.5 Reputation (usually a question of accreditation)

5. Accessibility

    5.1 By age cohort

    5.2 By sex

    5.3 By ethnic origin

    5.4 By political jurisdiction in which most recently lived

    5.5 By social class

    5.6 By previously attained academic qualification

    5.7 By previous work experience

6. Institutional finance

    6.1 Proportion of budget devoted to administrative salaries and benefits

    6.2 Proportion of budget devoted to library and teaching equipment (laboratory equipment, and so on)

    6.3 Proportion of budget devoted to instructional cost (salaries and benefits)

    6.4 Proportion of budget devoted to student services (direct services: counselling, food and lodging, and so on)

    6.5 Proportion of budget devoted to information technologies (computerization, Internet access rates)

    6.6 Strength ratio (from UK): number of days of total expenditure payable from general funds (before the institution starts accumulating deficit)

7. Student choices

    7.1 Enrolment by subject area (useful indicator only if in relation to other indicators)

    7.2 Physical and mental health (visits to health professionals, and so on)

8. Professorial choices

    8.1 Proportion of staff engaged in research (as measured by annual publication and/or grants)

    8.2 Proportion of staff engaged in teaching improvement (measured by attendance at workshops, and so on)

9. Administrative choices and performance

    9.1 Student/teacher ratios

    9.2 Size (in numbers of persons, "layers," or other) of administrative apparatus (staff, line)

    9.3 Level of financial support acquired from private sector (national, international)

    9.4 Accuracy of judgement in reaching financial/accounting objectives (budgeting on target, and so on)

    9.5 Proportion of tenured staff

    9.6 Proportion of sessional teaching staff

    9.7 Size of non-teaching staff

    9.8 Quality of labour relations (measured by time lost to strikes, and so on)

    9.9 Proportion of student fees to total income

    9.10   International student fees proportionate to total income

10. Public support

    10.1   Gallup polls, PDK polls, Decima, and the like

10.2   "League ranking": example of *Maclean's* annual ratings of Canadian
          universities

10.3   Election results (election/defeat of persons/parties committed to support
          higher education)

PART 5

In the Public Interest: Reclaiming Our Purpose

To not intend, or to intend not
...that is the question

JANICE A. NEWSON

Since the early 1980s, a handful of academics and commentators have written
about significant and potentially transformative changes taking place in the
social organisation[1] of higher education. Together, their work catalogues the
imminent dangers these changes pose to the public interest which the higher
education system in Canada is designed to serve.[2] Despite these collective
Cassandras' warnings, funding policies, reordered social relations, and
institutional practices have carried forward a corporate-serving, economic
competitiveness agenda for higher education which continues unabated.

The question to ask is not "Why do we oppose these trends?" but "Why
would concerned faculty members, students, and citizens *not* oppose these
trends?" What conception of "the public interest" is required *not* to view
commercialization and corporatization as endangering that interest? And
here's the rub! To *not* oppose these trends, we would have to abandon the
conception that universities and colleges exist to serve the larger public
interest, as well as the diverse interests of multiple publics.

THE TWO SIDES OF CORPORATIZATION

"Corporatization," as we have come to call it, has two sides. On one is the
increasing openness of universities and colleges to the special interests of the
corporate sector. In the guise of an economic policy that views international
competitiveness and technological innovation as the key to Canada's wel-l
being, governments' general underfunding of the higher education system is
matched by a multitude of funding "incentives" for collaborations between
post-secondary institutions and private sector corporations.[3] For example,
matched grant funding programmes such as the Ontario Challenge Fund, the
Innovation Fund, and many programmes supported by the three granting
councils, through which public dollars are matched to amounts raised from
private sector partners, strongly encourage academics to orient intellectual
interests to research questions that corporate clients will fund. Centres of

excellence, research parks, technology transfer centres, private in-house research companies, and cost-recovery academic research units have become the institutional infrastructure to support this corporate linking.

Universities and colleges thus compete for financial support from private sector "clients." In exchange, these clients have the means to acquire the intellectual property rights to research findings that lead to marketable products; or to ensure that knowledge discoveries that benefit their interests will be pursued, or that a work force will be trained to their specifications.

Less noticed but perhaps more important than these benefits, however, is that the association of corporations with university researchers provides them with a source of legitimation particularly important in an increasingly knowledge-intensive, global economy. A medical researcher recently told me that many of the scientific investigations which multinational pharmaceutical companies agree to fund through university-corporate partnerships are in fact directed toward the discovery of knowledge that is inconsequential and relatively unimportant, even for developing specific products. But, he argued, these companies acquire in return something much more valuable: the names and institutional affiliations of Canada's leading researchers to use in marketing their products competitively and assuring consumers of their safety and reliability.

Whatever the benefits, the funding provided by corporate clients by no means covers the full cost of the research and teaching activities involved. Several years ago, an NSERC (Natural Sciences and Engineering Research Council) newsletter advertised the financial advantages to corporations of participating in academic collaborations: it explained how, for a $15,000.00 before-tax donation, a corporate donor could gain access to $225,000.00 of research. (Contact (1990), p. 4). In other words, these contracted partnerships are heavily subsidised by Canadian tax payers, yet the knowledge they create serves a specific private interest.

Three overall observations can be made about this side of corporatization. First is that, even though recent figures indicate that corporate donations to institutions of higher education have increased, they are not in the main "free gifts." They do not represent a trend toward increased philanthropy. Rather, the funnel for these funds is complex, proprietary-protected contracts. Although specific provisions of these contracts are kept confidential, based on the cases exposed to public scrutiny, either they contain conditions attached to the "donation" or they are outright commercial exchanges.

Second, this increased level of corporate funding is by no means sufficient to counteract the effects of government under-funding, nor to support the full costs of research and teaching programmes. Universities and colleges continue to rely heavily on public funds and student fees and tuition, even though their activities are being diverted toward serving private interests.

Third, as universities and colleges compete with each other for a relatively "marginal" source of funding, they tend to orient their programmes of research and teaching to attract such funding, re-shaping their own activities to present what they imagine to be of interest and appeal to potential corporate clients.

This third general observation leads to the second side of corporatization; namely, that universities and colleges have begun to adopt the modus operandi of private sector businesses. Their institutional practices and self-representations have become isomorphic with those of private sector corporations. Moreover, as they become more deeply implicated in the first side of corporatization for example, acquiring shares in corporations that are exploiting the knowledge that their own researchers develop, or holding licenses on their own "bank" of intellectual property universities and colleges are engaging in profit-making ventures of their own. It is possible now to imagine publicly funded universities and colleges that are indistinguishable in important ways from private corporations.

SUBSTITUTING PRIVATE INTERESTS FOR PUBLIC INTERESTS

These two sides of corporatization map out the extent to which the public interests traditionally served by post-secondary institutions are being replaced by private interests. They demonstrate that funding per se is not the crucial issue: that is, the concern is not whether corporate money should be a source of funding for universities and colleges. On the contrary, since the private sector economy has long benefited from the knowledge creation and dissemination activities of the public-serving post-secondary system, by all means, private corporations should fund it! But they should do it in the manner of other Canadians: as tax payers through the tax system, rather than through proprietary contracts and special relationships which give them access, not available to other citizens, for shaping and defining the kind of research and teaching programmes that universities and colleges pursue.

Supporters of this agenda for higher education deny that corporate-linking and commercialization present inherent dangers to the broader public interest. They claim this re-orientation of post-secondary institutions has been made necessary by work re-structuring and heightened international competition for leading edge new products, and that through it, Canadian interests will be better served. But these claims are not sustained even on their own terms.

For example, advocates claim that commercialising academic research ensures innovation and makes knowledge more useful, thus benefiting all

Canadians. In fact, commercialization turns knowledge into privately owned intellectual property from which only a limited number of Canadians will benefit. Moreover, as Seth Shulman's recent book, *Owning the Future* (1999), graphically displays, the resulting restrictions on communicating new research findings in the making, and the financial burdens of licensed research discoveries, increasingly inhibit innovation and limit the usefulness of knowledge.

Advocates claim also that the new alliance between post-secondary institutions and the corporate sector will ensure that today's youth will be able to pursue secure and successful futures. In fact, it denies young people the opportunity to shape their own future; the futures that they are being prepared for have been pre-determined for them. Although the increasing vocationalizing of academic programmes and the overbearing emphasis on securing degrees offer the promise of employability, the very economic processes used to justify them are creating rapid dislocation in the work force and degrading the value even of skills acquired recently.

Equally important, the prevailing ideology of education[4] embraced by those who support the corporate and commercial direction of educational programme tends to minimise, if not outrightly repudiate, the notion that higher education should provide young people with opportunities to reflect upon the world as it is, and to conceive of how it could be.

Students are left only with the task of learning to accommodate themselves to a world that appears fixed and unyielding to their diverse aspirations, innovative ideas, and rich imaginations. In light of these consequences alone, it is difficult to see why the commercialization and corporatization of post-secondary education would *not* be opposed.

FROM DEFENSIVE TO OFFENSIVE STRATEGIES

Asking "Why do we oppose commercialization?" requires us to supply reasons for what we should take as our starting point—that the public-serving purposes of universities and colleges need to be preserved. We should be demanding that the advocates of commercialization and corporatization explain why they are *willing* to undermine and displace these public-serving purposes in order to serve private interests.

Asking "Why do we oppose?" places us in a defensive position from which we will never stop the commercial take-over of post-secondary education. Regrettably, defensiveness and accommodation have characterized the stance of the academic community from the early 1980s, when the "corporate agenda" for universities was first publicly advocated by the Corporate Higher Education Forum, and governments and administrations began to implement it. Defensiveness and accommodation have proved ineffective.

We must analyse what has been happening; rather than addressing ourselves only to the "what" of commercialization and corporatization, we need to attend to the "how."

HOW CORPORATIZATION AND COMMERCIALIZATION ARE ACCOMPLISHED

To be sure, government funding policies, the influence of "third party" bodies like the Corporate-Higher Education Forum, the Canadian Manufacturers Association and the Business Council on National Issues, and pressures arising from the complexities of globalization, trade agreements and the like, are aspects of the external context that have created pressures on university and college administrators and faculty to re-orient their institutions and activities. But these influences alone do not account for the changes that have taken place in the interior of universities and colleges: changes that include not only the re-direction of research and teaching programmes to serve economic and corporate objectives, but perhaps more significant because of their long term implications, subtle and fundamental transformations in academic practices, in ways of thinking, in language, and in research and teaching cultures. These interior changes have been not merely instrumental, but critical, in facilitating the dramatic and relatively rapid re-orientation of higher education institutions toward corporatism and commercialism.

In spite of the wide-spread perception that commercialization and corporatization are recent phenomena, they did not happen yesterday. What are recent are the visible manifestations of growing corporate influences: the buildings named after corporate donors, the commercial deals with soft drink companies, the advertisements in campus buildings, and the emergence of an academic culture in which the making of commercial contracts between corporations and academic researchers and even whole faculties have become taken for granted, everyday occurrences.

These visible manifestations have arisen from a complex array of changing relationships mapped onto higher education institutions throughout the 1980s. The publication of *Partnership for Growth* in 1984, the first of several reports sponsored by the Corporate Higher Education Forum, marked the beginning of a concerted effort to bring about significant changes in government policy toward higher education. These changes were advocated to achieve a "profitable marriage" between underfunded universities and leading edge knowledge-seeking Canadian corporations. Ten studies carried out in the 1980s by the now defunct Science Council of Canada filled in the details for bringing this profitable marriage into reality. They provided rationales and detailed guidelines for establishing Technology Transfer Offices and Innovation Centres on campus, advanced "Centres of Excellence" as the best way to join together academic and industrial researchers in pursuit of research objectives oriented toward marketable products and profitable ideas, and coined the term "the service university" to describe the new dynamic relations that need to exist between higher education and "society"(Enros and Farley, 1986).[5]

Government funding policies followed the recommendations of these quasi-public bodies as well as those of such corporate lobby groups as the Canadian Manufacturers Association and the Business Council on National Issues. At the same time, the three research councils – NSERC, SSHRC and MRC – were busily designing targeted research and matched grant funding programmes that virtually compel academic researchers to partner up with corporate clients, and to pursue desired, "strategic" research topics, or to face the possibility of not having their research funded.

Alongside these significant changes in funding priorities, the interior of universities and colleges began to change, not so much in "cause-effect" fashion as in mutual re-alignment. As universities and colleges "responded" to government funding policies, so government funding policies advanced further in the direction of Corporatization. As well, institutional cultures and associated practices have emerged to give new meaning to academic life and its activities and purposes, as exemplified in language that re-defines students as clients, faculty members as service providers, and research and teaching as educational product. This language not only describes the "new realities" on campus: it actually has helped to constitute them.

From the early stages, rather than strongly resist these changes, many academics, for different reasons, accommodated them. I will recount only a few uncovered by interviewing faculty members, reading higher education literature, surveying letters to editors and commentaries, and listening to responses at conferences.

Some faculty members embraced the new policy directions from the beginning. Some others remained unaware for a time that a new direction in higher education policy was being pursued. But many who were aware shared concerns about dangers implicit in them, such as shifting the balance between basic science and applied science and between the technologically and profes-sionally-oriented disciplines and the more academically oriented disciplines; undermining the sharing of knowledge, and the responsibility of academic researchers to adopt independent and critical stances; and displacing collegialism in favour of corporate-managerial practices of decision-making.

Even so, some believed that as scientists and intellectuals, their primary responsibility was to ensure continuation of their research and knowledge quests, even if doing so required them to accept changes in research funding practices and academic decision-making. Some perceived their own accommodations to these changes were inconsequential, or had no relationship to the "bigger" picture. And some believed it prudent to concede to at least some new demands, because to do otherwise might worsen the situation.

As changes in academic practices and cultures began to accumulate, university administrators and many faculty members maintained that the effects of these changes were marginal at worst; that they primarily involved applied sciences and professional schools that have traditionally worked more closely with industry and the corporate sector; and that the public serving teaching and research missions of universities and colleges would remain intact and not be undermined.

Their predictions were wrong. By the mid-1990s, changes on campuses across the country signalled a profound, institution-wide shift that has left few disciplines untouched by re-orientation toward the market and serving privatised interests. "Corporatization" and the "corporate-linked" campus can no longer be written off as exaggerated predictions of overly fearful critics. Indeed, the argument of the recently released report of the Expert Panel on the Commercialization of University Research—that "innovation" (meaning the production of marketable knowledge) should be made a fourth mission of universities alongside teaching, research and service—confirms how far and how fast the process has advanced. It would not have been possible to make such a bold claim on public sector services as little as two decades ago.

THE IMPORTANCE OF LEVERAGE

One important point stands out in this brief and necessarily simplified recounting of how commercialization and corporatization have gained momentum as powerfully transformative directions in post-secondary education. The dramatic shift in institutional practices and perspectives could not have been accomplished without the participation of members of the academic community, particularly the participation of members of the faculty. In fact, as someone who has been tracking the policy literature and position papers for some time now, I want to underscore the extent to which securing faculty participation and compliance was recognised from the beginning as the key to achieving this shift so much so that many of the strategies that have been employed have been designed specifically to overcome anticipated "faculty resistance."

But acknowledging the critical role that faculty members play in post-secondary institutions points us in two directions. First it points to the fact that, albeit often times inadvertently, the complicity of faculty members has been and continues to be part of the process of furthering the corporate-oriented agenda. But second, in spite of a seemingly daunting line-up of powerful agents who are promoting this agenda, it also underscores the extent to which the faculty have important leverage that can be used to resist these changes.

For one thing, the special expertise, accumulated knowledge, and highly trained intellectual skills of academics are the resources being sought after, to "add value" to the products and processes that are seen to be crucial to competitiveness in a globalized economy. Without academics' willingness to apply these resources to corporate and commercial ends, achieving this agenda becomes highly problematic. For another thing, the faculty have some (although diminished) power and influence over university and college programmes and objectives. And finally, as holders of expert authority, faculty members have considerable influence with the public or at least with key segments of the public.

This leverage can not be applied, however, unless it is recognised and effectively collectivised in a strategy explicitly directed toward stopping the commercial take-over. Some faculty members remain unconvinced of the dangers, or of the importance of (and their responsibility for) preserving the public interest.

Among those already persuaded are many faculty members who do not see the relationship between their own practices and the broader changes that are taking place. Although many of them have not intended to support commercialization and corporatization, they have often inadvertently done just that, both by their actions and through their inaction.[6] Rather than passively *not intending* to support these trends that are so harmful to the public interest, an effective strategy requires us to actively *intend not* to support them.

There are several projects currently underway that, at first glance, appear to have tangential, if any, relationship to changes that we will need to challenge if we want to stop the commercial take-over. Our participation in these projects can either contribute toward, or begin to undermine, the hold of corporatism and commercialism over our campuses. I refer, for example, to the accountability project inextricably tied to attempts to install performance indicators in universities and colleges. Claire Polster and I have argued elsewhere that performance indicators help to institutionalise a complex system of control over the content of academics' work that can operate, not only through the managerial apparatus of individual institutions, but also from outside these institutions at provincial, national and even international levels (Polster and Newson, 1998). Even well-intentioned attempts to minimise the negative effects of performance-based measurement contribute to the construction of this broad network of control.[7] This network of control, in turn, makes available an effective means for shaping the research and teaching activities carried out in universities and colleges in ways that support corporatization and commercialising academic activities.

The findings of a recent Ph.D. dissertation investigating the application of performance indicators in four Western Australian universities adds some evidence to our argument. One depressing conclusion of this study is that performance indicators do work—especially if financial rewards, including research money, are attached to them. Even though the faculty members surveyed were negative toward performance indicators in general, even though they were critical of the criteria being used and sceptical about the desirability and appropriateness of the types of activities that were rewarded (for example, acquiring a patent on their intellectual property), and even though the measurements were not meaningful to their own research and teaching objectives, the majority confessed they had altered their own practices and interests in order to improve their scores. (Taylor, 1999)

Yet another project that facilitates the micro- and macro-management of academic activities "from afar" is the newly introduced Tri-Council Code of Ethics, ostensibly designed to protect research subjects from unethical practices and to prevent plagiarism and unjustified claims to authorship. Research Ethics Committees which operate under the direction of the federal research councils are being established in local institutions according to the specifications of the Tri-Council document. Faculty members will be required to submit an ethics protocol for approval to their local committee whenever they apply to research programmes that are supported by federal level public funds. Failure to comply will mean that a university's faculty will be ineligible for funds from these sources.

I am not able to fully re-count here the three or four year struggle over the Tri-Council document and the controversy that erupted over many of its provisions. Some Learned Societies have vigorously objected to "biases" encouraging certain kinds of research relationships and research method-ologies while discouraging, if not outrightly preventing, others. As well as these issues, there are alarming implications for the ongoing role of the federal research councils and the surveillance that this initiative introduces over faculty members' research activities. Perhaps most relevant is the possibility that the overtly stated purpose of this initiative —to ensure "scientific integrity" in academic research—may be less important than a more covert desire to ensure that ownership of intellectual property is clearly established, in order to avoid disputes over commercially oriented patent claims.

Performance indicators and the new research ethics regime require the consent and participation of academics in local institutions. This means that they offer an opportunity to challenge their implementation, not only on the grounds that they undermine academic freedom and institutional autonomy, but because they potentially contribute to corporatization and commercialization. Similar opportunities will unfold if, for example, the Expert Panel's recommendations for commercialising academic research are adopted.

Most important, stopping the commercial take-over of post-secondary education is a practical political project: it will not be accomplished simply through further research and discussion. We need to look for the critical places to intervene, and to be alert to routine matters that are connected to the growing corporatism and commercialism on our campuses, as they come up in departmental meetings, faculty and senate discussions, and even in the ways we teach in classrooms.

Nor can we accomplish this project alone. We need to ally, and act in concert, with groups who share concerns and interest with us, whether grass roots, citizen based or occupationally and professionally based.

Most of all, although government policy, trade agreements, and the political influence of economic elites make up the defining context, we need to give equal weight to the fact that we who work inside Canada's post-secondary education system have a considerable degree of influence and leverage over what takes place. We also have a responsibility to the public interest. That responsibility requires us to do more than *not intend* to support an agenda that undermines that interest. We must firmly and actively *intend not* to support it. And we must do all that we can to stop it.

Bibliography

Axelrod, Paul (1986). Service or Captivity? Business-university relations in the 20th Century. In Nielson, Wm. and Gaffield, Chad (eds.) *Universities in Crisis*. Montreal: Institute for Research on Public Policy, 45–68.

Buchbinder, Howard, & Newson, Janice (1990). Corporate-university links in Canada: Transforming a public institution. *Higher Education*, 20, 355–379.

Buchbinder, Howard, & Newson, Janice (1985). University-corporate linkages and the scientific-technical revolution. Interchange 16, 37–53.

Calvert, John. (1993). NAFTA and Post-secondary Education in Canada. In Calvert, J. (with Larry Kuehn) *Pandora's Box: Corporate power, free trade and Canadian education* (chapter 6). Toronto: Our Schools/Our Selves Education Foundation.

Cassin, Marguerite, and Morgan, J. Graham. (1992). The professoriate and the market-driven university: transforming the control of work in the academy. In Carroll, Wm., Christiansen-Ruffman, Linda, Currie, Ray, and Harrison Deborah (Eds) *Fragile Truths: Twenty five years of sociology and anthropology in Canada* (pp. 247–260). Ottawa: Carleton University Press.

Enros, Philip. and Farley, Michael. (1986). *University offices for technology transfer: toward the service university*. Ottawa: Science Council of Canada.

Graham, Wm. (1989). From the President. *Ontario Confederation of University Faculty Associations Bulletin*, 6(22), 2.

Jeannette Taylor.(1999).The Impact of Performance Indicators on the Work of University Academics: A study of Four Australian Universities. Perth, Australia: Unpublished doctoral dissertation, Murdoch University.

Katz, Michael (1986). The Moral Crisis of the University, or, the Tension between Marketplace and Community in Higher Education. In Nielson, Wm. and Gaffield, Chad (eds.) *Universities in Crisis*. Montreal: Institute for Research on Public Policy, 3–28.

Maxwell, Judith and Currie, Stephanie (1984). *Partnership for Growth*. Montreal: The Corporate-Higher Education Forum.

McMurtry, John (1991) Education and the Market Model. *Journal of the Philosophy of Education*, 25, 209–217.

Newson, Janice, & Buchbinder, Howard. (1988). *The University Means Business: universities, corporations and academic work*. Toronto: Garamond Press.

Noble, David. (1982, Feb. 6) The Selling of the University. *Nation*, 129, 143–148.

Polster, Claire and Newson, Janice. (1998). Don't Count your Blessings: The Social Accomplishments of Performance Indicators. In Currie, Jan and Newson, Janice (Eds.) *The University and Globalisation: Critical Perspectives* (pp. 173–192). Thousand Oaks, California: Sage Publishers Inc.

Polster, Claire.(1994). Compromising Positions: The Federal Government and the Reorganisation of the Social Relations of Canadian Academic Research. North York: Unpublished Doctoral Dissertation, York University.

Scheffel, David. (1989). The academy's final surrender to the marketplace. *University Affairs*, 30(2), 20–21.

Shulman, Seth. (1999). *Owning the Future*. New York: Houghton Mifflin.

Shifting Gears: Creative Resistance to Corporatisation

CLAIRE POLSTER

There is no easy way to reclaim our universities as truly public serving institutions; but two shifts in our thinking may bring us a little closer to this goal. At the risk of sounding like a management consultant type, I have named these *the shift from accommodation to resistance* and *the shift from reactivity to creativity.*

It is vital that we move from a strategy of accommodation to the corporate agenda to a strategy of resistance to it. As Genovese notes, a strategy of accommodation avoids direct confrontation with a situation, instead attempting to manoeuvre within its parameters. A classic example is a secretary who spits in the coffee before bringing it to her sexist boss.

It is fair to say that many academics and academic organizations have attempted to accommodate rather than to resist the corporate agenda. For example, faced with the skewing of government research funds away from independents to targeted and industrial partnerships, many academics adjust their research programs to the dictates of government and business, hoping to squeeze their own research agendas into the plans of others. For fear that their voices will otherwise be marginalised, many academics participate in various forms of university consultation and planning which by-pass established governance structures, thus contributing to the erosion of collegial decision-making practices. In hopes of preserving access to higher education, many academics support on-line instruction instead of fighting cancellation of classes on satellite campuses. Rather than opposing external mechanisms such as performance indicators, many academics actually contribute to their production in the forlorn hope of making them either as meaningful or as harmless as possible.

Such strategies of accommodation require both intelligence and effort undertaken with the best of intentions. Nonetheless, we must abandon them. *Accommodation simply doesn't work.* Not only does it do nothing to challenge the new relations being established in the university, it actively reinforces them. Academics who accommodate shortfalls in public research funding by allying with industrial partners generally must cede intellectual property rights to the knowledge they produce. This increases the costs of research, forcing more academics to turn to industrial funding as public funding shrinks further. Likewise, where the *nature* of our assistance in developing performance indicators may make them fairer or more accurate, the *fact* of our participation advances and legitimizes the erosion of university autonomy.

Accommodation is based on a misguided and dis-empowering lack of faith in our colleagues and in the public. Many academics fear that their colleagues cannot be trusted to actively resist the corporate agenda. Thus, rather than initiating opposition and risking failure, many of us assume accommodation to be our only strategic option. My recent experience opposing performance indicators at the University of Regina, and inspiring examples like the York University strike, suggest that our colleagues will often surprise us—and one another—by the strength of their commitment to a public serving university and their willingness to defend it in a concerted and collective way. By adopting an accommodationist strategy as our first line of response, we deny ourselves the opportunity and context within which to rise to the challenge with solidarity.

We also underestimate the ability and willingness of the public to understand and resist the corporate agenda. As stories such as the Apotex scandal, various cases of scientific fraud, and the dangers of genetically modified food find their way into the mainstream press, people are increasingly concerned that corporatised universities may be compromising their interests. With a bit of effort on our part, this energy could be harnessed to a project of resistance. As the neoliberal agenda proceeds apace, many public interest groups see the links between the corporatisation of the university and their own struggles. As we learned when we successfully fought against the bid to bring the private International Space University to the York university campus, these groups are not only willing but *eager* to lend support.

When we adopt a strategy of accommodation to the corporate agenda, we actually aim too low. We underestimate our own power and resources, both individually and collectively. Resolutely and collectively resisting the corporate agenda will bring far higher returns. Not only are we far more likely to win particular battles, but even when we lose we will win—because we will reaffirm and defend the vision and values of a public serving university, rather than compromising them and ourselves in the process.

The second shift is from *reactivity* to *creativity*. It is important to understand the corporate agenda and how it is being put into place— not abstractly, but on the ground—but far more important for us to envision

196

building a public serving university suited to the particular demands of our times and our own agenda.

This means thinking very concretely about what a renovated public serving university would look like—its specific features and dimensions —and actually translating that vision into a reality. Just as the corporate university was not put into place overnight or according to a pre-conceived plan, it will take time and many different kinds of efforts from groups in different places to bring about this truly public serving university. A small but growing number of ideas in Canada and elsewhere aim precisely at achieving this goal.

A key aspect of a public serving university is making the research skills of its academics (and students) available to all citizens, regardless of ability to pay. The European science shop is one kind of institution set up to ensure broad public access to academic problem solving skills. Public groups can go to these shops in search of solutions to various technical, economic, environmental, and social problems—for free. They are the inspiration for the recent CURA program of the SSHRC, just one of many possible vehicles for establishing science shops in Canadian universities. These institutions, together with programs inspired by similar ideals, such as those which place students in community organizations rather than affluent corporations for their various practica, can help develop and enrich a public serving university in a myriad of ways. Prime among these is their ability to cultivate a vigorous public service ethic in academics and students, and to reinforce a view of the university as a public resource on which all groups not only have the right to draw, but are *encouraged* to draw.

A public serving university, it makes the knowledge produced by its scholars freely available to all citizens. As I suggested in a recent editorial in the *CAUT Bulletin*, a public serving university has no truck with the intellectual property business. Weaning the university from its involvement in intellectual property production and exploitation will be no easy task. One step towards this goal would be to cultivate and celebrate Canadian versions of Manuel Patarollo, the Columbian physician who developed the first synthetic malaria vaccine. Rather than selling his patent to a pharmaceutical company, he donated it to the World Health Organization, ensuring its broad accessibility to people in the third world. Publicly lauding Canadian academics who keep their knowledge in the public domain—and possibly exposing and shaming those who don't—is not the only strategy we can use to keep academic knowledge public. Another might be to develop knowledge collectives in which various academics pool their intellectual capital as a lever to free up yet more knowledge. Still another would be to negotiate clauses in faculty association contracts to vest some or all property rights to knowledge produced in the university with the public, as opposed to either individual academics or universities. Needless to say, all these proposals contradict those put forward by the Expert Panel on the Commercialization of University Research. We need creative methods to expose the flaws in, and special interests behind, these proposals.

A public serving university is autonomous in the sense that it is not beholden to or compromised by any single social sector or constituency. Of the many proposals to revitalize university autonomy, I have found a paper by Markey and Price particularly inspiring. They show how employing the principles of community economic development (or CED) would enable universities to free themselves from dependence on corporations and government while becoming more integrated with local communities and more responsive to their many and plural needs. Some of their specific suggestions demonstrate the potential for revitalizing a public serving university.

For instance, they suggest establishing university-run restaurants to displace corporate outlets. In line with the principles of CED, these restaurants, variously integrated into the studies and projects of students in a number of faculties, might serve organic food purchased from local farmers, and donate their compost to community food growing plots. In addition to enhancing the health and working conditions of many people on campus, such projects could reduce corporate presence and control on campus, promote numerous links between the university and surrounding communities, and revitalize both institutional democracy and true university accountability to the public.

There are many, many other seeds we can plant. We can establish prestigious public service awards for academics to ensure their work greater recognition and value in the university. We can devise a certification process for "uncompromised university research units" whose staffs and research results safeguard the public interest. University policy and policy making mechanisms, the media, and even the law offer further creative opportunities. For instance, there is the precedent of public groups such as farmers' organizations suing universities for practices that undermine local interests. I can imagine other suits launched by academics and/or students over suppression of democratic and consumer rights by university/industry partnerships invoking non-disparagement clauses or monopoly pouring or selling rights.

A creative approach can be extremely liberating for activists. It gives us a public opportunity to stand *for something* as opposed to being *against everything*. This can instigate productive resistance more effectively and easily than outright confrontation.

A creative approach can put advocates of the corporate agenda on the defensive for a change. As we learned in the struggle against the International Space University, one should never underestimate how big a wrench a little creative action can sometimes throw into the mechanism of the corporatised university.

In the long run, a creative approach can not simply obstruct the corporate agenda but make the university environment inhospitable to it. Just as introduction of new plants can transform an ecosystem so previously flourishing life forms can no longer survive, so the creation of new institutions, practices, and relations on our campuses may transform them in ways that make it difficult, if not impossible, for the corporate agenda to put down viable roots.

Strategies of creativity and resistance are not mutually exclusive but can complement, reinforce, and even produce the other when firmly centered in and resolutely moving toward a vision of a truly public serving university. Our training and practice as academics better prepare us for, or incline us more towards, critique and resistance over creativity. In the interests of redressing this imbalance, we must reaffirm our vision of a public university, share ideas about how to generate it, and dream bold new schemes and plans for our own particular institutions and communities.

What is to Be Done? Envisioning the University's Future

PAUL AXELROD

I come to the subject of commercialization from three points of academic interest: my research on the political economy of higher education; my particular concern with the fate of liberal education in the university; and my empathy for the voice and experiences of youth.[1] Perhaps a fourth concern is simple self-interest. As a faculty member in the arts, I wonder what the future holds for me, my colleagues, my colleagues yet to be, my colleagues who may never be.

My entire adult life has been spent studying and teaching history and social science. I can't imagine the university world without them. Unfortunately, many politicians, businessmen, and university administrators evidently can. This is the sobering reality behind this anthology. My following comments seek to bridge these concerns in a way that encourages action, not merely lament, about the state of the university. What, indeed, can be done about the pervasive and growing commercialization of higher education?

Perhaps our greatest challenge is a broadly political one: confronting the forces of neo-conservatism, neo-liberalism, and (it must be said) neo-social democracy. These envision the university as a mere instrument of economic life, its only important goal to prepare people for their special slots in the global economy. From this perspective other academic activities hardly matter. Governments thus introduce insidious managerial schemes such as performance indicators in order, allegedly, to make universities more efficient, and cut university budgets to make them more competitive, forcing them into the world of privatization.

Private and public funding agencies increasingly seek to reshape the purpose of research to define curiosity-based scholarship right out of the equation. If the results of our labours are not judged market-worthy, they are deemed to be of minor importance—a perspective that appears to have embraced virtually the entire political class in Canada.

201

The federal Liberals have stripped away resources while simultaneously reallocating those that remain to "Centres of Excellence" schemes, and to such monsters as the eight billion dollar Canada Foundation on Innovation, designed to privilege science, health, and engineering under the probable guidance of the private sector. The Social Sciences and Humanities Research Council is increasingly driven by utilitarian priorities. SSHRC's Strategic Grants Program channels research to projects on such themes as "managing global competitiveness" and "challenges and opportunities in a knowledge-based economy." Similarly, British Columbia's NDP government recently created two major post-secondary educational initiatives—Royal Roads University, and the Technical University of British Columbia—both designed explicitly to serve economic needs. The arts have no obvious role in this mission. All of this is to say nothing of the market-driven educational schemes of the Tories in Ontario designed, among other things, to steer enrolments away from the arts and into the high technology and business fields.

Those pushing higher education in these directions have a great public relations advantage: they appear to own the new language that embodies their goals. When they talk about the needs of the "global economy" and the purpose of the "knowledge" economy, they sound so non-partisan, so sophisticated and logical, as to seem to represent the new "common sense" of what higher education should be all about. That these ideas evidently cut across political and ideological boundaries only increases their legitimacy. Those who teach or research in other fields are immediately put on the defensive—"What are *you* contributing to the needs of the global economy?" The public funds which have enabled the arts to thrive in Canada then go elsewhere.

Our real problem lies with the political forces controlling this agenda, and shrinking the space in universities for the humanities, the social sciences, and basic scientific research. In organizing, lobbying, and other actions, we must stay focussed on this target. In a curious form of trickle-down politics, the new academic agenda is being played out through various conflicts on university campuses, notably collective bargaining. I think that faculty associations at the campus, provincial, and national levels should make faculty control of the university's academic life a major priority. This is an old issue with a new sense of urgency.

Securing control of academic planning will not, of course, be easy. From the time bicameral systems of university governance were created, with business-dominated boards of governors in charge of finance, and academic senates responsible for curriculum, it has not really been possible to separate administratively the academic and financial functions of higher education. In good economic times, the power struggles between boards and senates could be papered over—everyone's needs could be met during the 1960s when enrolments and budgets ballooned. Now, with intense competition for resources, academic choices are usually made to the disadvantage of the humanities and social sciences. Loss of university autonomy to the centralizing authority of provincial governments only compounds the problem.

University administrations may choose to wield the heavy hand, closing down those programs considered to be anachronistic, costly, and impractical in favour of "market-worthy" ones. Using the big stick, however, is not generally the Canadian way. We prefer to be more subtle and benign, achieving such change by attrition. Given the huge number of retirements on the horizon, universities can simply replace humanities and social science retirees with faculty in business, applied science, and high technology fields. Faculty associations on every campus must therefore carefully monitor and confront the centralization of decision making, and the degree to which institutional appointments are being reallocated from the arts to other fields.

Those of us committed to securing the health of the humanities and social sciences must argue more persuasively for the intrinsic value of the liberal arts, in clear and accessible language, and to a broad audience. I can't speak to the policies of his university, but James O. Freedman, president of Dartmouth College, has written poignantly and eloquently about the virtues of liberal education:

> A liberal education...stirs students to probe the mysteries of the natural world, to reflect on the rise and fall of cultures, to find meaning in the enduring achievements of Western and Eastern civilizations, and to consider ambiguities and arguable lessons of human history.... Further, a liberal education encourages students to seek the affirmation of their most authentic selves. It sets in motion a process of critical examination and imaginative introspection that leads students towards personal definition. It helps students to develop an independent perspective for reflecting on the nature and the texture of their lives...More than any historical datum, any experimental result, or any textual explication, a liberal education conveys to students a sense of joy in learning— joy in participating in the life of the mind..."[2]

We must make this case in ways not conventionally élitist, respecting the intelligence of the public. Liberal education, after all, was never designed for the masses, and it is no wonder that many citizens still view these subjects, and the people who teach them, with some suspicion. David Strangeway, the former president of UBC, proposes to save liberal education in traditionally exclusivist terms, by creating a private arts university which will charge students some $25,000 in annual tuitions. This may indeed help preserve liberal education, but not in an especially democratic form; in my view, it is no model for the future.

Even in publicly funded universities, we academics too often condescend to our audiences, or ignore potential audiences. More youth than ever attend universities today, and Canada shares with the United States by far the world's top higher education participation rates. At the very moment, then, that a critical mass of the population is in a position to reap the benefits of curiosity-based, scholarly endeavour, our universities' practices, if not their rhetorical missions, are being skewed towards those subjects considered narrowly valuable in the marketplace. We must counteract this trend by demonstrating to students, their families, and their communities the social importance and personal rewards that flow from exploring "the life of the mind."

One cannot simply ignore the pervasive utilitarian mind-set. Higher education has an undeniable role to play in preparing graduates for the labour market. In fact, as it turns out, the arts have much to contribute to this mission. Several recent studies demonstrate that relatively impressive employment record of liberal arts graduates, assessed over the long term.[3] Census data reveal that for 25- to 29-year-old university graduates, the unemployment rate in 1996 by field of study was 6.5% for fine arts, 9.4% for humanities, 7.9% for social sciences, 5.9% for commerce, 7.4% for engineering, and 7.7% for math and physical sciences—indicating a marginal advantage for those in business and sciences. For those graduates 30 years old and up, the unemployment rates declined to 6.4 % for fine arts, 6% for humanities, 4.5% for social sciences, 3.9% for commerce, and 5.2% for engineering. (Note that the unemployment rate for social science graduates was lower than for engineers. Engineering, as it turns out, is a notoriously volatile employment field, exceedingly difficult to predict, and universities attempting to tie their futures to that supposedly market-proof discipline may be outsmarting themselves.) Overall, these statistics demonstrate that the long term employment outcomes for university graduates is positive, with very little distinction between the applied and liberal arts fields.

Income by fields of study shows significant gaps between arts students and commerce and engineering students at the 25- to 29-year-old level, but those close considerably for those over age 30. I do not want to deny or even understate the problem of underemployment for university and college graduates, which sociologist D.W. Livingstone has recently analysed with considerable insight.[4] Our economy, after all, has been on a roller coaster over the past two decades. Part-time work has grown, and underemployment has become a reality for many of the university-trained. But where it has occurred, underemployment has not been confined to those in the liberal arts, and has tended to be of temporary, not permanent duration.

One field which merits specific comment is the fine arts. Relatively speaking, census results show, incomes of graduates in this field are low— an average of $17.7 thousand dollars for those 30 years and up, making this group probably the least advantaged in income terms of all university graduates. Yet the overall contribution of arts and cultural activities to the Canadian economy is considerable. In 1992–93, these sectors employed 660,000 people "directly and indirectly," and contributed $23.8 billion to Canada's gross domestic product. The seasonal and contract nature of such work in all likelihood explains the low individual incomes; at the same time, these graduates willingly encompass the vibrant community of writers, performers and producers that enriches the country's cultural and artistic life, not to mention its tourist industry. Support for the fine arts in institutions of higher education appears to be a terrific economic bargain for society as a whole.

To be even more crudely utilitarian, we could echo Michael Useem's argument that in a world of globalization and corporate restructuring, the broadly trained have a viable place. Its employees' understanding of languages, cultures, and environmental concerns can help smooth a company's path to foreign markets. Domestic corporations require managers to "cultivate relations" with politicians and community leaders. Academic backgrounds in such areas as politics, religion, and ethnic relations prove materially valuable in the world of investment and commerce.[5]

Testimony from liberal arts graduates who have obtained fulfilling employment in a variety of fields also might aid the cause. As one psychology graduate put it,

> I don't think there is one psychology course that [offered] actual material I use day to day, but the general concepts and the skills I have learned—the research skills, the presentation skills, the analytical skills—weekly, daily, hourly, I am using those skills.

Other employee traits attributed by graduates to a liberal arts education included critical thinking, flexibility, tolerance, and the ability to integrate new information and to "grasp the big picture."[6]

These are useful arguments on behalf of liberal education, echoed by most university spokespersons, although somewhat risky . If the arts are promoted largely on the basis of economic utility, what happens to the argument when an economy stagnates, and arts underemployment increases? If we choose to live by the investment discourse, we risk dying by it as well. The liberal arts can and at times should be justified economically, but the case can and must be made more effectively in terms that speak to broader social and cultural concerns.

We might, for example, point to the ways in which liberal education has proven to be innovative and intelligently adaptable to the world around it. Contrary to myth, the humanities and social sciences do not constitute a static intellectual universe. Ironically, at the very time "pragmatic" disciplines are being hailed as economic saviours, there is a growing literature which points to the dissolution of disciplinary boundaries among the arts, between the arts and sciences, and between the professions and the arts. For example, the venerable University of Toronto's medical school now requires students to take a community health program designed to broaden their knowledge beyond the technical, and it employs social science literature in the classroom. McMaster University's medical school, renowned internationally for its policy of admitting students with strong humanities and social science backgrounds, irrespective of their science training, uses a problem solving, holistic approach to medical education. The assumption in both cases is that students with broad intellectual interests and experience should make better physicians than those merely technically proficient.

The same is true in other applied fields such as engineering and business. A biology professor has argued that

> an engineer who can design a cost-effective dam that can hold a
> mighty river, yet [who] is unaware of the environmental conse-
> quences of building it is dangerous.[7]

Similarly, ethical issues from "whistle blowing" to "product safety" compel business persons to "wrestle with their own standards of right and wrong, their self conceptions and character, and their perceptions of their roles in complex commercial enterprises"—again, issues central to liberal education.[8] Social science and humanities faculties should attempt to penetrate professional education and training programs by stressing the importance of exploring the worlds of technology, health, and business in a social context. And we should continue to argue for the critical importance of liberal education as a foundation for *all* specialized and professional training. After all, could anyone actually *oppose* the concept of being served by "humane" professionals whose skills go well beyond the technical?

We can point to the increasing significance of the humanities and social sciences as subjects of interest and edification for maturing, and eventually retiring, baby boomers who will no longer need to link their schooling with career aspirations. This is one important and potentially enduring aspect of "life-long" learning in which liberal education plays a vital role.

At the same time, we cannot ignore the demands of contemporary students, increasingly pragmatic in their academic choices. From our usually safe positions as tenured professors, we are too quick to dismiss students' bread and butter preoccupations while bemoaning their failure to love learning for its own sake. In our own self-interest, we must make our arts courses as engaging, exciting, and innovative as possible, in order to retain student enthusiasm for the humanities and social sciences. This may mean changing how we teach. Arts faculties may also have to address thoughtfully the relevance of their courses to the world of employment.

Familiarising themselves with contemporary student learning styles is an equally important challenge for faculty. A study by Charles Schroeder concluded that today's students succeed best in an academic environment based on "direct, concrete, experience, moderate to high degrees of structure and a linear approach to learning."[9] On the other hand, the majority of faculty are inspired by the "realm of concepts, ideas and abstractions;" they wrongly assume that students, like themselves, favour a high level of individual autonomy in their academic work, and [faculty] generally depend on passive forms of classroom learning.[10]

But the authors also contend that, rather than lamenting students' excessive pragmatism or anti-intellectualism, faculty should help bridge the pedagogical gap between professor and student through effective liberal education instruction. Students seek clear, detailed instruction in assignments, and helpful feedback in grading. Faculty can provide these without compromising their academic ideals. Students are increasingly oriented to group learning, which, effectively practised, can enrich discussion of ideas and concepts. Initial assignments can be based on concrete events, and move, in a logical fashion, to more abstract notions, thus presenting "experience earlier, theory later."[11] To sustain students' interest in the liberal arts, and to teach more effectively, the authors suggest that faculty should "learn more about who their students are, how they learn, and how they may be taught."[12]

Bridging programs between universities and colleges can respond to students' practical interests while ensuring technically trained students have some exposure to the humanities and social sciences. A number of universities, including my own (York), sponsor work placements for students in mass communications, urban studies, and labour studies, thus underlining the links between theory and practice, and providing students with valuable workforce experience. Students almost always speak highly of these courses.

Matson and Matson report on similar programs in a number of American universities. At Wichita State University, for example, some 250 students in the Liberal Arts and Sciences college are placed each year in jobs related to their majors. Social science students generally work in social agencies such as Big Brothers and Sisters, correctional settings, adoption centres, women's crisis centres, and law offices, while humanities students are assigned to cultural centres such as museums. Math and natural science students work for actuaries, or businesses with an environmental focus. Computer science students find placements in large companies such as AT&T and IBM, or in federal agencies. The University sees these programs as an important part of its strategy to exploit the institution's "metropolitan advantage," and to raise its profile within the community.[13]

One of the most unique placement programs is in the College of Humanities at Ottawa's Carleton University. The College offers a select number of high-achieving students a set of courses that covers, in thematic form, the fields of literature, languages, philosophy, and religion. Designed to contribute to the development of the "whole person," the curriculum explores in successive years "myth and symbol," "reason and revelation," "culture and imagination," and "science, technology and power." Students are then placed in internships with businesses and community organizations (from law firms to non-profit agencies such as Amnesty International), where employers and employees can, ideally, witness and experience the mutually enriching relationship between intellectual and working life.[14]

We must address other pedagogical questions. Do traditional lectures in huge classes maintain students' interest in our subjects or alienate them? Can the Internet be used in a creative way to inspire interest in the arts, or is it mostly a gimmick and a threat to high quality education? One thing is certain: the new technology will not go away, and if we do not learn how to use it effectively and responsibly, high-tech programs and applied disciplines may, by default, continue to attract students at the expense of the arts. Furthermore, if we ignore the question of how students learn, and its differences from how we as faculty learned, then we deny them a legitimate voice in the shaping of their own educations. Unless we teach liberal education courses creatively, we may lose the academic battle from the bottom up, not just from the top down.

In the face of these ominous trends, we have to do more than merely circle our academic wagons in resistance, or fold up our tents in surrender. For one thing, those of us in the liberal arts may run out of wagons and tents, as students continue to register in the programs that they think will reap the highest material rewards. In the face of such challenges, I think that there are some creative pedagogical initiatives that arts and social science faculty can take. It is a delicate exercise: we risk being co-opted by the very forces we are trying to contain. But perhaps, through a combination of political engagement, effective public communication, and imaginative teaching, we can avoid this fate. The unpalatable alternative is unpalatable is unfortunately not unimaginable.

Notes

INTRODUCTION

Introduction - What Commercialization Means for Education
[1]Science Council of Canada, *Winning in a World Economy: University-Industry Interaction and Economic Renewal In Canada,* Report 39 (Ottawa: Minister of Supply and Services, 1988), x-xi.

[2]Expert Panel on the Commercialization of University Research, *Public Investment in University Research: Reaping the Benefits.* Presented to the Prime Minister's Advisory Council on Science and Technology, 4 May 1999.

[3]Lehman Brothers, *Investment Opportunity in the Education Industry.* Research Report. New York, February 9, 1996, 4.

[4] William G. Symonds, "Education Industry Outlook," *Business Week,* 10 January 2000.

[5] http://www.wemex.com/index2.html

[6]See David F. Noble's discussion of the commodification of teaching in "Digital Diploma Mills: Rehearsal for the Revolution", pp. 101-121 in this volume and Langdon Winner's parody, "Introducing the Automatic Professor Machine, pp. 89-99.

[7]Courtney Leatherman, "Part-Timers Continue to Replace Full-Timers on College Faculties," *Chronicle of Higher Education,* 28 January 2000, A18.

[8] http://www.aaup.org/ptlink.htm

[9] National Association of Teachers in Further and Higher Education, *Working Paper #19,* July 1996, 17.

[10]William F. Massy is Professor Emeritus of Education and Business Administration at Stanford University and former Director of the Stanford Institute for Higher Education Research. Robert Zemsky is Professor of Education at the University of Pennsylvania, Chair of the Higher Education Division, and Director of the Institute for Research on Higher Education.

[11]William F. Massey and Robert Zemsky, "Using Information Technology to Enhance Academic Productivity," 2. http://www.educause.edu/nlii/massy.html

[12]Ibid., 4.

[13]Ibid., 6.

[14] "Finally, technology provides more flexibility than traditional teaching methods once one moves beyond minor changes that can be instituted by individual professors. The 'career' of a workstation may well be less than five years, whereas that of a professor often exceeds 30 years. Workstations don't get tenure, and delegations are less likely to wait on the provost when particular equipment items are 'laid off.' The 'retraining' of IT equipment (for example, reprogramming), while not inexpensive, is easier and more predictable than retraining a tenured professor. Within limits, departments will gain a

larger zone of flexibility as the capital-labor ratio grows. The benefits of shifting away from handicraft methods, coupled with scale economies and increased flexibility, argue for the adoption of IT even when one cannot demonstrate immediate cost advantages. For example, the ability to break even during the first few years provides strong justification for going ahead with an IT solution, provided the effects on quality are not harmful." Ibid., 7.

[15]"A small core of traditional institutions will probably remain buffered from these changes: these are the well-endowed institutions with many more applicants than student places. A small core of traditional learners, those who can afford it and those whose abilities are rewarded with scholarships. will continue to seek out the traditional handicraft-oriented education that has been the hallmark of our system. For these students, traditional education provides acculturation as well as learning. The public has begun to question, however, whether this model is extendible to the whole of higher education. Already the criticism of higher education's rising costs suggests that society finds this educational model too expensive for massified higher education." Ibid, 9.

[16]D. Bruce Johnstone with Alka Arora and William Experton, *The Financing and Management of Higher Education: A Status Report on Worldwide Reforms* (Washington: The World Bank, 1998), 26.

[17]Ibid., 22.

[18] Robert Wilson, "Presentation on behalf of the Nepean Chamber of Commerce to the Ontario Standing Committee on Social Development," Ottawa, 17 March 1997.

[19]See William Graham, "Academic Freedom or Commercial Licence?" pp. 23-30.

[20] Expert Panel on the Commercialization of University Research, *op sit.* CAUT's commentary on the Report is available on the CAUT Web site (www.caut.ca).

[21]"Letter to the Prime Minister." 13 March 2000. Available at www.caut.ca under "Public Policy and Issues."

[22]Kathryn May, "'Misguided' policies driving out scientists," *The Ottawa Citizen*, 21 November 1999, A1.

[23]Quoted in Eyal Press and Jennifer Washburn, "The Kept University," *The Atlantic Monthly*, March 2000, 54.

[24]See Nancy Olivieri, "When Money and Truth Collide," pp. 53-62.

[25]Henry Thomas Stelfox, Grace Chua, Keith O'Rourke, and Allan Detsky, "Conflict of Interest in the Debate over Calcium-Channel Antagonists," *The New England Journal of Medicine* 338(1998): 101-106.

[26]Bill Readings, *The University in Ruins* (Cambridge: Harvard University Press, 1996), 5.

[27]George Martell, "The Labelling, Streaming and Programming of Working Class Kids in School," in *It's Our Own Knowledge*, ed. James L. Turk (Toronto: Our Schools/Our Selves Education Foundation, 1989), 29.

WHAT IS AT STAKE?

Academic Freedom or Commercial Licence?

[1]"Donation and Charitable Trust Agreement, December 6, 1996, between the Joseph Louis Rotman Charitable Foundation and the Governing Council of the University of Toronto." See also, Bill Graham, "Corporatism and the University Part 2: Donor Agreements and Academic Freedom," *UTFA Newsletter*, February 25, 1998; Bill

Graham, Memorandum to the Academic Board, University of Toronto, December 12, 1996 and December 19, 1996; *The Varsity*, Vol. 117, No. 34, January 27, 1997.

[2]"University of Toronto Statement of Institutional Purpose," passed by the Governing Council of the University of Toronto, October 15, 1992.

[3]Memorandum from the Acting Vice-President and Provost, Carolyn Tuohy, to the University of Toronto Policy and Budget Committee, Academic Board, Business Board, and Governing Council, December 5, 1996.

[4]"Donation and Charitable Trust Agreement, made as of the 27th day of September, 1996 among Horsham Corporation, Barrick Gold Corporation and Peter Munk, and Peter Munk Charitable Foundation, and the Governing Council of the University of Toronto." See also, Bill Graham, "Corporatism and the University Part 2: Donor Agreements and Academic Freedom," *loc.cit.*; "U of T to Change Barrick Contract," *The Toronto Star*, November 26, 1997; *The Varsity*, Vol. 118, No. 24, November 24, 1997, and Vol. 118, No. 25, November 27, 1997.

[5]"Agreement between Bell Northern Research Ltd. and the Governing Council of the University of Toronto, February, 1997." See also, Bill Graham, "Corporatism and the University Part 2: Donor Agreements and Academic Freedom," *loc. cit.*

[6]*Public Investments in University Research: Reaping the Benefits*. Report of the Expert Panel on the Commercialization of University Research. Ottawa, May 4, 1999.

[7]John C. Polanyi, "Knowledge as property in universities," *The Toronto Star*, April 5, 1999: also, Peter Calamai, "Profit-first research plan outrages professors," *The Toronto Star*, September 19, 1999.

[8]See Medical Research Council of Canada, 1999-2000 General Information Guide, *http://www.mrc.ca/library/gag/intro.*

[9]Michael Gibbons, *The New Production of Knowledge*, Sage: 1994.

[10]Second International Symposium on Research Funding, "Measuring the Impact," Ottawa, 13-15, 1995.

[11]*Winning in a World Economy: University-Industry Interaction and Economic Renewal In Canada*, Report 39, Science Council of Canada, April 1988; see also, Healthy, Wealthy and Wise: A Framework for an Integrated Federal Science and Technology Strategy, Report of the National Advisory Board on Science and Technology, Ottawa, April 1995. The main theme was application: "Canada's ability to apply research results should attain a level of excellence that matches our current level of excellence in research. Canadians must be developers and exporters of the products of R & D, not just producers of the knowledge itself." It recommends:

> improve the business climate by revising the overall tax structures;
> provide incentives to support entrepreneurs and new companies that commercialize research results from universities and government labs;
> emphasize the need for training in entrepreneurial and technological skills;
> Canadian universities must increase diversification of their funding sources. All granting councils should increase their exploration of new ways of levering funds from other science and technology stakeholders;
> encourage and strengthen collaborative research arrangements among government, university and industrial laboratories, and promote cross-sectoral and multi-disciplinary partnerships.

[12]"Agreement between Bell Emergis, a Division of Bell Canada, and the Governing Council of the University of Toronto, November 12, 1998." See also *The Varsity*, Vol. 120, No. 13, October 18, 1999.

Commercialization and Resistance: Commercial Take-over of Post-Secondary Education

[1]The views in this paper are the author's own and should not be taken to reflect the views of the Association of Academic Staff of the University of Alberta.

[2]In deference to future sociological work, I shall avoid an exploration of the rhetorical and political constitution of the "commercialization of post-secondary education" as an issue. See J. Best, "Rhetoric in Claims Making: Constructing the Missing Children Problem" (1987), 34:2 *Social Problems* 101.

[3]One of the great challenges that Deans face is balancing their roles as academic leaders with their increasingly emphasized roles as entrepreneurs in the fund-raising business.

[4]N. E. Bowie, *University-Business Partnerships: An Assessment* (Lanham, Maryland: Rowman & Littlefield, 1994) 52, 83; T. Caulfield, "The Commercialization of Human Genetics: A Discussion of Issues Relevant to the Canadian Consumer" (1998), 21.

[5]S. Slaughter and L.L. Leslie, Academic Capitalism: Politics, Policies, and the Entrepreneurial University (Baltimore: Johns Hopkins University Press, 1997) 5; "Parajo Dunes Conference Draft Statement," in Bowie, *supra* note 4 at 160; N. Wade, "The Erosion of the Academic Ethos: The Case of Biology" in Bowie, *supra* note 4 at 143.

[6]Indeed, some corporations extend considerable autonomy to their own in-house scientists: R. Varma, "Professional Autonony vs. Industrial Control" (1999), 8:1 *Science as Culture* 23.

[7]A. Geddes, "Newell Blasts Class Cuts," the [Edmonton] *Journal* (April 25, 1999) A1.

[8]See Bowie, *supra* note 4 at 91, for a discussion of "distributive justice" issues bearing on private funding availability.

[9]M. Foucault, *Discipline and Punishment: The Birth of the Prison*, trans. A. Sheridan (New York: Vintage Books, 1979) 26, 27.

[10]Ibid.

[11]My notions of "need" and the role of "vendors" in fabricating and satisfying needs are drawn from the work of Ivan Illich. See, for example, "The War Against Subsistence," in *Shadow Work* (Boston: Marion Boyers, 1981) 53; and "Disabling Professions" in *Disabling Professions* (London: Marion Boyers, 1977) 11.

[12]The Faculties of Extension, Engineering, and Agriculture have had relationships with the external business communities and with provincial government-sponsored research initiatives throughout the history of the University of Alberta: W. H. Johns, *A History of the University of Alberta, 1908–1969* (Edmonton: University of Alberta Press, 1981) 30, 75-77, 82-83. In the United States, business investment in university research has a long history. American Association of University Professors, "Corporate Funding of Academic Research" in Bowie, *supra* note 4 at 225; Government-University-Industry Research Roundtable: New Alliances and Partnerships in American Science and Engineering, in Bowie, ibid. at 194.

[13]"The Networks of Centres of Excellence program is a federal initiative which links academics with industry and government to promote and enhance collaborative research and development in Canada." University of Alberta, 1998–2001 Strategic Business Plan: Building Intellectual Capital Beyond 2000 (June 1998) 19.

[14]Facts About the University of Alberta 1999/2000, online:
 http://www.ualberta.ca/UALBERTA/About/Facts/index.html.
[15]Ibid.
[16]Ibid.
[17]General Faculties Council Policy Manual, s. 35. On the conflict of interest/conflict of commitment distinction, see Bowie, *supra* note 4 at 69; and The University of Minnesota: Disclosure of Conflict of Interest (1991) in Bowie, ibid. at 242.
[18]General Faculties Council Policy Manual, s. 120.
[19]Ibid., s. 96.2.
[20]Ibid., s. 96.2.5 (1) and (9).
[21]See, for example, Article 8 of the Faculty Agreement.
[22]University of Alberta Budget and Statistics, Data Book 97–98, online: *http://www.budstat.ualberta.ca/databook/97-98/w978t64.htm.*
[23]I note that students at other universities have rejected single source soft-drink supply deals: C. Campbell, "Student protest of pop deal costs university $10M," National Post (December 8, 1999) A10.
[24]Some examples include recent University of Alberta winners of the Alberta Science and Technology Foundation Awards including a spinoff company, Biotools Inc., a "bioinformatics" company that applies computational power to biological problems, and has developed software permitting the interpretation of gene sequences as part of the human genome project; Dr. David Schindler, whose research concerns human impacts on freshwater ecosystems; Dr. Wayne Grover, whose research concerns "self-healing and self-organizing telecommunications networks;" and Dr. Gary Stringham, whose research concerns canola: G. McMaster, "U of A shines at ASTech Awards" 37:5 *Folio* (October 29, 1999) 1. Another example is PENCE Inc. (the Protein Engineering Network of Centres of Excellence), whose researchers are concerned with innovative protein technologies.
[25]N. Rose, "Beyond the Public/Private Division: Law, Power and the Family" in P. Fitzpatrick and A. Hunt, eds., *Critical Legal Studies* (Oxford: Basil Blackwell, 1987) 61 at 71.
[26]Faculty of Law, Report of the Ad Hoc Committee on Student Evaluations (University of Alberta, 1988); General Faculties Council Policy Manual, s. 111.2(2): "Evaluation of teaching shall be multifaceted. Multifaceted evaluation shall include the Universal Student Ratings of Instruction . . . and other methods of assessing teaching designed within the individual Faculties to respond to the particular conditions of the Faculty. Such assessments shall include one or more of the following: input from administrators, peers, self, undergraduate and graduate students, and alumni."
[27]M. Foucault, *The History of Sexuality, Volume I*, trans. R. Hurley (New York: Pantheon Books, 1978) 95.
[28]P. Miller and N. Rose, "Governing Economic Life" in M. Gane and T. Johnson, eds., *Foucault's New Domains* (New York: Routledge, 1993) 75 at 77.
[29]Slaughter and Leslie, *supra* note 5 at 128–131.
[30]Ibid. at 5, 239.
[31]Such policies should address such matters as the prior approval of private externally-funded research (is it appropriate for the institution?), disclosure of bases for conflicts of interest (such as share ownership in the funder), compensation for the institution for overheads connected with the project, limitations on the delay of publication of findings, limitations on licensing of intellectual property to corporations

to which staff are connected, assurances that graduate students will not be misused to promote the funded research, assurances that duties other than those to the funded research are not shirked, and assurances that academic decisions will not be improperly influenced by the desire for personal gain. See also D. Noble, "Technology Transfer at MIT: A Critical View" in Bowie at 130; and Wade, *supra* note 5 at 143.

[32]B. Barber, *A Place for Us: How to Make Society Civil and Democracy Strong* (New York: Hill and Wang, 1998) 4.

[33]Ibid. at 61.

Academia in the Service of Industry: the Ag Biotech model

[1]Not tied to industry, in the form of matching fund restrictions

[2]Originally known as BGH or bovine growth hormone, although "to avoid the stigma associated with hormones, the industry agreed to change its name to bovine somatotropin" (Butler, 1999)

[3]As explained by Kronfeld (1993), milk production follows a normal cycle with an initial 12-week period of rising lactation, fuelled in part by catabolic processes where body reserves are mobilized to support yields in excess of what can be accounted for by intake alone. Normally, this phase is followed by an interval of declining productivity, in which body reserves are replenished, to keep the cow in good health and capable of timely re-breeding. Use of rBST has the effect of prolonging peak lactation by up to another 12 weeks (24 weeks in total), further depleting body condition, compromising fertility, and leaving the cow vulnerable to disease and even death

[4]Snowdrop lectin is not known to be toxic to mammalian systems, which is why it was used, unlike ConA lectin (taken from Jackbean) which is known to be toxic to mammals. Like alkaloids or tannins, lectins are ubiquitous vehicles to deter herbivory, can be isolated from many types of organisms, and have been widely explored for potential use in transgenic plants. According to Cummins (internet communication 19 September 1998), patents have been issued for lectin genes in jacalin, elderberry, osage orange, and more than 50 other species (US Patent 5,407,454), in barley ((US Patent 5,276,269), in soybean (US Patent 5,604,121), in snowdrop (US Patent 5,545,820), in pea (US Patent EP-A-0351924), and other lectins (US Patent EP-A-0427529). He further reported that field trials of transgenic lectin-modified crops have already been conducted for potatoes, maize, walnut, sunflower, and grapes.

TEACHING AS A COMMODITY

Trading Away the Public System: The WTO and Post-secondary Education

[1]Charlene Barshefsky, "Services in the Trading System," Speech at the World Services Conference, Washington, DC, June 19, 1999.

[2]Post-secondary institutions, including universities, are frequently referred to as 'colleges' in the U.S.

[3] WTO, Council for Trade in Services, "Education Services: Background Note by the Secretariat," Sept. 23, 1998; Industry Canada, International Investment and Services Directorate, "The Commercial Education and Training Services Industry: A Discussion

Paper in preparation for the World Trade Organization General Agreement on Trade in Services (GATS) Negotiations," nd.

[4]The Canada-U.S. Free Trade Agreement (FTA) was the first major international bilateral agreement to include services. The subsequent North American Free Trade Agreement (NAFTA) between Mexico, Canada, and the US replicated the FTA provisions on services and serves as a model for WTO negotiations.

[5] When the GATS was negotiated and then added to the GATT, the WTO was thereby created.

[6]WTO, "The design and underlying principles of the GATS" (see WTO website)

[7]Richard Langlois, "The WTO and the Millennium Round: What is at Stake for Public Education," (Brussels: Education International, March 1999), p. 7.

[8]These are Australia, Congo RP, Costa Rica, Czech Republic, European Community, Hungary, Jamaica, Japan, Lesotho, Lichtenstein, Mexico, New Zealand, Norway, Panama, Poland, Sierra Leone, Slovak Republic, Slovenia, Switzerland, Trinidad and Tobago, Turkey.

[9] Article XIX of the GATS provides for the ongoing negotiations. "In pursuance of the objectives of this Agreement, Members shall enter into successive rounds of negotiations, beginning not later than five years from the date of entry into force of the WTO Agreement and periodically thereafter, with a view to achieving a progressively higher level of liberalization."

[10]Ibid.

[11]Industry Canada, International Investment and Services Directorate, "The Commercial Education and Training Services Industry: A Discussion Paper in preparation for the World Trade Organization General Agreement on Trade in Services (GATS) Negotiations." 1999.

[12]Government consultation on women, Ottawa, December 1999.

[13]Industry Canada, op cit., pp. 12–13.

[14]The information which follows is from WTO, Council for Trade in Services, "Education Services: Background Notes by the Secretariat," Sept. 23, 1998.

[15] WTO, "Education Services," Table 9.

[16]"Natural persons" are human beings. The term is used to differentiate people from "legal" and "juridical" persons, terms that can apply to corporations as well as human beings.

[17]Its website further explains its mission: "Committed to developing and promoting transnational education as a viable means of delivering education to the world population, GATE plans to involve country accreditation parties, college and university bodies, commercial institution, multinational corporations, and government agencies to face the challenge of evaluating degree programs and other academic standards from countries around the world." (See *www.edugate.org*.)

[18]It should be noted that the claim for discriminatory treatment could only be made by foreign competitors.

[19]The ability of the private sector to dominate university priorities through this process is obvious. One example of this at Simon Fraser University is the recent establishment of a program of Scottish Studies. This occurred only because wealthy Scots in the community wanted it to happen. It was not a priority of the university in the three-year planning process (as was a centre for Race and Gender Studies), but because someone would fund it, the university very rapidly acquired a program in Scottish Studies.

[20]WTO, "Education Services," op. cit.

[21]The attempt to introduce the voucher system in the school system is a similar attempt.

[22] NAFTA, Chapter 15, Article 1502.

[23]Ibid.

[24]Shawn MacCarthy, "Public must be persuaded open markets are beneficial," *Globe and Mail*, Sept. 10, 1999.

[25]Scott Sinclair, *What Happened in Seattle? What's Next in Geneva* (Ottawa: CCPA, January 17, 2000).

[26]WTO, Draft Ministerial Text, Dec. 3, 1999, paragraph 28.

[27]Anonymous government official.

[28]J. Robert Vastine, President, United States Coalition of Service IndUstries, "Services 2000: Innovative approaches to Services Trade Liberalization," Symposium on the Agenda for the Next WTO Negotiation," organized by Japan External Trade Organization, Tokyo, May 13, 1998.

CORPORATE MANAGEMENT AND ITS CONSEQUENCES

Bettrayal of the Public Trust: Corporate Governance of Canadian Universities
[1]By corporate governance I mean both the style of management and the dominance of the corporate community on board of governors.

[2]The predominance of corporate interest on boards of governors is empirically documented in the research of: Beaton, James B. (1998). The Commercialization of Universities in Canada: Corporate University Relations. MA Thesis, York University, Toronto. And Universities and colleges in the public interest. Research Report 1 and 2 (1999). Canadian Association of University Teachers.

[3]Federal Spending on Post-Secondary Education Transfers to Provinces: Trends and Consequences. (1999). Ministry of Advanced Education, Training and Technology.

[4]Beaton, James B. (1998). The Commercialization of Universities in Canada: Corporate University Relations. Introduction. MA Thesis, York University, Toronto.

[5]In a recent *60 Minutes* episode (December 19, 1999) a representative for Apotex denied there was a smear campaign against Olivieri, including the allegation that company spread rumours about Olivieri's mental health. However, during a portion of the show in which the company representative thought the camera was off, he leaned over to Leslie Stahl and said, in reference to Dr. Olivieri, "She's crazy, you know."

[6]Newson, J. and H. Buchbinder. (1988). *The University Means Business*. pp. 59. Garamond Press, Toronto.

[7]Average debt load for student graduating from a four year program. Source: "Take on the Future: Canadian Youth in the World of Work," Human Resources Development Canada report, 1996. Tuition fees for undergraduate Arts students have increased on average 126% between 1990/91 and 1999/2000. Statistics Canada, the Daily, August 25, 1999.

[8]The risk premium of 5% is based on the value of the loans at borrower's consolidation and is equal to approximately $75 million a year.

[9]Trent University's Board of Governors recently voted to close down its downtown Arts campus. One of the major reasons cited for the decision was the fact that the sale of the land would generate the funds that would allow Trent to tap into matching fund programs

216

offered by the federal and provincial governments. See Trent to Sell Colleges, page 1, *CAUT Bulletin*, Vol. 46, No. 10. December 1999.

[10]Grayson, J. Paul. (1999). Who Goes to University and Why? pp. 37–39. *Education Canada*. Vol. 39, No. 2.

[11]Noble, D. (1997). Digital Diploma Mills, www.journet.com/twu/deplomamills.

[12]Misguided polices driving out scientist: Government has pushed 'industrialized' research too far: Nobel laureate. Kathryn May. *Ottawa Citizen*, November 21, 1999, page A1.

Shall We Perform or Shall We Be Free?

[1]For a discussion of the CMEC rationale for PIs, see Canadian Education Statistics Council, *Education Indicators in Canada: Report of the Pan-Canadian Education Indicators Program 1999* (Ottawa and Toronto: Canadian Education Statistics Council, 2000), pp. 1–7.

[2]See Sid Gilbert, "Performance indicators for universities: Ogres or opportunities?" *OCUFA Forum*, Spring 1999, at Web site: *http://www.ocufa.on.ca/*.

[3]At the First National Consultation, Council of Ministers of Education, Canada, Edmonton, Alberta, 1994, claims for performance indicators were surprisingly muted, especially considering that the meeting took place in a province where Key Performance Indicators already decided at least some of the curricular and administrative structure of work in provincial community colleges. See J. Hodder, unpublished manuscript talk, First National Consultation, Council of Ministers of Education, Canada, Edmonton, Alberta, 1994, pp. 1–4, for an illustration of a "soft" approach to performance measures.

[4]For variable definitions of "economy" and "market," see E.G. West, *Higher Education in Canada: An Analysis* (Vancouver: Fraser Institute, 1988), an early and well-written argument for vouchers and indicators in publicly-supported (but not publicly-funded) higher education.

[5]Jonathan Swift, *Gulliver's Travels*, ed. J.F. Ross (New York: Rinehart, 1948), p. 5.

[6] "How to upgrade education: Ontario needs higher standards, more focus and more challenges for kids," *Ottawa Citizen*, 1994 November 1, pp. 58–9.

[7]See Mary Burgan, "The Corporate University and Its New Ways," unpublished manuscript, Spring Council, Canadian Association of University Teachers, Ottawa, 1997, for a survey of contemporary business management theories of university governance, and their requirements that academics and universities become nimble and responsive to economic change and rapidly changing market demands.

[8]See James G. Greenlee's *Sir Robert Falconer: A Biography* (Toronto : University of Toronto Press, 1988), for examples of direct provincial interference on the basis of admission statistics, budget information, and the like, especially after 1910.

[9]The search for the Holy Grail of economic utility was helped by the publication of careful economic policy research that might have argued against as for PIs. See, for example, Robert C. Allen, "The Economic Benefits of Post-Secondary Education and Training in B.C.: An Outcomes Assessment," Centre for Research on Economic and Social Policy, University of British Columbia, April 1996, CRESP Discussion Paper DP

[10]From the Canada Foundation for Innovation Web site, at:

http://www.innovation.ca/english/about/index.html

[11]From the CAUT Web site at:

http://www.caut.ca/English/PublicPolicy/Commercialization/

comment_commercialization.htm

[12]Science Council of Canada, *Winning in a World Economy* (Ottawa: Science Council of Canada, 1988), p. 1.

[13]Quoted in R. Callahan, *The Cult of Efficiency* (Chicago: University of Chicago Press, 1962), p. 24.

[14]F.W. Taylor, *The Principles of Scientific Management*, p. 37, qu. in Callahan, p. 27.

[15]*School Review*, XXIII (1915 October): pp. 505–34.

[16]See Frank McKinnon, *The Politics of Education in Canada* (Toronto: University of Toronto Press, 1962). McKinnon offers horror stories about graduate theses in education on the optimal sizes of school toilets and the correlation of toilet-construction with (a) pupil performance and (b) voter satisfaction.

[17]See Ontario Council on University Affairs, *Sustaining Quality in Changing Times: Funding Ontario Universities, A Discussion Paper* (Toronto: The Council, 1994), esp. pp. 23ff.

[18]It's worth noting that the UK began in 1987–1988 by ranking whole universities on a set of several dozen global PIs. By 1993, the system had reached down to department and institute level, and the number and types of PIs had increased substantially. The UK began with a ranking of 45 universities on a PI called "UFC research rating" (roughly equivalent to what would be a SSHRCC or NSERC ranking in this country). By 1993, the ranking was on bibliometric measures—numbers of articles, books, and commercially paid reports per person—and the listing and verification of publications had become a large-ish, self-standing industry. On the early period, see Jill Johnes and Jim Taylor, *Performance Indicators in Higher Education: UK Universities* (Buckingham: Open University Press, 1990), esp. the table at pp. 10–11, and Ch. 1, *passim.*

[19]Ernst Benjamin, "The Decline of Academic Autonomy in Higher Education," *Academe*, 80, 4 (1994 July/August): 34–6.

[20]The recent announcement of Canada Research Chairs, too few of which will go to smaller and medium-sized universities, merely intensifies this phenomenon.

[21]Burton Bollag, "University Leaders in Europe Uneasy Over Moves to Assess Quality," *The Chronicle of Higher Education*, 1994 September 21, p. A46.

22 Burton Bollag, p. A46.

[23]C. Sanders, "Welsh aim for single quality agency," *Times Higher Education Supplement*, 1994 October 21, p. 1.

[24]For the South Carolina system and its attitude to PIs, see the State web site at: *http://www.che400.state.sc.us/web/chemis/wintro.htm.*

[25]CAUT Information Service Reference: 51-28, approved by CAUT Council, November 1996.

IN THE PUBLIC INTEREST: RECLAIMING OUR PURPOSE

To not intend, or to intend not , that is the question

[1]I am referring not only to changes in the social relationships within institutions of higher education, but also between institutions of higher education and the corporate sector, governments, and academically-oriented funding agencies such as the federal research councils.

[2]Some of these people are represented in this anthology: Paul Axelrod, Ursula Franklin, Bill Graham, David Noble, and Claire Polster. Others include Howard Buchbinder, John

Calvert, Marguerite Cassin, Michael Katz, John McMurtry, Dianne Meaghan, Graham Morgan, and David Scheffle, Neil Tudiver, and Howard Woodhouse. See the bibliography for a listing of some early publications that warned about the dangers of corporate linking.

[3]Claire Polster's doctoral dissertation (1994) tracks the federal government funding shifts that have taken place over the past two decades. It convincingly demonstrates that the money withdrawn from general public research council programmes has re-appeared in targeted and matched funding type research programmes. In fact, some of this funding has been allocated to special research programmes of economically and industrially oriented government ministries.

[4]We should expect, rather than an ideology, that a new "philosophy of education" would motivate the changes that are being introduced. But it is precisely the absence of any guiding philosophy of education that makes them so disturbing: educational institutions are being appropriated, not for a new educational agenda, but rather for a particular economic agenda.

[5]The Enros and Farley study that advanced the notion of the service university referred to dynamic relations with "society" but the content of their recommendations was limited to relations between corporations and institutions of higher education.

[6]Claire Polster and I have recently written a paper, "Re-claiming our centre: Towards a robust defence of academic autonomy," that explores the theme of faculty accommodation in detail.

[7]For example, rather than outrightly resist them, some attempts have been made to "capture" performance indicators through ensuring that the criteria that are used in them promote better teaching and research practices.

What is to Be Done? Envisioning the University's Future

[1]Signified in part, by a course I teach called "Youth and Society."

[2]James O. Freedman, *Idealism and Liberal Education* (Ann Arbor: University of Michigan Press, 1996), 2.

[3] Paul Anisef, Paul Axelrod and Zeng Lin, "Universities, Liberal Education and the Labour Market: Trends and Prospects" (York University: Centre for Research on Work and Society, Working Paper Series), 1999. Other studies reaching similar conclusions: Robert C. Allen, "The Employability of University Graduates in the Humanities, Social Sciences and Education: Recent Statistical Evidence" (Unpublished, 1998); Neil Guppy and Scott Davies, *Education in Canada: Recent Trends and Future Prospects* (Ottawa: Minister of Industry, 1998); and various reports from the National Graduate Survey, including Michael Paju, "The Class of 1990 Revisited: Report of the 1995 Follow-up Survey of 1990 Graduates," *Education Quarterly Review* 4, no. 4: 9-29.

[4]D.W. Livingstone. *The Education-Jobs Gap: Unemployment or Economic Democracy* (Toronto: Garamond, 1999).

[5]Michael Useem, "Corporate Restructuring and Liberal Learning," *Liberal Education*, (Winter, 1995): 18-23.

[6]Sharon D. Crozier and Patrick Grassick, "I Love My B.A.: The Employment Experience of Successful Bachelor of Arts Graduates," *Guidance and Counselling* 11, no. 1 (Winter 1996): 19-26.

[7] George Sorger, quoted in *Toronto Star*, Dec. 15, 1997.

[8] Jeffrey Nesteruk, "Business Teaching and Liberal Learning," *Liberal Education* 85, no. 2 (Spring 1999): 56-59.

[9] Cited in Christina Elliot Sorum, "'Vortex, Clouds, and Tongue': New Problems in the Humanities?" *Daedalus* 128, no. 1 (Winter 1999): 254.

[10] Ibid, 254.

[11] Marjorie T. Davis and Charles C. Schroeder, "New Students in Liberal Arts Colleges: Threat or Challenge?" In JoAnna M. Watson and Rex P. Stevens, eds. *Pioneers and Pallbearers: Perspectives on Liberal Education* (Macon, Ga.: Mercer University Press, 1982), 147–68.

[12] Ibid, 166.

[13] Linda Casey Matson and Ron Matson, "Changing Times in Higher Education: An Empirical Look at Cooperative Education and Liberal Arts Faculty," *Journal of Cooperative Education* XXXI, no. 1 (Fall 1995): 13–24.

[14] Blayne Haggart, "Picture a Privately Funded, Classical Education on a Public Campus," *Catholic New Times*. 22, no. 9 (May 17, 1998): 1–2.

About the authors

Paul Axelrod is Professor in the Division of Social Science at York University and has written widely on the history and political economy of higher education. His publications include *Scholars and Dollars: Politics, Economics, and the Universities of Ontario, 1945-1980; Making a Middle Class: Student Life in English Canada during the Thirties; and The Promise of Schooling: Education in Canada, 1800-1914.*

Michèle Brill-Edwards is a pediatrician and specialist in drug development. Formerly Canada's senior physician responsible for prescription drugs approvals, Dr. Brill-Edwards resigned from Health Canada in 1996 to publicly object to excessive influence of the pharmaceutical industry in Canada's drug safety system, jeopardizing lives to bow to political and industry pressures. She is an authority on the use of Canada's *Food and Drug Act* to protect the public interest in drug research.

Bill Bruneau is Professor in the Department of Educational Studies at the University of British Columbia. He is a social historian, particularly interested in the development of universities. Professor Bruneau has been an elected trustee to the Vancouver School Board (1990-1993), President of the UBC Faculty Association (1992-1994), and President of the Canadian Association of University Teachers (1996-1998). He is Co-Editor of the journal, *Historical Studies in Education.*

Ann Clark is an Associate Professor in the Plant Agriculture Department at the University of Guelph. Her specific interests are in pasture and grazing management and in the design of ecologically sustainable production systems. She has written one book and several book chapters and more than 120 articles. In addition to her teaching and research responsibilities, she is also a frequent invited speaker at scholarly and producer conferences throughout Canada and the northern United States. Recent presentations in the areas of genetic engineering and sustainable agriculture may be found at (http://www.oac.uoguelph.ca/www/CRS/faculty/eac.htm).

Marjorie Griffin Cohen is an economist who is a Professor of Political Science and Women's Studies at Simon Fraser University. She is an activist who has served on the Executive Board of the National Action Committee on the Status of Women, the Coalition Against Free Trade and the Canadian Centre for Policy Alternatives. She is

Century Ontario; *Free Trade and the Future of Women's Work*; and is co-author of a two volume series, *Canadian Women's Issues*.

Michael Conlon is National Chairperson of the Canadian Federation of Students. He has previously served as the National Executive Representative for British Columbia (1998-1999), Chair of the National Graduate Council (1998-1999), and President of the University of Victoria Graduate Student Society (1996-1998). In addition, he served as chair of the organizing committee for the unionization of teaching assistants at the University of Victoria. Mr. Conlon is completing his Ph.D. in the Department of English at the University of Victoria.

Ursula Franklin is University Professor Emerita at the University of Toronto and a Senior Fellow of Massey College. She has been a member of the Science Council of Canada and served on the Boards of National Research Council and Natural Sciences and Engineering Research Council. In addition to her teaching and research in the field of Metallurgy and Materials Science, Dr. Franklin has been active in the areas of peace and justice, the social responsibility of science and scientists and issues affecting women. She has received numerous honours and tributes including the Order of Canada, Order of Ontario, the Civic Medal of Merit from the City of Toronto and numerous honorary degrees. During the past decade she has written extensively about the impact of modern technology on various facets of life including education. A new and enlarged edition of her book *The Real World of Technology* was published in 1999.

Bill Graham is Professor Emeritus of Philosophy at the University of Toronto. He was awarded a Doctor, Honoris Causa, by the International Institute for Advanced Studies in 1997. He is Past President of the Canadian Association of University Teachers. He has also served as President of the Ontario Confederation of University Faculty Associations and the University of Toronto Faculty Association.

Janice Newson is Associate Professor of Sociology at York University in Toronto. She has been the President of the Canadian Sociology and Anthropology Association, on the Board of the Social Sciences Federation of Canada, member of the CAUT Council and Chairperson of the CAUT Status of Women Committee. She is co-author with Howard Buchbinder of *The University Means Business: Universities, Corporations and Academic Work* and the co-editor of *Universities and Globalisation: Critical Perspectives*.

David Noble is Professor of History at York University. He has also taught at the Massachusetts Institute of Technology (MIT) and Drexel University. His books include *American By Design: Science, Technology, and the Rise of Corporate Capitalism;*

Forces of Production: A Social History of Industrial Automation; Progress Without People: In Defence of Luddism; A World Without Women: The Christian Clerical Culture of Western Science; The Religion of Technology: The Divinity of Man and the Spirit of Invention.

Nancy Olivieri is Professor of Pediatrics and Medicine at the University of Toronto, Director of the Hemoglobinopathy Program at the Toronto Hospital, and Program Head of Hemoglobinopathies at the University of Toronto. She is on the editorial boards for several medical journals and a consultant to the Provincial DNA Disagnostic Laboratory for Hemoglobin Disorders, McMaster University.

Claire Polster is Assistant Professor in the Department of Sociology and Social Studies at the University of Regina. She has written a number of articles on federal government policy related to academic research. Her current research focuses on the development and extension of national and international intellectual property regimes and their implications for universities in particular and the public interest more generally.

Wayne Renke is Associate Professor in the Faculty of Law, University of Alberta and author of numerous articles published in legal journals. He is a Past President of the Association of Academic Staff: University of Alberta (1998-1999) and has been involved for several years in the negotiation of a proposed intellectual property policy for University of Alberta staff. In 1997, he was Visiting Professor of Law at Niigata University in Japan

Maureen Shaw is President of the College Institute Educators' Association of BC (CIEA). Previously she served as Secretary-Treasurer of CIEA and as an English instructor at Kwantlen University College in Surrey, British Columbia.

James L. Turk is Executive Director of the Canadian Association of University Teachers. Previously, he was Director of Education for the Ontario Federation of Labour and was an Associate Professor of Sociology at the University of Toronto.

Langdon Winner is Professor of Political Science in the Department of Science and Technology Studies at Rensselaer Polytechnic Institute in Troy, New York. He is a political theorist who focuses upon social and political issues that surround modern technological change. He is the author of *Autonomous Technology, The Whale and the Reactor: A Search for Limits in an Age of High Technology* , and editor of *Democracy in a Technological Society.*

223